CRUISING: SAIL OR POWER

Peter Heaton

CRUISING:
SAIL OR POWER

KAYE & WARD LTD · LONDON

First published 1970 by
Kaye & Ward Ltd
194–200 Bishopsgate, London EC2

© Kaye & Ward Ltd 1970

ISBN 0 7182 0791 2

Printed in Great Britain by
Richard Clay (The Chaucer Press) Ltd
Bungay, Suffolk

ACKNOWLEDGEMENTS

I wish to thank the following for permission to include photographs and in some
cases drawings of the craft discussed in chapter two: Russell Marine Ltd, Calvira
Works, Southend-on-Sea, Essex; Carl Ziegler Yacht Agency, 37 Great Cumber-
land Place, London W1; Penryn Boatbuilding and Engineering Co Ltd,
Ponsharden, Cornwall; M. S. Redman Esq, Woodham Ferrers, Essex; Interyacht,
Woodbridge, Suffolk; City Centre Boatyard Ltd, Glasgow; Offshore Yachts Ltd,
Great Wakering, Essex; Illingworth and Associates, Emsworth, Hants; Camper
and Nicholson Ltd, Southampton, Hants; G. Prout and Sons Ltd, Canvey Island,
Essex; Musters Marine Ltd, Poole, Dorset; Jachtwerf 'Victoria' CNP Vader,
Alkmaar, Holland; David Cheverton (Sales) Ltd, Cowes, Isle of Wight; Beagle
Boats Ltd, Woodbridge, Suffolk; The Whitehall Shipyard, Whitby, Yorkshire;
Senior Marine Ltd, Bitterne, Southampton, Hants; Jones Buckie Shipyard Ltd,
Buckie, Banffshire, Scotland; The South Coast Catamaran Co Ltd, Whites
Shipyard, Southampton, Hants; Walter F. Rayner Ltd, Poole, Dorset; Dixon
Kerly Ltd, Maldon, Essex; Dell Quay Sales Ltd, Itchenor Shipyard, Chichester,
Sussex.

I also wish to thank the editor of *Motor Boat and Yachting* for permission to
include material published in that magazine.

Contents

5

6

CONTENTS

7

List of Illustrations

List of Plates

What is Cruising?

With all forms of sailing there is, apart from the excitement of the sport, the awareness of being in a new element, quite different from land sports. Each weekend spent sailing induces a feeling of being 'on holiday', of pleasurable escape from the work-a-day world. In no branch of sailing is this more pronounced than in cruising.

This book is about cruising in small boats under sail or under power. In addition to helping you to select the right boat for your purpose (and your means), it is intended to provide the basic information whereby a man, or woman, or a family can make passages at sea for pleasure and in safety. That is a definition of cruising and while technically correct it misses the reality by a distance greater than the width of the Pacific Ocean at its widest.

The very early morning start in the cold air when the only sounds as you step on deck are sea sounds and bird sounds; then the small stove hisses to life and the smell of eggs and bacon frying rises from the hatchway — that is cruising. The very real fear when the weather blows up a little too quickly and you are fighting much bigger seas than you had ever pictured and your gradual confidence in your boat and in yourself and the triumph as you enter harbour with the world suddenly at your feet – that is cruising. The ever-changing weather and the problems that keep you on your toes the whole time and the skipper's pride when his workings-out bring the landfall exactly where it should be; only to suffer a salutary degree of humiliation when he makes a 'nonsense' of anchoring or picking up a mooring – that too is cruising. And all the post-mortems and the plans, as you sit round the cabin table, while outside it is dark and silent and night-fresh. And before turning in when you go on deck to check that the anchor light is burning, you notice that already she is swinging to the ebb and you remember that on the morning flood you must be under way, bound for new horizons.

For cruising is a way of life and this book is written to try and help you to know it too. And you are lucky; for the last fifteen years has seen a revolution in sailing. The sport of yachting, once the preserve of the rich, is now available virtually to all. The enormous increase in the number of dinghies and dinghy sailors alone bears witness to this. As these young men and women grow older it is very natural that they should want to try their hand at larger boats. This happened and is happening, and of the two main branches of sailing – racing and cruising – it is the cruising world (although the racing yachts get the publicity) that has seen the greatest expansion.

But with larger boats come increased expense and it is here that modern techniques in reinforced plastics and resin glues used in sheet or moulded ply construction help to keep prices within reasonable levels. Most people with young families have little enough to spend on sport, and it is no good pretending that running even a small cruiser costs nothing. Certainly dinghy sailing, just as having fun with a small boat with an outboard motor on the transom, can be indulged in for very modest figures, but cruisers, whether sail or power, cost more the larger they get and the more gadgets they carry. It is for this reason that I have directed that part of this book in which costs figure, mainly at people of modest means, to try and show that whether she be your floating weekend cottage or a means of adventure and exploration, the small modern cruiser can cost you much less than your car.

However, those who can go to any boat show, pick out an ocean cruiser/racer for £9,000 or a lavishly equipped motor cruiser for $20,000 and sit down and write a cheque there and then, can still I hope, learn from this book for I have tried to make its range as wide as possible. While assuming that most readers possess a certain amount of knowledge already, I have included a section on how to sail for the benefit of the complete beginner.

CHAPTER ONE

The Boat

Sizes, Types, Multihull Yachts, Rigs, Engines and Materials

Let us begin with the first essential, the boat. You can cruise in small boats or large ones; using sail or power or both as your driving force. Your vessel can have one, two or three masts – or one, two or three hulls – and she can be driven by a number and variety of engines. The choice today is immense. The world is shrinking under the tightening lines of modern communication, and ideas and styles once local, become world wide. The three-sided sail of the Bermuda Islands is now seen alongside the Chinese lugsail of the Junk. The old English predilection for narrow racing yachts withered before the reality of successive ocean-racing victories by beamy American yachts; and now beam is firmly with us.

But the traffic is never all one way. Each country contributes something from its experience of the sea and ships and what emerges is the meeting-point of many sea-lanes. It is not the differences that matter, it is what common agreement has decided is best (although let me quickly add we are always still learning). It is with this thought in mind, that is to say the idea of a number of styles of vessel now generally accepted internationally, that I have approached this chapter, and the succeeding chapter on types. The fact that they are mostly British does not matter; being myself British, and sailing in British waters mainly, it would be surprising if they were not; but these vessels sell readily overseas and are representative of modern trends to be found universally. Were I to include a selection of yachts from every sailing country there would be room for nothing else in this book.

15

Sail

(i) Comparison and Advantages of Size

Obviously finance has got a lot to do with this, but I would emphasise the domestic aspect of getting the largest boat you can afford. I am talking, as I said in the introduction, to people of relatively modest means. This statement about size is not intended for those who can afford to buy second-hand Cunard liners. In other words if you can afford a 5-tonner, get that in preference to a 3-tonner. Let me hastily add that I am well aware that all sorts of magnificent cruises have been made in very small boats – John Guzzwell careered all round the world in the Giles-designed *Trekka* and her water-line length was only 18ft 6ins. There are many good cruisers on the market of even smaller dimensions too. The Russell Marine *Alacrity*, designed by Peter Stephenson has a water-line length of only 17 feet, and the Wayside Marine, Crighton-designed *Alouette* has a water-line of one inch less than that! Designers nowadays need no tuition in getting quarts into pint pots. A great advantage of these very small craft is that mainly they are cheap. The 3-ton *Alacrity* will set you back about £745 and the 16-foot LWL *Alouette* £825. These two little boats, both built in glassfibre-reinforced plastics represent good value for money up to a point. Take now the Thames Marine designed and built *Snapdragon 26*. This vessel has a LWL of 21 ft 8 ins. Her Thames measurement is 6 tons, so she is therefore about twice as big from the point of view of space below as *Alacrity*. *Alacrity* has a beam of 6 ft 11 ins while *Snapdragon*'s beam is 8 ft 6 ins. Headroom in the former is 4 ft 2 ins, in the latter it is 6 ft. These differences may not seem much, but you try living aboard for a week and see the difference! Of course the price of *Snapdragon* is twice as much as *Alacrity*, being just over £2,000.

These particular vessels quoted at random are British, but the same arguments apply to small cruising vessels the world over. There will always be people who having very little to spend, will bless the foresight of designers and builders who can produce these very small but seaworthy craft for such a low price.

The reasons why I stress buying as big a boat as you can afford are many. Take first the domestic side. Somewhere below decks there has to be space for dry clothes, oilskins, shoes, bedding, sails, charts, navigational instruments, water cans, radio, cushions, food of all kinds and the stove on which to cook it, etc. Do you see what I mean? The list could continue. Again try putting on or taking off your clothes in the cabin of a 2- or 3-tonner with 4-foot headroom. After a week you get more proficient at it, but you never really get to like it. I know, I've done it in a 2½-tonner I owned some years back. I even went cruising in January in the English Channel in the little boat *and* enjoyed it. So there's nothing against very small boats. It's just that a bit more room below goes such a long way to make life easier on board. Larger boats are less tiring at sea too. Boats of a very short water-line tend to 'dip' into every hole in the ocean!

On this question of size, you may be wondering whether it is better to buy a larger second-hand boat than a new small boat. In some cases, yes. A lot depends on your own plans. For example whether you are married and have any small children you will want to take with you sailing. Also the area in which you will be sailing will affect your decision. Those who wish to venture offshore will be wiser to buy as large as they can afford. Again the *number* of people sailing the boat will dictate her size. If you are likely to be a single-hander at all then your largest boat will be about 8 tons ideally. It is difficult to lay down rules for the price of second-hand craft; but as a rough guide a boat costing new £655 will be going for about £625 when a year old; and will depreciate by less and less each successive year. When about six years old she would probably cost a little over £400. (Foreign and overseas readers please accept my apologies; but I cannot spare the space here to list equivalent prices in Dollars, Marks, Yen, Francs, Escudos, Pesos, Pesetas, Roubles, etc. May I ask you to do your own currency conversion?)

It is very difficulty to generalise, but a little research shows that the depreciation is not so very much. For example a 4½-tonner costing new £1,400 will fall to about £1,140 after one year, and after three to four years will be standing at about £970. When you consider that the boat is now between three and four years old (and that means her gear, sails and engine as well as her hull) the saving in price is doubtful. With more expensive craft, for example, the £3,150 South Coast *One Design* (a 6-tonner, 21-foot water-line) will, after say three years' use have fallen to around £2,520, a drop of £650, and this may well turn the balance in favour of the older boat. As a general rule then with the cheaper boats, better buy new. More expensive craft, desirable as they may be when brand new, can still represent good value when three or four years old and the drop in price may bring them within our budget.

(ii) Types

Unlike a dinghy, or a small half-decked keel racing yacht, a cruising yacht, in addition to taking you wherever you want to go, is also your home. You will be spending nights on board both under way, and at anchor and in connection with this comes the question of the locality in which you would be doing most of your sailing. For example, if you are planning to cruise in estuaries and in places where there are quiet creeks much of which dry out at low water, you should choose a type of hull which will sit happily on the ground under such circumstances. Such a vessel will be relatively flat bottomed and will have either a centreboard or bilge keels. This may at first sound like a rather odd way to go cruising – to set sail and leave the shore only to end up on it again – but it is in the secluded creeks of the world's river mouths that some of the most lovely and unspoiled anchorages can be found. One of the snags of the ever-increasing popularity of sailing is that, while the number of boats multiply, the available harbours remain the same. Deep-draught vessels, while having certain advantages, especially in rough weather, are often unable, because of their draught, to visit these delightful places, where one really can 'get away from it all' and anchor quietly with only the call of the local birds and the magic sound of the tide gurgling past. Compare this with the transistor radios of the two adjacent yachts in the average marina and maybe you'll see what I mean!

From the foregoing it will be clear that just as the general sport of sailing divides into racing and cruising; so cruising divides into the two distinct types we have been discussing. A shoal-draught boat will have more initial stability than a keel boat. She will have what is known as a 'firmer' bilge and may also have more beam, although this last fact is truer of British yachts than of American. American designers have always liked beam (in my opinion rightly). As a shoal-draught boat heels under the wind her bilge, being immersed, causes the centre of gravity to rise, thus giving her a righting moment. The keel boat with her lead ballast deeper in the water does not have the same righting moment so she has much less initial stability. However, it cannot be denied that as the wind increases and the two yachts heel further, while the lead on the deep keel of the keel boat then acquires a steadily increasing (and righting) leverage; the shallow-draught boat may be pushed over beyond her critical angle of heel, a situation obviously with unattractive possibilities! It is therefore obvious that for the man who wishes to venture well offshore into deep and probably very rough waters, the keel boat has the edge. But let me add at once that this kind of argument 'deep draught versus shoal' is like ketch versus yawl, inboard versus outboard, more suitable for the subject of one of those endless and fascinating discussions wherever seamen gather which has no hard and fast conclusion.

It is a fact, however, that with boats up to say, 9 tons, the bilge keel and the centreboard are increasing in popularity. This is especially true of the USA, indeed shoal-draught boats have been popular there long before their merits were appreciated in Britain.

Multihull Yachts

There is a lot of interest in multihulls – catamarans, trimarans – these days and many people think they are a modern invention. This is not so. Most people know that the chief advantage of one or more additional hulls is to achieve greater average speeds. Anyone who reads the newspapers knew by the finish of the round Britain race of 1966 that a properly designed and built multihull was more than a match for the single-hull boats in that race as far as pure speed was concerned. This method of getting speed, that is by so arranging matters that a large area of sail can be carried without additional ballast weight, was well known to the Pacific islanders who, most naval historians claim, invented the outrigger – the first double hull. When exactly is not known but when the Pacific Islands began to be explored, vessels of this type were in common use. In the reign of Charles II of England, a double hull was built, but was lost in the Bay of Biscay while on passage to the West Indies. The word catamaran is in fact Indian and is used to describe two-hull craft. The Pacific Island vessels consisted of a single hull with one or more buoyant smaller hulls called outriggers; but the principle was of supporting sail by widely spread beam.

Since those early days the problem has been how to produce a safe sea-going catamaran. In 1870 Nathaniel Herreshoff in North America experimented with twin 30-foot (9·14 m) hulls of 1 ft 6 ins (0·457 m) beam, spaced 15 feet (4·57 m) apart. The hulls were hinged so that each could pitch independently of the other. Herreshoff, an influential designer, while admitting that the twin-hull craft would always be capable of maintaining a higher average speed than the conventional single hull; laid stress on the dangers attendant on twin-hull craft at sea and he and other yacht designers concentrated on single hulls.

In 1936 a Frenchman, by name Eric de Bisschop, built a 38-foot (34·74 m) catamaran with 3-foot (0·914 m) draft and 17-foot (5·18 m) beam. She was called *Kaimiloa*. Her Polynesian name reflected the origins of her design; double-ended 'V'd hulls, flexibly attached with an open platform between. She was Junk rigged. This remarkably successful pioneer sailed from Hawaii to Cannes in the South of France, round the Cape of Good Hope in the winter, averaging some 130 miles a day. The next 'cat' development of note was in 1947 after the Second World War, when Woody Brown, an American glider champion launched the 38-foot (11·58 m) *Manu Kai*. This vessel ply built and weighing only 1½ tons (1,524 kg) achieved speeds of 25 knots, but was not an ocean-cruising boat. She had no accommodation and was used for beach chartering. In 1955 a still larger American 'cat' *Waikiki Surf* appeared on the scene. She was 40 feet (12·19 m) in length and her displacement was less than two tons (2,032 kg) – about one-seventh of a conventional keel yacht of equivalent length. On one Pacific cruise it was recorded in her log that for six hours her speed never dropped below 15 knots. Her average speeds however were less impressive and on passage from Honolulu to Santa Monica only 7½ knots was maintained; once again high-lighting the problem that although a catamaran will have three times the speed potential of the single huller; when allowance is made for calms, light airs, and especially for long beats to windward the cat's superiority over the solo hulls is not so very marked. There remains, too, the danger of capsize. Can a vessel which is not able to right herself when thrown on her beam ends be called seaworthy? Many would say 'no'!

We have so far talked of American 'cat' pioneering but in Europe, after the Second World War, much began to happen.

In 1956 Bill O'Brien and the Prout brothers were designing fast
16-foot (4·87 m) inshore cats, dinghy style. But these were not
cruising vessels. All the time, however, designers were seeking to
solve the problem of giving a catamaran enough ballast in
shallow keels so as to give positive stability at 90 degrees and
with it the desired ability to right herself. To combine the
stabilising characteristics of the single hull with those peculiar
to the multihull it was necessary to reduce the sail area/weight
ratio of the catamaran and of course, as a result, of her potential
speed. But designers today (and there are many) are producing
cruising catamarans that combine great comfort below with
perfect stability, the 'cat' can be safely said to have 'come to
stay'.

For the readers of this book then, what can I suggest by way
of advice? In chapter two I am giving the details of three
multihull craft; two catamarans, one by Prout and one by the
South Coast Catamaran Company (Bill O'Brien) and one
trimaran from Musters Marine, and these three excellent
cruising multihull craft will give as good an idea as you will get
of the look, accommodation and general specification of such
vessels. It would be a brave man who would set down on paper
any definite advantages of the 'tri' over the 'cat' or the 'cat' over
the monohull. But you my reader having paid (I hope) for this
volume, deserve a little more than that cowardly running
behind a platitude for shelter – so here goes! With a reaching
wind the multihull is faster than the mono as we have already
seen. When sails are correctly trimmed, a multihull will sail
herself for hours on end; a great advantage. On a very close
windward leg, punching into short seas, the monohull is
superior (although wetter). The lightweight multihull will be
slowed by the short head seas. When running, however, the
multihulls come again into their own. There is no problem of
broaching to, that ever-present worry with the monohull when
running before large seas. The 'cat' cuts along in her own twin
grooves. There is no yawing about; no rolling. As far as any
great difference between the 'cat' and the 'tri' this really only
manifests itself when running. The twin floats outside the large
central hull could present a problem in that one or the other
might dig in with obviously undesirable results, and in consequence steering before large following seas would need as
much care and attention as with the single hull. Cruising

yachtsmen, used to single hulls and who have in their time ridden out many a gale successfully, tend to favour the latter design and mistrust the 'cat'. As far as accommodation goes, a glance at the photographs and the plans in chapter two will show you more vividly than I could describe the 'roominess' of the multihull below decks. Multihull craft will take the ground safely and upright on each tide. As for power, either outboard or inboard engines can be fitted without presenting any problems. It is a matter of personal taste. On the question of expense – the figures must speak for themselves. They aren't exactly cheap, but you get a lot for your money. To conclude: Bill O'Brien, who knows as much about these vessels as anyone you'll meet has gone on record as saying that there is '. . . little doubt in my mind that the catamaran is the safe family cruising yacht of the future . . .'

Rigs

In the sailing boat, surely one of men's most attractive creations, we see the physical laws put to a practical and universal application. Over the years various combinations of sails (as well as types of sail) have been evolved. The yacht designer has nowadays a wide choice and so have you. Let us take a look at this choice.

Most yachts nowadays have three-cornered mainsails which as we have already seen are often called Bermudan or Marconi. The four-sided 'gaff' rig is still found, however, and for certain craft it has advantages. All the vessels mentioned in this book have however three-sided mainsails and I will in consequence confine my remarks to that particular rig. As far as the principles of sailing go, there is little difference anyway. The simplest form of rig is that of the single sail like the famous 'cat' boats of North America. The International 'Finn' class, designed by R. Sarby of Sweden for the Olympic Games of 1952, is a single-sail boat, so too is the National 'Solo' class designed by Jack Holt of England. Cruising boats *can* be rigged with a single sail – for example, Colonel Haslar rigged his *Folkboat* with a single Chinese lugsail (Junk type) for a single-handed transatlantic race.

Small craft, up to about 3 tons, sometimes use a lugsail. This is illustrated in figure 1. It can be either a standing lug (*a*) (incidentally a four-sided sail as will be seen) or (*b*) a sliding

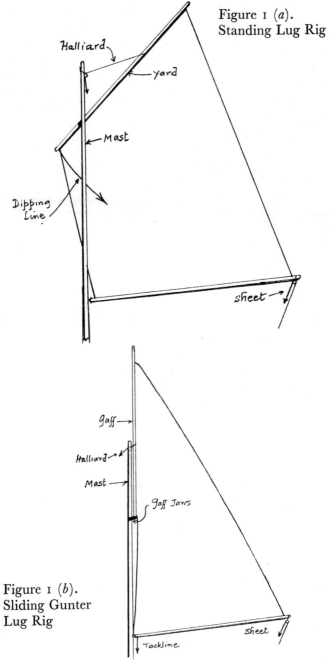

Figure 1 (*a*).
Standing Lug Rig

Halliard

yard

Mast

Dipping
Line

sheet

gaff

Halliard

Mast

gaff Jaws

Figure 1 (*b*).
Sliding Gunter
Lug Rig

Tackline

sheet

23

gunter lug. The main advantage of such a rig, the shortness of the mast (enabling you to pass under bridges, etc, when river or canal cruising) is nowadays largely cancelled out by the device of housing the mast in what is called a 'tabernacle'. This enables it to be lowered and raised easily. I don't think here we need consider these rigs for long as most of the small cruisers seen today have a two-sail rig; one sail abaft (behind) the mast, the mainsail; and the other (the headsail), before it. This brings me to the simplest of such rigs – the sloop.

Figure 2 shows a sloop. It has the advantage of simplicity and cheapness. The mast is often stepped fairly well forward in the boat. This tendency is actually less prevalent today. The forward position of the mast gives rise to the criticism that sloops in steep headseas have a tendency to 'dip' their bows. So designers for some time have stepped the mast further into the boat. Since this often results in the mast being in the same

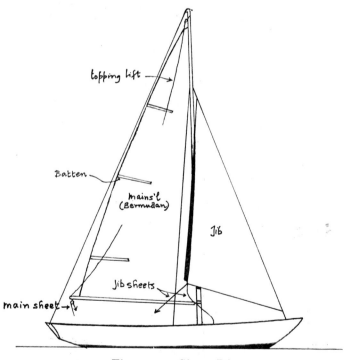

Figure 2. Sloop Rig

position as a cutter (a two headsail rig) the rig is sometimes (but fortunately not often) called the 'slutter' rig. Like most things in life, of course, the explanation for stepping the mast further aft is not as simple as that. The ocean racing rules, which tax the mainsail rather than the foretriangle, have produced vessels with larger headsails and smaller mainsails and a little thought will show you that for balance in such a case the mast must be well 'into' the boat and not right forward. As racing car experience benefits the touring motorist everywhere, so racing yacht design and experience continually benefit the cruising man. This becomes abundantly clear when one sails one of today's small cruisers of, say, 18 feet on the water-line. The speed and manoeuvrability is remarkable by comparison to the older sisters (often converted workboats), and this all round efficiency owes much to experiences and experiments with racing craft of all sizes. The next rig (see figure 3), the cutter, is

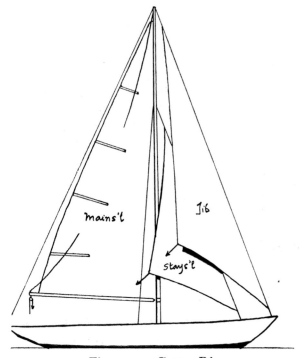

Figure 3.   Cutter Rig

as a general rule found in larger craft than that of the sloop; although the 'slutter' rig has done much to confuse (or perhaps eventually simplify?) the issue. The cutter has two headsails, a main staysail (nearest to the mast), and (ahead of that) a jib. Sails are called after the spar or stay from which they pivot. The mainsail pivots from the main mast. The main staysail from the main mast stay (the mainstay). The jib is a tricky one though since in the days of square rig the jib was set from a spar called the jibboom and the stay involved was the fore-top-mast-stay! Nowadays in yachts we call it the jib stay. With smaller and greatly simplified (and more efficent to windward) rigs the traditional nomenclature suffers a bit of a sea change at times. But most of the old terms survive, and sailors, being conservative minded as a whole, like this. You don't have to be a 'square' to like the look of square rig, although probably favouring the most up-to-date fore-and-aft rig for your own ship.

The cutter is a very efficient rig if the only criterion is

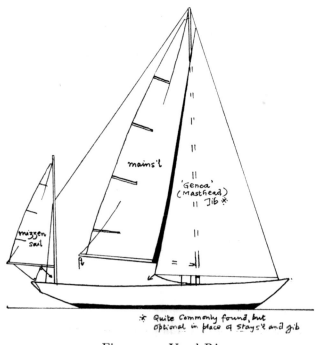

Figure 4. Yawl Rig

performance to windward. In larger yachts the size of the mainsail can become a major problem, however, and so we find in these yachts that the sail plan is broken down into a number of smaller sails by the addition of a second mast.

Figure 4 shows how this is done in the case of the 'yawl' rig. Here the mainsail is smaller and a small mizzensail has been added. In figure 5 we see the mainsail is smaller but the mizzen is not only larger, it is stepped further forward, in front of the steering position in fact, and not, as is the case with the yawl rig, abaft it. This is the ketch rig and many people favour it. William Robinson chose this rig for his *Svaap* in which he sailed round the world. A yawl is a little more close-winded as a rule than a ketch and most two-masted ocean racers carry the yawl rig; although the cutter (or slutter) is the most popular.

The romantically minded reader may by now be saying to himself – 'yes, but what about the schooner – surely the prettiest of all rigs?' I agree, it is! But it is a rig for a large

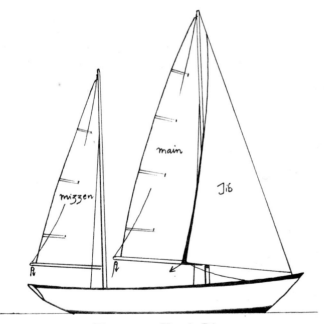

Figure 5.   Ketch Rig

vessel really. Schooner rig on a vessel of less than 40 feet LWL looks a bit silly to my mind, although in theory you can rig any vessel as a schooner. Figure 6 shows typical schooner rig.

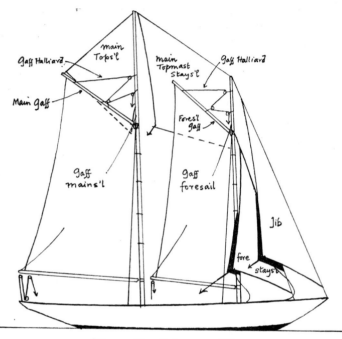

Figure 6.   Schooner Rig

Engines

It is thought by many that the cheapest engine to install in a yacht is one made up from castings of car engines. This is a fallacy. Marine engines have one great difference from car engines – they make use of materials that are resistant to erosion by sea-water and salt-laden atmosphere. There are of course some excellent professionally converted car engines but this is a different matter, and not at all the same as those engines one finds alas too often which are merely car engines with the essential conversion parts omitted. Avoid such engines. Another fallacy is that concerned with horse-power. As a hull moves faster through the water, friction increases between the boat's hull surface and the water. At slow speeds the whole resistance comes from this skin friction. As the hull moves faster a second factor comes into operation; that of waves caused by the inertia of the water which the yacht's hull pushes out of her way. This wave factor varies first as the square of the speed. As the boat continues to move faster, the wave factor increases rapidly until the point of critical speed is reached. From now on any increase in speed can only be obtained by making the boat plane on the surface of the water, thus reducing the friction and wave factors. This is not primarily a technical book and the above is a simplified explanation of the difference between the displacement hull and the planing hull from the point of view of speed.

A cruising sailing yacht may have a light-displacement hull; indeed length for length, some bilge-keel cruisers can have less displacement than a motor-cruiser.

Generally speaking a sailing yacht will use her engine in calms and to facilitate getting in and out of harbours in crowded (or windless) conditions. The motor-cruiser whose sole means of propulsion is her engine (or engines) will tend to have much more horse-power at her disposal. The lighter their displacement and the flatter the after sections of their hulls, the faster they will go. In between the two we have the motor-sailers – often called a 50/50; and unfairly so, as they often represent the best of both worlds. In them, the displacement is likely to be such as to prevent anything much in the way of speed. The maximum speed of a displacement hull is roughly calculable by the following formula $1 \cdot 4\sqrt{\text{load water-line}}$ (in feet) $=$ maximum speed in knots. I say 'roughly' calculable because, with different hull forms the figure '$1 \cdot 4$' varies quite a lot; but it gives a rough idea; and also reveals the important truth that speed is closely related to length.

If you design your boat so that she has a wide 'V'-shaped and almost flat bottom aft and a sharp entry forward, so that she will plane on the surface of the water, you can install much more horse-power without wastage since you will get speed far in excess of the theoretical maximum. However, if your boat is of that shape in which a considerable proportion of the hull is under water, this question of 'wastage' becomes very relevant. Let us take an example.

Suppose you have a 10-hp petrol engine in your boat, which drives her at a maximum speed of 5 knots. For some reason you become dissatisfied with the rate of progress and so you find the money to buy an engine of double the horse-power and install it hopefully. But do you get double the performance? You do not! If you are lucky you may get an extra knot. Now you experience a win on the pools and out goes the 20-hp engine and in its place is installed a 60-hp engine. Eagerly you go on trials, only to find that your new engine will only succeed in giving you 8 knots at the most. The lesson is – when buying a boat look at the engine from the point of view of the use to which it will be put, and relate its size and power to the length and shape of the hull. For the flat-sectioned high-speed motor-cruiser, horse-power will pay off, but for the displacement hull of the 50/50 or the auxiliary sailing yacht, if the engine has power to drive her at her theoretical maximum speed, then she has power enough; anything more is a waste of money (and weight where you least want it!).

Marine engines today are basically petrol or diesel and the arguments for and against each are as long (and often as nebulous) as the Milky Way. The same can be said about the controversy concerning inboard versus outboard engines; and to add to the fun we now have the very popular half in-, half outboard engine, about which I shall have more to say at the end of this section. Most (but not all) outboards make use of the two-stroke principle. In this type of engine there are no valves, and the explosion occurs once in each revolution. Such engines work on a mixture of petrol and oil in a proportion of half to one pint of oil to a gallon of petrol, and are self-lubricating. A two-stroke engine thus has the merits of simplicity and of lightness, but does not run as efficiently as a four-stroke. A two-stroke engine is also cheaper.

The diesel engine has the cycle of induction, compression, explosion and exhaust as the four-stroke petrol engine, but works on the principle that if you compress air sufficiently it will generate enough heat to ignite oil fuel. There is no carburet-tor and no sparking plugs. The induction stroke simply draws air into the cylinder, which is then compressed, and at the moment of highest compression a small amount of fuel is injected at the top of the cylinder. The heat of the compressed air causes the fuel to ignite immediately, power and exhaust strokes following in the same manner as the petrol engine. There are a very large number of marine engines available today with a wide range of power. For example, Ailsa Craig Ltd have petrol engines ranging from 4 bhp to 40 bhp. In diesel their range is smaller consisting of two, the 16 bhp and the 20 bhp. The following list of makes may be of use. Petrol: Ailsa Craig; Aquapower; British Marine; Chrysler; Coventry Victor; Ford; Kelvin-Ricardo; Newage/BMC; Parsons; PNP Duerr Coaster; Renault; Seawitch; Stuart; Sutton Star Class; Universal; Vire; Volvo Penta and Watermota; while in Diesel you have Ailsa Craig; British-International; Caterpillar; Coventry Victor; DAF; Foden; Ford; Fiat; Gardner; General Motors; Gleniffer; Kelvin; Blackstone; Mercedes-Benz; Newage/BMC; Parsons; Perkins; Petter; PNP Duerr Coaster; Rolls-Royce; Saab; Stuart; Sutton Star Class; Thornycroft; Volvo Penta; Watermota; Yannicar and Wortham Blake.

This list, while containing Swedish, Norwegian, Italian, USA, Japanese and West German makes as well as British, is not comprehensive, but will give some idea of the number of makes available and all the makes quoted are known to be reliable. I apologise in advance if I have omitted any reader's favourite! With outboard engines, the list is equally impressive; Albin Husqvarna; AP; Vire; British Anzani; Crescent Marine; Chrysler; Evinrude; Homelite; Johnson; McCulloch; Mercury; Penta and Sea Bee. Finally, the following firms are among those who make sterndrives (or outdrives); that is the inboard engine, outboard screw unit type (very popular for small cruisers today); Chrysler; Crescent; Delta Drive; Evinrude; Johnson; and Mercruiser and Volvo Penta.

With many modern small sailing cruisers the engine is optional and may be inboard or outboard. In the case of motor-cruisers it can again be optional; for example, for the Bertram 25 twin sterndrives are stipulated but the make is left to choice. On the other hand for the Scoresby 32-footer, the designer stipulates a 70-bhp Thornycroft engine driving through a 'V' drive. For the beautiful little Nicholson 26 auxiliary sailing cruiser, Campers will install either a 10-hp Albin Cadet or, if you prefer it, the 8-hp Saab; both of them capable of driving this vessel at a fair speed in calm water; and perfectly adequate for the job. Any larger engine would be a waste of power; which brings me back to my original point.

This would seem to be the right spot for a discussion on that relative newcomer; the inboard/outboard engine (sometimes called 'sterndrives', 'outdrives' or just I/O units). First introduced in Sweden in 1959, it has gained a wide popularity because it combines the advantages of an inboard engine and an outboard engine while managing to eliminate of most the disadvantages. An I/O unit is installed through the boat's transom. It consists of an engine, which is inboard and can be either petrol or diesel, and an outboard drive unit containing a reverse/reduction gearbox, steering swivel, bevel drives and propellor-shaft. In some cases water for cooling is sucked through the outdrive unit, and discharged back through it with the exhaust gases. The propellor thrust steers the vessel (as with the conventional outboard). The propellor unit may be tilted to clear rock or avoid weed. The advantages should be obvious. Here is a protected yet accessible economical inboard four-stroke engine with the steering and propulsion and tilting advantages of an outboard, which makes light of such things as shallow water, rocks and mud berths.

Another relative newcomer is the jet engine. This propels the vessel by means of a directed jet of water. Their popularity is increasing, especially for boats used in waters where the conventional external propellor is in danger of being fouled be weeds or debris. One example is the 'Deflectajet' made by Buckfast outboards. This is a single-cylinder, hand-started engine of 15-inch shaft, running at 3,500 rpm. It weighs 23 lb and costs £35. A larger jet engine is the 'sailjet', 3,600–5,000 rpm. The model known as the BE 150 weighs only 21 lb and costs £55. The makers are Shipelle Ltd. A larger model still, the BE 250, weighs 39 lb and costs £110.

Materials – Wood versus GRP

A visit to a boat showroom nowadays will reveal the continually increasing number of glass-reinforced plastic yachts, commonly called 'GRP' for convenience. This does not mean that wood is going out of fashion for boat building. There are advantages and disadvantages on both sides, however, and I will try and state them briefly. Let us take wood first as it is the traditional material for building boats. There have been great technical advances in glue making and this has brought about a revolution in wooden boat construction. The techniques of hot and cold moulding, using layer upon layer to build up a hull, produces great strength and resilience. Remember Sir Francis Chichester's *Gipsy Moth IV*? She was built this way, and no one can doubt her strength! Again, the lamination of structural members from thinner sections of wood, produces members shaped exactly right for the design. In former times such members had to be made from naturally grown shapes. Another innovation made possible by modern glues is marine plywood. There is, too, a much wider variety of timbers available to the boat builder today; much more is imported than hitherto. Everyone knows of oak, ash, pine, elm and teak; but did you know of afrormosia for planking and decks, guavea for frames, of opepe or danta for keels? They are all good durable woods. Wood has for many great aesthetic appeal. Have you noticed how many glassfibre hulls are 'trimmed' with wood for this very reason? But what are the disadvantages?

The enemies of wood are rot and what are called 'marine borers', small worms that bore into the wood. These latter can cause considerable damage. Modern anti-fouling paint will protect the hull to a large extent and some modern woods like afrormosia and opepe have, like teak, considerable resistance to worm. Nevertheless, one thing you can say about GRP is that wood rot and worms make no impression on it; so let's take a look at GRP.

Its advantage is that it can be moulded easily into any desired shape. It is quite impervious to water and it is very strong. Its disadvantage is that the laminate is, though strong, flexible by comparison with a piece of wood of equal thickness. However, the greater the curvature the stronger, and one particular advantage is that, since GRP can be moulded to any shape, the designer has a very free hand.

Now what exactly is GRP? The laminate is composed of two basic components, resin and glassfibre. To describe a yacht as being of glassfibre or 'fibreglass' is misleading because only about 40 per cent by weight is of glass. The function of the glass is to strengthen, being used in the form of a chopped strand mat, woven rovings or woven cloth. Two types of resin are suitable for laminating; polyesters and epoxides, the most common being the former. To the resin is added an accelerator and afterwards a catalyst whose function is to cause polymerisation. Probably the most obvious advantage of GRP is the ease with which both repairs and maintenance can be carried out. No more scraping or caulking! You can leave a GRP hull afloat all winter if you want to. Of course it is wrong to imagine that no painting of the hull is necessary, perhaps not after one season, but it will be after two! However, this is purely a matter of aesthetics rather than a structural necessity as it is with wood.

To conclude, wood has been used in yacht building for a very much longer time than GRP has, and for this reason alone GRP may still have some prejudice against it; it shouldn't have. The firm of Camper and Nicholson build jointly with the firm of Halmatic some very strong and proven cruisers in GRP. (The 32 ft and the 36 ft, 38 ft and 43 ft for example) and C and N have always been renowned for craftmanship and producing tough, seaworthy vessels. On the other hand, when Sir Francis Chichester wanted a 'world-circler' he chose wood! It has become more a matter of taste!

CHAPTER TWO

The Boat

A selection to choose from

In presenting this selection of cruising boats, including some power cruisers, motor-sailers and multihulls, I am aware of the dangers of obsolescence. Just as it can be said that a man starts dying the day he is born; so a yacht begins to grow out of date the day she leaves the launching slipway. In point of fact these are all up-to-date craft at the time of writing; but that is not of first importance and I hope the exaggerated maxim above will cast enough ridicule on the notion that, because a vessel may be three or four years old, she is of no interest and has no use. The basic principles of the design of cruising yachts don't change all that quickly. In this collection I am seeking to give the reader an idea of the variety of craft available; so that he can compare dimensions, rigs, hull forms, accommodation, etc. It is *not* suggested that he should make his choice from my selection (there are many craft not included which are just as good), but that having read this chapter his ideas, perhaps vague to start with, will crystallise into a definite form. He will, I hope, know more the *sort* of boat he wants. Having got that very necessary proviso off my chest, let us now look at the boats.

Barbel I and Barbel II

I cannot believe that you can get a sailing cruiser much smaller than this! I would even bet that *Barbel II* is just about the smallest two-berth sailing yacht in production. Mr M. S. Redman of Woodham Ferrers in Essex is the man we must thank for giving us a workmanlike little cruiser for as little as

BARBEL I
Round bilge twin keel
L.O.A. 12 ft (3658 mm)
Beam 5 ft (1524 mm)
Draft 1 ft (305 mm)
Sail Area 50 to 60 sq ft
(5·58 sq m)
Wt. 350 lbs (158 kg env)

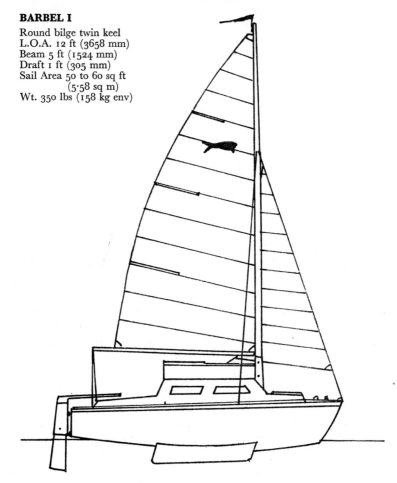

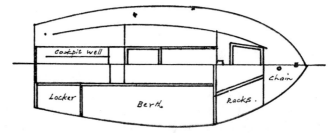

Figure 7 (*a*). Sail plan of *Barbel I*

BARBEL II

Double chine twin keel
L.O.A. 14 ft (4267 mm)
Beam 5 ft 1 in (1549 mm)
Draft 1 ft (305 mm)
Sail Area 90 to 100 sq ft
        (9·29 sq m)
Wt. 350 lbs 158 kg env

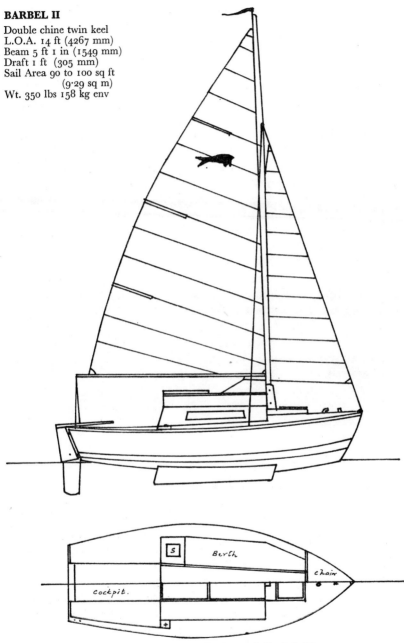

Figure 7 (*b*). Sail plan of *Barbel II*

37

£300! Let us start by checking her measurements: LOA 12 ft
(3·65 m); LWL 11 ft 3 ins (3·42 m); beam 5 ft (1·52 m); draft
1 ft (0·305 m); sail area 60 sq ft (5·57 sq m); headroom 3 ft 3 ins
(0·990 m) (ouch! – never mind – the late E. F. Knight, of
'Falcon on the Baltic' fame, said 'if you want to stand up you
can always go on deck!'). If you are thinking that 12-foot
LOA is perhaps a tiny bit small, Mr Redman has already
anticipated you in *Barbel II*, measuring as follows: LOA 14 ft
(4·267 m); beam 5 ft 1 in (1·54 m); draft 1 ft (0·305 m); sail area
100 sq ft (9·29 sq m). *Barbel II* will cost you £100 more (£400).
The drawing (figure 7) shows the sail plan of both boats, and
the coachroof arrangement of *Barbel II*. *Barbel I* is round bilge
construction; her larger sister, double chine. This sister's
advantage to most people will be the greater space both below
and in the cockpit. Planking and decking are in ¼-in plywood.
Mast and boom are Columbian or Panama pine. According to
Mr Redman the basic cost of materials, including ropes and
sails, is £125, takes about 300 hours to build from basic wood.
You can buy her plans (five sheets) for £3 3s (which includes
the royalty for one boat). This is in Britain; abroad add 5s.
Accommodation plan can be modified to suit the owner, for
example a family with small children – (but not, I should
imagine quintuplets). With their shallow draft (1 foot) and
twin keels the *Barbel* sisters can go anywhere and take the
ground happily. Buoyancy is built in. You can of course trail
her – almost with a bicycle. Time off; to raise a glass and
toast the thanks of all sailors of small means to Mr M. S.
Redman!

Alacrity Mk II

This little cruiser (and I mean 'little') first introduced in 1961,
can now be found happily cruising the seas and lakes of
Canada, the United States, Sweden, Denmark, Germany,
Holland, Switzerland, France, Italy and South Africa as well as
all round the coasts of the British Isles. Peter Stephenson is the
designer and in giving the hull twin bilge keels he was well in
the tradition of the British East Coast for he was a designer at
Burnham-on-Crouch at the time of the conception of the
vessel. Twin bilge keels are of enormous advantage in such
tidal waters. They allow the boat to sit upright on the mud at

low water. But Stephenson claims that bilge keels, as fitted to *Alacrity*, not only fulfil this function but also give a good performance to windward, since the lee keel is more deeply immersed when the vessel is heeled while the weather keel develops a righting moment. It is the same principle as the East Coast sailing barge with her twin leeboards; and who can doubt that Stephenson is right?

Let's look at measurements: LOA 18 ft 6 ins (5·70 m); LWL 17 ft (5·20 m); beam 6 ft 11 ins (2·10 m); draft 1 ft 10 ins (0·55 m). The areas of the working sails are: mainsail 95 sq ft (9·0 sq m); headsail 55 sq ft (5·20 sq m); and she carries a Genoa jib of 90 sq ft (8·50 sq m). Notice that she is only 17 feet on the water-line because it is then all the more remarkable that she can accommodate three berths. Headroom in a vessel this size is bound to be limited but the 4 ft 2 in (1·50 m) is good for her size. She has a toilet and a galley. There is a fitting for an outboard engine on the transom which allows the engine to be tilted clear of the water when sailing; but in a handy little vessel like this, I can't see one often needing an engine!

Now a word about specification. The hull is of Lloyds approved GRP, using four 1½-oz glass cloths above the water-line and six cloths below. The deck is also of GRP as is the coachroof. Hatches are of GRP but there are wooden hand-rails either side of the coachroof in addition to the usual wood trimming to be found in GRP hulls. There are those who dislike wood trim, holding that 'a glassfibre yacht is a glassfibre yacht dammit! and why pretend it's made of wood?' However, a large number of people do seem to like the blank plastic to be relieved with a little iroko or mahogany or what have you. The decks of *Alacrity* are impressed with *Trakmark* to give a non-slip surface. In the saloon below bulkheads and interior fittings are in marine-ply. Mast and boom are of aluminium alloy. A final point in favour of this economically maintained vessel is the basic price of £745.

Vivacity

Another small vessel, just 6 inches longer on the load water-line, is *Vivacity*. She is a good-looking craft as a glance at the photograph (Plate 3) will show. The now typical round bilge hull in GRP can be fitted with either single fin keel or hydrofoil twin keels, according to the taste of the new owner and suitability for the area in which he will be doing most of his sailing. Like *Alacrity*, this vessel is easily trailed with all the advantages of holiday planning that it brings. It needs little imagination to picture the difference in time between trailing a yacht from England to the Mediterranean and sailing her round via Biscay, the west Spanish coast and through the Strait of Gibraltar or even of making the passage through the French canals. This latter evolution takes about a month (although it *can* be done in three weeks if you're lucky with the locks) while to trail from Boulogne to Nice will only take a very few days. But what is of more importance is that the journey back to England by French waterways is far harder. The Rhône river runs at a speed to make the average auxiliary engine useless and it is necessary to engage in the considerable expense of a tow. Whereas behind your car the return passage is simplicity itself. On arrival at Boulogne you simply trail the boat on board one of the ferry steamers and in well under two hours you are back on British soil. This whole exciting question of the way in which small modern yachts can cruise in waters may hundreds of miles from the home port within the compass of the average summer holiday is dealt with more fully in chapter three. The point I am making here is that craft like *Alacrity* and *Vivacity* are not only of a size to permit easy trailing, but are sufficiently seaworthy to make quite long passages once the new cruising ground has been reached.

Let us now take a look at *Vivacity*'s measurements and general specification. LOA 20 ft (6·096 m); LWL 18 ft 6 ins (5·634 m); beam 7 ft (2·134 m); draft 2 ft 4 ins (0·711 m). Yacht measurement tonnage works out at 3·4 while displacement is 1,800 lbs (816·47 kg). Her mainsail is 100 sq ft (9·29 sq m) and working headsail 75 sq ft (6·97 sq m). In addition a storm jib and Genoa are specified. All these sails are in 5-oz Terylene. The hull is Lloyds approved GRP using the hand-laid chopped strand mat 6 oz above water-line and 10 oz below. Deck, doghouse, etc are also of GRP and so are the hatches. Mast and boom are of aluminium, the mast being stepped on a laminated mahogany main beam. The standing rigging which supports the mast (masthead rig) is of stainless steel and running rigging is of Terylene.

Below decks are four full length (6 ft 2 ins) berths. The galley is located amidships, cooker to port, sink to starboard. The WC is right forward at the point where the two forward berths meet and under the forehatch. To starboard of the self-draining cockpit is stowage for an outboard motor, which when in use ships on the port side of the (outboard) rudder fitting, sliding into tracks on the transom.

The little vessel is well within the average man's pocket and is economical to maintain. It is difficult to give hard figures but as a guide a glassfibre sloop of this type should cost little more than 30s a week to run including insurance and fuel, while depreciation rates are almost negligible. Standard basic cost at time of writing is £945.

The 4-hp Seagull outboard for either *Alacrity* or *Vivacity* costs about £57.

Victoire 22

From Holland in 1660 the first yacht came to England; a gift from that great seafaring country to King Charles II on his restoration to the English throne. Yacht is a word of Dutch origin and the Hollanders invented yachting; so it is fitting that I include here this personable little sailing cruiser, the 21 ft 8 ins overall *Victoire 22*. Jachtwerf Victoria of Alkmaar are responsible for this tough little class, members of which have carried off a lot of offshore racing prices. *Victoire 22* is a glassfibre boat trimmed with mahogany. The hull is round bilge and she has a fin keel and separate rudder and there is an alternative centreboard model. Under each quarter berth, she carries an air chamber and with a third air chamber in the forepeak she can be said to be unsinkable. If you want to sail round the world and you don't mind much about headroom (4 ft 6 ins (1·371 m)) and you've only got £1,000 to spend; an unsinkable yacht with all the Dutch know-how is surely a good proposition. The price in fact, at time of writing, is £1,090 standard version. For what is called the 'luxury' version £1,250 is the figure. As with all these prices and specifications there are of course the usual 'extras' available; among the extras are: pulpit stanchions and life-lines (important for extended cruising); Dacron Genoa jib and storm jib, nylon spinnaker and roller reefing (standard version has points or lacing). Another extra you may want is an outboard (make optional) but, with a working sail area of 175 sq ft (16·25 sq m) on just under 19-ft LWL, an engine may be an extra, it is not a necessity.

Dimensions are as follows: LOA 21 ft 8 ins (6·60 m); LWL 18 ft 8 ins (5·70 m); displacement is 2,550 lbs (1,150 kg). This little ship is obviously a good bet for the cruising man of moderate means. She sleeps four (two settee berths and two quarter berths). She is well designed, seaworthy and fun to sail. I was going to add that she is a good-looker, but you've got the photograph (Plate 4) to show that. She's going well too isn't she? And look at the Genoa doing its work!

Kestrel 22

Look now at *Kestrel 22*. The photograph (Plate 5) gives a good idea of this handy little vessel and figure 8 shows her hull and sail plan. First of all, measurements: LOA 22 ft (6·70 m); LWL 19 ft 8 ins (6·00 m); beam 7 ft 1 in (2·16 m); draft single (deep) keel 3 ft 3 ins (0·99 m); draft (twin keels) 2 ft 3 ins (0·68 m). Her yacht measurement tonnage works out at 4 tons, and her displacement tonnage at 1·33 tons (1,471 kg), and her working sail area (mainsail and headsail) is 227 sq ft (21 sq m). As for materials – she is built of glass-reinforced plastic – a one-piece moulding. Her plastic deck and coachroof are bonded to the hull, the joint protected by a wooden rubbing piece. As is frequently the case with plastic yachts, to avoid an appearance of starkness wood is used for hatches, hand-rails and trimming, the wood being iroko or mahogany. Below decks woodwork is of mahogany and mahogany-faced ply. Mast and spars are hollow spruce and the mast is supported by stays and shrouds (the arrangement of which can easily be seen in the drawing) of stainless steel. Running rigging is of Terylene. The single keel weighs 1,000 lbs (454 kg) or if you prefer the twin-keel version – the weight is divided, the two keels weighing 500 lbs each. In either case the keels are of cast iron. It will be noticed that the rig is masthead.

This little vessel is a proven success. Her very experienced designer, Francis Jones produced a design originally for a wooden vessel, and this glass-reinforced plastic version is the logical development. Indeed improvements are being added or replaced all the time and the newest models will include gold anodised alloy spars instead of spruce, a Lloyds certificate with

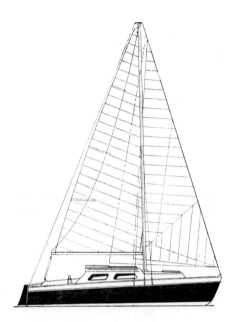

Figure 8.   Sail plan of *Kestrel 22*

each boat (certifying that the yacht is built to Lloyd's specifications) and external woodwork will be available in afrormosia.
Over 170 *Kestrels* have been built. In the 1968 yacht world
rally *Kestrel* was included in the 'top ten'. You can be sure
that this is a tried and trusted vessel should she meet your
requirements.

For accommodation four full-sized berths are carried in two
separate compartments; two in the saloon and two in the
forward cabin. The space between the forward berths can be
filled in to make either a double bunk or to make room for three
children. The two compartments, saloon and fo'c'sle are
separated by a good-sized toilet compartment.

The basic model is not fitted with an engine and this helps to
keep the price down, but an engine can be supplied, the make
being either the Vire model BVK 6-hp petrol engine, or the
BVR model which has the addition of a reverse, neutral and
ahead gearbox with 2–1 reduction gear; the cheaper engine
having ahead and neutral only. In this connection, that of
extra costs, etc, it is always difficult if not dangerous to quote
prices in a book of this sort. At the time of writing the twin-keel
Kestrel sells at around £1,400 and the single keel for a little more.
The two engine models are about £168 and £230 extra; and
there is a host of other optional extras ranging from additional
sails, Genoa jib and spinnaker for example, to electric lighting
in the cabin. You can for just over £100 buy a trailer to take
Kestrel around by land which can be of great advantage where
time is at a premium. But all these prices can and probably will
rise as everything in sailing seems to cost a little more each
succeeding year. For all that one can see with half an eye that
this is good value for money. *Kestrel 22* is a sturdy little ship and
you can see from the plans and photograph, she is a good-looker
too!

Islander 23

Let us now take a look at another small sloop, *Islander 23*, again
an attractive little vessel as the photograph (Plate 6) will show.
Again the popular masthead rig carries in the working sails no
more than two people can handle with ease. Indeed for those
who like to go it alone; single-handed sailing is perfectly possible
in all these small cruisers. Careful planning has produced snug

interior accommodation with berths for four. I am including *Islander 23* here because she is a small cruiser which you can build yourself; not by any means the only one; but she provides a very fair example of a boat of this sort for home assembly. From the specification issued by Russell Marine of Southend-on-Sea, Essex, in England, it is easy to see the various stages of construction and to work out for oneself how much time is required and what is done by the yard already and what you have to do. The prospective amateur builder receives the hull (in GRP) complete with deck and superstructure with the following already fitted: tabernacle (for the mast), king post, coachroof hand-rails, rudder, stem-head fittings, chain plates (for the shrouds) and deck-rubbing strakes. Together with this comes separately all fastenings, fittings, wooden parts, mast, boom, rigging and the following sails: Mainsail 125 sq ft (11·60 sq m); working headsail 85 sq ft (7·90 sq m); Genoa 120 sq ft (10·80 sq m) and spinnaker 270 sq ft (24·30 sq m). Storm jib and ghoster can also be supplied. All the woodwork is supplied sanded ready for varnishing and made rig; and they even drill and countersink screw and bolt holes! If this is by now giving you the idea that you have little left to do, let me correct that impression by telling you that twenty-four separate stages have been worked out for you, stages which it would be wise to follow as they have clearly involved a lot of thought. The time of completion of each stage is also given, but this must be an approximation depending on the speed of working and experience of the amateur builder, for although there is nothing very complicated in the work those accustomed to carpentry and jobs about the home will get along faster than the complete novice to construction of any kind. The time estimated, adding up all the stages is 27½ hours – I like that '½' hour and wording of the final stage (number 24) – 'immediately after launching and before having the party, check all skin fittings for water-tightness then – have fun and happy sailing'. In conclusion a brief look at *Islander*'s measurements: LOA 22 ft 6 ins (6·86 m); LWL 20 ft (6·10 m); beam 7 ft 6 ins (2·29 m); draft 2 ft 9 ins (0·84 m); displacement tonnage is 2,688 lbs (1,220 kg).

Of course if you want to you can buy *Islander* already built and she will set you back £1,395 (at the time of writing that is) – but if you build her yourself you'll knock quite a bit off that.

Mapleleaf

The design on the sail, as seen in the attractive photograph (Plate 7) taken by Miss Linda Norman, tells passing yachts that they are in the company of a *Mapleleaf* class yacht, a 4½-ton shoal-draft sloop-rigged centreboarder. Designed and built by Chandler and Smith of Great Wakering, Essex, in England, this little vessel (18 foot water-line) costs only £1,595. Since making her début in 1959, *Mapleleaf* has proved herself fast, weatherly and comfortable below – an ideal little family cruiser. She is easy to handle and can be sailed easily by one person: Let's look at her dimensions: LOA 22 ft 9 ins (6·93 m); LWL 18 ft 1 in (5·51 m); beam 7 ft 6 ins (2·28 m); draft (board raised) 2 ft 6 ins (0·76 m); (board lowered) 5 ft (1·52 m). Displacement is 2·15 tons (2,794 kg); working sail area is 230 sq ft (21·36 sq m). For engine a Stuart Turner 5 hp is specified. Below decks she can sleep three people. Headroom in the cabin is 4 ft 3 ins and in the doghouse 4 ft 9 ins. *Mapleleaf* is planked in mahogany in the clinker method; her timbers being Canadian rock elm. Deck is ⅜-in marine ply covered with Trakmark. Both engine and working sails are part of standard equipment. Indeed *Mapleleaf* comes very adequately fitted and as bargains go she must be well up the list of favourites.

Magyar 7

If my reader is one, and there are many such, of those who prefer wood to plastics, and who tend to equate (however unfairly) GRP boats with bath-tubs, here is something to raise his spirits. From a country in the heart of Europe comes this delightful little cruiser able to take open sea as well as river and lake sailing and with her raising rudder and shallow draft equally at home in creeks, estuaries and shoal waters. It might be expected that such an all-purpose vessel would come from a race of people with both flair and capability and *Magyar 7* 'hails' in every sense of the word from Hungary.

Magyar 7 is a twin-keel fast cruiser, built of wood in the traditional method, using ¾-inch pine planking on oak frames and non-ferrous fastenings. The hull is of carvel construction but is round-bilged, having a double chine amidships tapering to a single chine at bow and stern. The deck is in marine ply

or pine planking, canvas covered. Coachroof is pine and
mahogany; coamings, mahogany. Mast and spars are spruce
and the ballast keel, cast iron. All in all a thoroughly traditional
specification of high quality. Dimensions are: LOA 23 ft 9 ins
(7·23 m); LWL 22 ft (6·7 m); beam 7 ft 9 ins (2·36 m); draft
2 ft 3 ins (0·68 m); displacement tonnage 3,086 lbs (1,399·7 kg).
Standard (Terylene) sails are: mainsail 150 sq ft (13·93 sq m);
working headsail 65 sq ft (6·03 sq m) and Genoa 91 sq ft
(8·45 sq m).

There are enough *Magyar 7* owners around the world for a
pretty impressive survey of yachting opinion and it appears to
be uniformly good. There is now a Mark II version of the
Magyar 7 in which the coachroof has been extended forward and
the mast stepped on the reinforced coachroof and a doghouse
has been included. The effect of this is to open up accommodation below decks and a WC is standard fitting in the Mark II.
There is space for a WC amidships in the *Magyar 7*, but it (a
'baby' Blake) is an optional extra, costing in British money
£75 19*s*, a slightly cheaper WC the 'Lavac' costs £52 11*s*. The
galley installation is also an extra. The Mark II vessel is not
intended as a replacement for the original *Magyar 7*; it is for
the yachtsman who prefers standing headroom, even if it means
a little sacrifice of performance. For this added top-hamper
must be compensated by additional ballast (550 kg) and, since
the hull form is unchanged, the Mark II will sit slightly deeper
in the water and a little more surface friction will result. The
two prices are *Magyar 7* basic hull, sails and gear £1,095; while
Mark II costs £1,195. Both are clearly good value. An engine is
another optional item and consists of a Vire 6-hp outboard
which rides up and down two runners on the port hand side of
the transom. An attractive feature is the deck room; there is
good space forward and on the side decks for reefing the main;
changing headsail, anchoring and all such pleasant tasks. From
any angle *Magyar 7* is a good-looker. Glance at that photo (Plate
8) once again!

If you feel like an extra 7 feet overall length in the same basic
design; the *Magyar 9* may well interest you. In this vessel there
is a fitted Volvo Penta 15½-hp engine and of course much more
space below. You don't get that for nothing and you'll have to
find £3,500! But for a vessel that sleeps five that's still pretty
good.

East Anglian

Here is a vessel from a good stable if I may be allowed that equestrian phrase. When Alan Buchanan designs and Dixon Kerly of Maldon (Essex) build, you can be sure that the design and construction are good. In this case, the *East Anglians* are built of mahogany, copper fastened, on oak frames and with laid decks. For a 21-foot water-line yacht the price (£3,450 basic) may seem high but it is not. This is a beautifully built little ship to a high specification. Furthermore, she is not all that 'little', her yacht measurement tonnage working out at 6½ tons. Of course by the time you have acquired those extras she'll come to nearer £4,000 if not more and the price of a fully equipped (and I mean very *fully*) *East Anglian* today will be around £4,250. Even so, the price, if you can afford it, is by today's standards by no means high; and you are getting a little gem for your money. Let's have a look at measurements: LOA 27 ft 9 ins (8·45 m); LWL 21 ft (6·40 m); beam 8 ft (2·43 m); draft 4 ft 6 ins (1·371 m); displacement 3·7 tons; sails are Terylene, main 206 sq ft (19·13 sq m); headsail 101 sq ft (9·38 sq m); spinnaker 404 sq ft (37·53 sq m). For engine an 8-hp two cylinder Stuart Turner is specified.

I suppose I am open to accusations of 'squareness', but there is something very attractive about a wooden ship built by craftsmen. Accommodation below is by no means square, however, being light and airy and well planned. The large galley area is a feature always appreciated as one seems so often to be eating when cruising, and the cook must have room to operate. What a delightful little yacht, with her jaunty sheer, this is!

Contest 25

Here's an interesting boat from Holland, a fin keel family cruiser, called *Contest 25* (*Mark III*). *Contest 25* is built in the Conyplex factory at Medemblik, in the Netherlands; a Lloyds approved yard for the building of GRP (glass-reinforced plastic yachts, and construction is to Lloyds approved standards). Let's look first at measurements. LOA 25 ft (7·62 m); LWL 20 ft 6 ins (6·24 m); beam 7 ft 3 ins (2·20 m); draft 3 ft 11¼ ins (1·20 m). The displacement tonnage is about 4,400 lbs (2,013 kg) and this includes the engine, a four-stroke 5-hp slow-revving Marstal engine, giving about 6 knots in smooth water. It has electric starting. The cast-iron ballast keel weighs 1,900 lbs (861 kg). Sail areas are as follows: mainsail 134 sq ft (12·44 sq m); working jib 105 sq ft (9·75 sq m); storm jib 52 sq ft (4·83 sq m); Genoa 180 sq ft (16·72 sq m); No. 2 Genoa 137 sq ft (12·72 sq m); spinnaker 430 sq ft (39·94 sq m) and spinnaker staysail 86 sq ft (7·99 sq m). Quite an inventory of sails! And they are made by Ratsey and Lapthorne in Terylene. This yacht is the newest version of a very popular class indeed. Hull, deck and superstructure are of GRP. Large windows and a translucent glassfibre top to the forehatch give plenty of light below decks.

Mast and spars are of spruce. Standing rigging is stainless steel and running rigging Terylene. The main boom is fitted with roller reefing. General gear includes Danforth anchor and 100 foot of ¼-inch chain, the sheet winches, whale bilge pump, halyard mast winch, etc. I could go on, but the point I am making is that this little ship is well found. There are of course a large number of optional extras, like echo sounder, barometer, clock and even such refinements as an insulated backstay and (anti-chafe) plastic tube round the shrouds! All this of course costs money. The basic price of *Contest 25* is about £3,000 in Great Britain – a figure which includes the 8 per cent import duty, discounts may or may not be given according to Government policy; but is must be appreciated that this figure applies *only to Great Britain* and will clearly differ slightly in other countries. While with rising costs, *Contest* is unlikely to get any cheaper over the years; she represents to my mind excellent value. Nearly 300 *Contest 25*'s have been built at the time of writing. Once again we have been examining a well-tried vessel. The *Contest* was first introduced in Britian in 1963 at the Earls Court Boat Show. The original design had five berths, but experience showed this to be too cramped, and the vessel now has four. Accommodation below is now excellent; in addition to the four berths there is hanging space for oilskins, chart table with a good-sized chart drawer, and a serviceable galley. As with many glassfibre yachts, there is a fair amount of mahogany and teak trimming on deck.

Folkboat

The Scandinavian-designed *Folkboat* is a very well-known International Class and is probably the most popular 5-tonner in

Europe, and there are hundreds of *Folkboats* in use all over the world. There are several variations of the 'cruising' *Folkboat* and without wishing to make any particular inference I have selected the German-built version as imported by City Centre Boatyard of Glasgow. It is not the cheapest of the versions, but it is an attractive design as the photograph (Plate 11) shows and is well-fitted below decks so that a family can live aboard in comfort. The exhilarating sailing qualities of these beautiful little vessels come as near as you can get to achieving the difficult combination of handling almost like a dinghy and yet being able to venture offshore in safety.

This version is carvel built of mahogany planking, unlike many other early versions which were clinker built. Frames are of oak and fastenings are bronze screws. Mast and spars are pine or spruce. There are four berths in two cabins and 5 ft 9 ins headroom under the doghouse; the WC is between the two forward berths, and the galley in the right place slightly aft of amidships where the vessel is wide and the motion at sea the least. Measurements are: LOA 25 ft (7·62 m); LWL 19 ft 8¼ ins (5·695 m); beam 7 ft 2½ ins (2·196 m); draft 3 ft 10¾ ins (1·181 m); the working sail area (sloop rig) is 258 sq ft (23·97 sq m). You can select your own make of engine; City Centre suggest a number ranging from a Seagull Century long-shaft outboard for £60 to a 10-hp Volvo Penta for £325. Working sails come in the basic price of £1,990 (at time of writing) but storm jib, Genoa and spinnaker are extra. I should mention (and I make no apology when I repeat this) that when buying a new vessel you will almost always find that you will both need and desire a number of extras which will raise the final figure up quite a bit above the basic price. The prices I give in this book are to give a general idea of the sort of money needed to purchase a given type of yacht at the time of writing. With this *Folkboat*, of one thing you may be certain; it represents thoroughly proven value for money!

Queen Bee

The pleasing lines of this 6½-tonner designed by A. K. Balfour can be followed in Figure 9 which shows her plans. *Queen Bee* yachts are of carvel construction in mahogany strip plank. The designer's intention to produce a comfortable, 6-ft

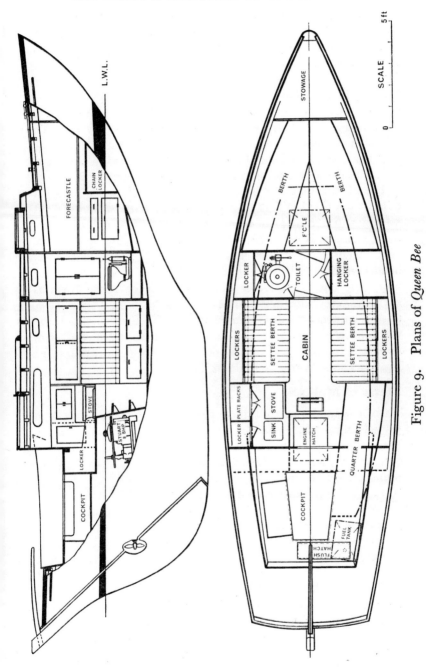

Figure 9. Plans of *Queen Bee*

headroom, four to six berth cruising yacht has resulted in these yachts which meet the needs of an increasing sector of the cruising public. For a man who can afford £3,290 or thereabouts, this yacht (which comes with standard 6-hp Penta MD1 diesel engine and working sails for that figure) takes a lot of beating. She is an ideal family cruiser with room for additional guests if your family is not all that big and she is of a size and seaworthiness to make extended and interesting cruises. To follow in the footsteps of E. F. Knight to the Baltic or sail to the west coast of Ireland should represent no problem, provided of course that the seamanship and navigation are up to it!

The proportions of this compact little vessel are: LOA 27 ft 6 ins (8·382 m); LWL 21 ft (6·40 m); beam 8 ft (2·438 m); draft 5 ft 6 ins (1·676 m); sail area 309 sq ft (28·70 sq m); displacement tonnage is 4·25. The absence of a doghouse adds to the attractiveness of her design and you still get 6-ft (1·828 m) headroom below. With 20-gallon (90·919 lit) tanks aboard for both fuel and fresh water and good storage space there is nothing, except the limitations of the time available for cruising, to stop your nosing into many a far port in this yacht; and she will look after you with her sea-kindly lines and 3,000 lbs of ballast on the way there too. If you want to know more about the *Bee*, try Dixon Kerly of Maldon, Essex.

Merle of Malham

There cannot be many sailing people who have not heard of John Illingworth. Formerly a successful ocean racing man he has for some years now made a reputation as a most original designer of yachts. *Merle of Malham* is typical. Just look at her plans (figure 10) and the photograph (Plate 12). Certain features stand out. Notice the bow; the tall thin high-aspect-ratio mainsail; the mast stepped right into the boat (a 'slutter' rig if ever there was one) and the great foretriangle in which a variety of head-sail may be set. This boat looks fast and she is, and when you are at the helm you know you have a thoroughbred in your hands.

She is not large (about 3½ tons yacht measurement), her dimensions being: LOA 26 ft 6 ins (8·07 m); LWL 21 ft (6·40 m); beam 8 ft 2 ins (2·48 m); draft 4 ft 4 ins (1·32 m); sail area is 237 sq ft (22·01 sq m). No particular engine is specified but the designers Illingworth and Associates of Emsworth in

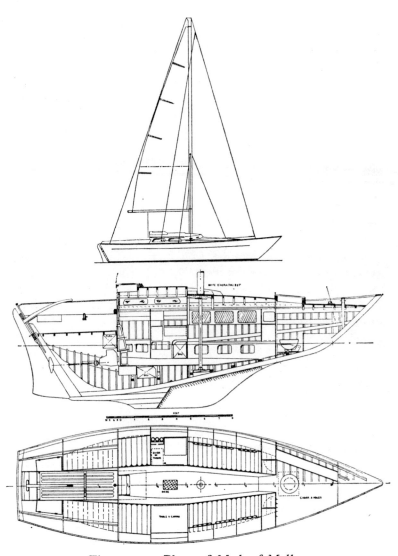

Figure 10. Plans of *Merle of Malham*

Hampshire will help you make a suitable choice. *Merle of Malham* (remember the 'Myth'?) is built of mahogany carvel planking on rock elm bent frames. Decks and superstructure are ply. She sleeps four people and, as usual with Illingworth, has proved to be sound practice by all who go well offshore, the galley and chart table are allotted generous space amidships. This vessel at the time of writing costs around £2,800. A sister ship *Alacrity III* (a very successful racer) has a somewhat larger coachroof. And before you say that this sort of fast cruiser/racer is hard to handle, may I assure you that she is just exactly the opposite!

Nicholson 26

From the well-known firm of designers and builders, Camper and Nicholson, comes this, the smallest of their offshore cruiser-racer range, the *Nicholson 26*. As one would expect from this firm, we have here a handsome yacht, seaworthy, thoroughly well-appointed. She handles well being easily sailed by the average family crew, and is ideal for our purposes here. The hull and deck are all moulded in GRP, the coachroof top being of sandwich construction and able to provide insulation as well as being very strong. She has a lead keel, moulded inside the hull (2·286 kg). This is a yacht of high specification and she is going to cost you that much more; the starting price being around £4,660. No one would expect otherwise, and for what you get she is good value. A feature of the design is the arrangement of two quarter (over 6 feet) berths and two settee berths in the saloon (with galley and sink between them amidships), in such a way as to leave a good space up forward to house a WC, a wash-basin to port and a good cupboard to starboard. There is good headroom (6 feet) under the long raised part of the coachroof, the extent of it being quite an unusual feature in a vessel of this size. She has the complement of Terylene sails that we expect nowadays in vessels of this type and size, ie, main 150 sq ft (13·94 sq m); working headsail 152 sq ft (14·12 sq m). (Notice it is larger than the very modern, high-aspect-ratio mainsail); Genoa 230 sq ft (21·37 sq m) and of course spinnaker and storm jib are available. Rig, as can be seen from the illustration (Plate 13), is mast head.

Mast and spars are gold anodised aluminium (Ian Proctor);

standing rigging is stainless-steel wire and the halyards are flexible galvanised wire with Terylene tails; other running rigging is Terylene. For motor power she can have either the 10-hp Albin Cadet or if you prefer diesel – the Saab 8 hp. Her measurements are: LOA 26 ft 7 ins (8·10 m); LWL 20 ft (6·09 m); beam 7 ft 9 ins (2·36 m); displacement tonnage 4·21 tons (4,073 kg) and the yacht measurement tonnage works out at 6. This is a vessel not only good to look at but fully competent to go offshore.

Hillyard 9 Tonner

In the days before the war, a gentleman in Littlehampton called David Hillyard became the young and impecunious yachtman's benefactor by building sea-going craft for very moderate prices. Although the blue-eyed, white-haired David has passed to a better world (where I hope he can still sail) the yard continues to flourish under first-class management and to maintain its traditions. The 9-tonner chosen here is fairly typical – and when I say that she comes fitted with a BMC Navigator engine (electric starting) and Terylene working sails for £4,100 you will see what I mean. For this is a full 9-tonner. LOA 32 ft (9·75 m); beam 8 ft 6 ins (2·59 m) and draft 4 ft 6 ins (1·37 m). Berths are for six, the design being centre cockpit. Materials are: planking mahogany (carvel laid) on oak timbers and frames. Decks are ply covered with GRP; fastenings are copper. Brightwork is in mahogany. The photograph (Plate 14) gives a good idea of her pleasing appearance. There are of course extras for those who want them – Petter or Perkins diesel in place of the Navigator engine – Terylene Genoa (well worth having at £45), but as always with a Hillyard boat, the specification is plain and workmanlike and you get your money's worth. You can go places in them too – I know – I sailed many sea miles in a Hillyard 9-tonner some years ago.

Apache 37

The name Chris-Craft is universally associated with power boats – a huge range from small fast craft to large luxury cruisers, and so it is with great interest that we can take a look at this fine sloop-rigged sailing cruiser. Take a look at the photograph (Plate 15). Sparkman and Stephens designed this yacht – I could not very well not include an 'S and S' design could I? – and she has many interesting features. Sparkman and Stephens designers of many an ocean racer, to say nothing of successful America's Cup defenders have created here a most individual cruiser/racer. This yacht is of light displacement, the underwater body carrying a fin keel, a blade rudder hung on an integral skeg. The displacement (16,600 lbs) to ballast ratio is high. The aspect ratio of the mainsail is typically high and her mast head rig supports a large Genoa, that will get you where you're going fast as surely as it will win you races. The working sail area is 606 sq ft (56·29 sq m). Dimensions are: LOA 37 ft (11·27 m); LWL 26 ft 3 ins (8·68 m); beam 10 ft 2½ ins (3·67 m); draft 5 ft 9 ins (1·75 m). The hull and deck are of GRP trimmed with teak (hatches are also GRP). Mast and spars are extruded aluminium. Standing rigging stainless steel and running rigging is Dacron (hallyards stainless-steel wire with Dacron tails). For motor power a 30-hp universal *Atomic 4* is specified, but a diesel engine is an optional extra. As one might expect from Chris-Craft, *Apache 37* is distinctly smooth below! The accommodation comprises 6 ft 6 ins berths for six people. Headroom in saloons is 6 ft 3½ ins that should do for most people! And in the fore cabin the headroom is 5 ft 11 ins. The builders specify 'turquoise vinyl materials with satin-finished natural Philippine mahogany' for below decks décor. But don't let that fool you – this is a tough yacht and really seaworthy in every sense. She is a superb cruising yacht and her price, £9,990, reflects the fact! But then I can't keep them all in the lower brackets and, although I may not be writing this for many wealthy readers, it does none of us any harm to dream – or window-shop – and there's always the pools – or roulette – or even bingo if you stick at it! If you're lucky, or just rich, Carl Ziegler yacht agency (Great Cumberland Place) are the London agents. In Europe the Burson-Marsteller Association (9 rue Charles-Humbert in Geneva) will help you; and I surely don't need to tell Western Hemisphere readers that the Chris-Craft sail division hangs out on Pompano Beach, Florida.

Nicholson 38

It used to be fashionable to decry the motor-sailer; the yacht designed to sail as well under power as under sail, having a much larger than usual engine by comparison with the average auxiliary sailing yatch. Such craft were referred to as fifty-fifties and sixty-forties, etc. Indeed there was frequently cause for such derogation of motor vessels which were ugly and cumbersome and both their added sails and their motors were often

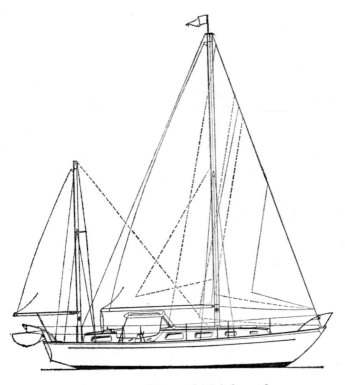

Figure 11. Plans of *Nicholson 38*

pretty useless. The true motor-sailer, a comparatively recent breed of yacht, not only carries ample power but can really sail especially to windward. Such a vessel is almost more of a ninety-ninety! It represents for many people that elusive cliché, the best of both worlds. Such a vessel is the *Nicholson 38*.

This is an expensive boat: perhaps before I write anything further I had better reveal the basic price – £13,750. Now for

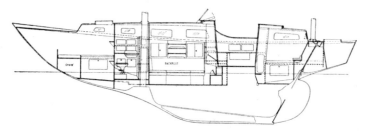

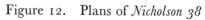

Figure 12.   Plans of *Nicholson 38*

those who are still with me, I will try to show why this is not expensive in relation to what you get for it and why it may be worth burning some midnight oil on new methods of pool winning, race betting, robbery, extortion and so forth. For this vessel is, of her kind, a masterpiece.

Let us start with measurements to get a good idea of the size of the boat. LOA 37 ft 10 ins (11·53 m); LWL 27 ft (8·23 m); beam 10 ft 6 ins (3·20 m); draft 5 ft 2 ins (1·57 m). The yacht measurement tonnage works out at 13 and the displacement tonnage at 7·1. Sails and sail areas are as follows: main 234 sq ft (21·73 sq m); mizzen 72 sq ft (6·68 sq m); working headsail 189 sq ft (17·55 sq m); Genoa 355 sq ft (32·98 sq m). Her ample motive power is supplied by a Perkins 4107 diesel of 47 hp with 2:1 reduction gear which gives 7½ knots maximum speed. The *38* is built in GRP. Halmatic Ltd – who have worked for some years now with Camper and Nicholson on such fine vessels as the *26*, *32* and *36* had a mould for a 38-foot design by the well-known American yacht architect John Alden. It was almost perfect for their requirements and negotiation and some modification resulted in C and N's design number A 352 – the *38*. The plans shown in figures 11 and 12 will give the reader an excellent idea of rig, sail plan and the very well-thought-out and roomy accommodation. There are now many lucky owners internationally of this fine little ship. In her you can live the year round and sail anywhere. Are you tempted?

Spey 35

Here is another modern motor-sailer but of a different design, being based on that of a fishing vessel. The designer is G. L. Watson of Glasgow. The accent here is on rugged seaworthiness combined with a high-class specification. The *Spey 35* is truly a yacht in which you can sail safely anywhere in the world. Moreover, like the *Nicholson 38*, the *Spey* motor-sailer can really sail. Jones Buckie Shipyard of Buckie, Banffshire, Scotland, build a 40-foot overall as well as a *35*, but I have selected the *35* because, while still providing comfortable berths for six, she costs £12,360 as opposed to £15,400. The first price is for sloop rig, if you have ketch rig you must pay £240 more; and personally I think you would be wise to, for, although the sloop rig might be a bit closer-winded, the ketch rig for this type of vessel is handier and more versatile.

Accommodation from aft includes double cabin, saloon with two seat berths, wheelhouse (which offers good protection in bad weather), galley to port, WC and washbasin to starboard; and a forward cabin with two berths. Headroom is 6 ft 1 in (1·85 m). Motor power comes from a Lister Blackstone 36-hp diesel with 2:1 reduction gear; a speed of 7½ knots being obtained. The sloop rig measures 475 sq ft (44·12 sq m) and the ketch rig 450 sq ft (41·80 sq m); and both can carry a Genoa jib of approximately 350 sq ft (32·51 sq m). Cruising range, under power alone, is 500 miles (804·670 km). The builders are quite happy to install twin engines if that should be desired, but the necessity for this is obviously of less importance in vessels like the *Spey* that can really get places under sail. For the second engine in a reasonably heavy displacement vessel of this nature is a safety-factor rather than a speed increaser. Let's take a look at measurements now: LOA 35 ft (10·66 m); LWL 32 ft (9·75 m); draft 5 ft (1·52 m); beam 11 ft 3 ins (3·429 m). Yacht measurement tonnage works out at 16 for the *35* and 23 for the *40*. Construction follows traditional fishing-boat pattern with larch planking below the water-line and mahogany above on grown oak frames. Decks are laid teak and brightwork is mahogany. Masts and spars are *Sparlight* aluminium alloy. Sails, made by Leitch of Tarbert, are in Terylene. The photograph shows clearly the pleasing, powerful lines of this deservedly popular motor-sailer. Although of fishing vessel origin, the *Spey*, as we have seen, has a high yacht specification, but perhaps the first reaction on going aboard is this is a real *ship*, and that alone will set many people searching for that twelve thousand pounds!

Gipsy II

Gipsy II is an interesting type of motor-sailer. She is hard chine with a modest draft (2 ft 9 ins) so that she can roam about in creeks and estuaries but yet is thoroughly seaworthy with a good beam and 1,000 lbs of ballast keel. She comes from the drawing-board of Rodney Warington Smyth and is built by the Penryn Boatbuilding and Engineering Company of Penryn in Cornwall.

One associates Warington Smyth with West Country-type boats like the *Falmouth Pilot* motor-sailer and a goodly number of other craft suitable for the long seas of the Western Ocean rather than shallow-draft vessels. But this is a clever compromise as we have seen. *Gipsy II*'s dimensions are: LOA 24 ft (7·315 m); LWL 20 ft (6·096 m); beam 8 ft 6 ins (2·590 m); and draft 2 ft 9 ins (0·838 m). She has a very respectable sail area of 240 sq ft (22·29 sq m) and this is a 'sailer' as well as a 'motorer' in truth. With the wide side decks that her beam gives, working on deck at sea is much facilitated while there is still good space below and a maximum headroom of 5 ft 6 ins (1·676 m). For motor power you can choose between a 10-hp Stuart Turner petrol or if you prefer diesel an Ailsa Craig 10 hp or a Saab 10 hp. She has berths for four or five according to owners' needs in the layout below decks. Twin bilge keels allow her to take the ground and dry out in comfort and safety. This is a versatile little ship. Price is £2,440 at time of writing and the inventory includes mainsail, headsail and Genoa (Terylene), pulpit, twin life-lines, sheet winches, anchor, 15 fathoms cable, WC (in fo'c'sle), stove, sink unit, engine (with electric start), cabin and fo'c'sle lights. This is all good value for money. By the time you read this the prices quoted may well have risen. However, some figures are necessary for purposes of comparison and within limits I hope they will provide at least a useful guide.

Lundy

This attractive motor fishing vessel type is built mainly by J. Hinks and Son of Appledore to the design of Walter F. 'Tom' Rayner, naval architect of Poole. Mr Rayner has had a great deal of experience in designing these sort of vessels; powerful sea-going motor-sailers (ketch rigged). As a glance at the sail plan will show (figure 13) these *Lundy*s carry sufficient sail to be able to make reasonable speeds when the wind is free. They are, however, mainly dependent upon their single Sutton Power/ Ford 62 (bhp) diesel, achieving 9½ knots under power while not more than about 5 under sail. Nevertheless the sails act as a steadier and it is always useful to know that should anything go amiss in the engine you can still carry on. Some of the *Lundy* class have been given twin engines in the form of two Perkins 36 bhp diesels. The boats are supremely seaworthy; owners who have experienced gale conditions for several days, comment on this fact.

Accommodation includes two separate sleeping cabins, galley, toilet and large deck saloon which houses two berths and

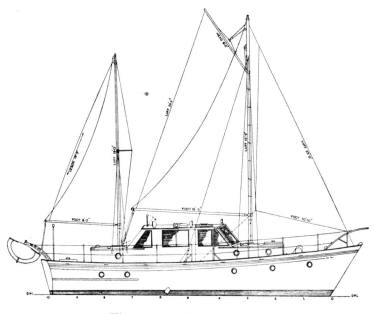

Figure 13. Plan of *Lundy*

the chart table. Bottom planking is of larch; topsides are mahogany. Decks are marine ply glass-covered. Dimensions are: LOA 37 ft 3 ins (11·353 m); LWL 32 ft 6 ins (9·906 m); beam 11 ft (3·353 m); draft 4 ft 6 ins (1·371 m). Yacht measurement tonnage works out at 14·75. The three working sails, headsail, mainsail and mizzensail measure 98, 158, and 72 sq ft (9·10, 14·68 and 6·68 sq m) respectively. It is good to see the traditional gaff rig for the mainsail and as both plan and photograph show in *Lundy*, Mr Rayner has produced a beautiful version of the now popular type of MFV yacht. The price at

time of writing is £10,500. In this boat you could sail anywhere and not be in a hurry to rush ashore as it is so comfortable
on board!

Jaunty 22

Jaunty 22 (and what a well-named boat!) is described by her
designer, J. Francis Jones, as a 'fishing cruiser' and, although
she is supremely well-suited to fishing rivers, estuaries and
around the shores of the North Sea, it is perhaps unfair to limit
her to these activities in one's mind because she is also a first-
rate little boat for coastal cruising. Of course there are 'fishing
cruisers' and 'fishing cruisers'. *Jaunty 22* (and her sisters the *20*
and the *24*) bear little resemblance to those fast predatory craft
that flourish in the Mediterranean for tunny fishers to indulge
their favourite sport or more particularly to the still larger
versions of the same type that seek the marlin in Gulf Stream
seas in the Hemingway tradition. Such craft have often to go
many miles offshore to their fishing grounds and speed and
seaworthiness are essential. The *Jaunty* is a 'potterer'. Her
native fishing grounds are to hand and her Saab 8/10-hp diesel
engine is exactly right for the purpose. Economical and reliable,
with her you can fish with line, or use a small beam or other
trawl, or just potter about and – dare one say it in this English
climate of ours – sunbathe! Let's look at her measurements:
LOA 22 ft (6·7 m); LWL 19 ft 10 ins (6·0 m); beam 8 ft 3½ ins
(2·53 m); draft 2 ft (0·61 m) (very useful for 'ditch crawling');
displacement tonnage is 2·3 (2,336 kg) and the yacht measurement tonnage works out at 5. Mahogany is specified for her
planking and she is built in traditional clinker fashion. The
drawing in figure 14 shows her accommodation. If, as she may
well do, she measures up to your dream boat, you will have to
find about £2,200 to buy her; and there are many extras
available.

If she is not quite large enough for your purpose, but you like
the design and general specification, the *24* costing about
£2,800 (depending on choice of engine) will be the answer.
That extra two feet makes a lot of difference. Again, the
Jaunty 20 (LOA 19 ft 6 ins (5·94 m)) will cost only £1,375
and this little vessel, unlike her sisters, sports a sailing rig of
lugsail and single headsail, and very attractive she looks! And if

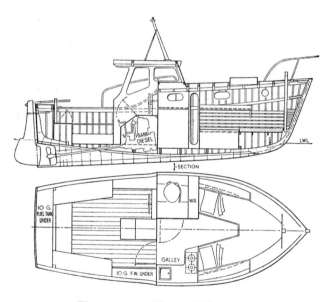

Figure 14. Plans of *Jaunty 22*

Plate 1   *Barbel II*

Plate 2   *Alacrity Mk II*

Plate 3   *Vivacity*

Plate 4   *Victoire 22*

Plate 5 *Kestrel 22*

Plate 6 *Islander 23*

Plate 7 *Mapleleaf*

Plate 8   *Magyar 7*

Plate 9   *East Anglian*

you prefer GRP to wood you can find your desire in this clever range of fishing cruisers in the *Jaunty 'Jolly boat'* (LOA 19 ft 6 ins again) but with the wheel shelter (see illustration (Plate 20)) of the *22* and the *24* and not open cockpit like the *20*, price £1,685.

Francis Jones is an experienced designer and in the *Jaunty* class he has, I think, added a touch of genius.

Scoresby 32

The Whitehall shipyard in Whitby, Yorkshire, asked designer Robert Tucker to take a look at traditional North Sea fishing-boats like the Yorkshire Coble, and then fashion a hull incorporating such features as he thought worth while. This, according to Whitehall shipyard, is how the *Scoresby* class began. The builders wanted, above all, two things: first, a good sea boat; secondly, a good-looker. For my part Tucker has come up trumps. The *Scoresby 32* has a tough elegance that is most attractive. From any angle she not only looks the fine sea boat she is but she looks a real thoroughbred of her kind with her very deeply flared clipper bow and generous sheer to the marked tumble home and curved transom aft. She has a good beam too 10 ft 10 ins (3·30 m), on an overall length of 32 ft (9·75 m) draft (amidships) is 2 ft 4 ins (0·71 m) and draft (aft) is 3 ft 4 ins (1·01 m). She is built of mahogany on grown oak frames and steamed oak timbers. Deck beams are oak and decking is of ½-in marine ply overlaid with ½-in teak. Sleeping capacity is for five or three single and one double berth. She is single screw and choice is to the owner but the builders specify the 240 D Thornycroft 70-hp diesel driving through ENV drive unit. Price at time of writing this is from £3,250.

The *Scoresby 32* has a larger sister, the *35* (beam 11 ft 4 ins) (3·45 m). Although for this vessel, too, the 240 D Thornycroft is specified (the standard vessel costing £4,250), you can if you want more power (and of course security) have twin Perkins 4·107 diesels for an additional £500. Had I the money, and wanted to do extended cruising, I would consider that extra £500 well worth it.

The basic *Scoresby* hull can be built to a variety of layouts. For example, a two-berth forward wheelhouse pure fisherman type or again a centre wheelhouse fore-and-aft cabin, cruising version. Either way this Yorkshire lass clinker built (and no other construction is somehow thinkable for this boat), is a vessel of real character.

Senior 32

Here we have an excellent example of a reasonably priced long-range power cruiser – the *Senior 32*. The names derives from Senior Marines Ltd of Bitterne, Southampton, England, who build a series, the *26*, the *31* and this the *32*; the figure denoting the approximate overall length. By long range, I mean that this yacht has a fuel range of over 500 miles. She is powered by twin Perkins 4·107 diesels. These are housed well aft and engine noise and smell are kept to the minimum. Power is transmitted to the screws through V or transom drive. Accommodation is for six people. This is a good-looking vessel having a centre cockpit, little or no sheer and a very pleasing bow. The general effect has a simplicity of line that is most attractive. Construction is in GRP.

The completed vessel will cost you £4,168 and that is not expensive for the accommodation, range of operation and very adequate motor power. Hull and superstructure only can be had for as little as £885, but before you get too excited about that remember that a marine engine of adequate power (the Perkins 4·107 diesel by the way is 47 bhp, has four cylinders, rpm 4,000 and cubic capacity 107 cc) is not cheap to buy and for this boat you need two. If you want to spend less in the same range; the *Senior 31* costs £3,969 and the *26* costs £2,010 – all this at the time of writing of course. Dimensions of the *32* are LOA 32 ft 6 ins (9·90 m); beam 9 ft 8 ins (2·94 m) and draft 2 ft 2 ins (0·66 m).

Cheverton Champ 27

If you can afford to spend between £3,000 and £4,000, and you are looking for a power boat about 27 feet (8·23 m) long which will maintain speeds of 15 knots plus being able to take rough weather in her stride, then the *Cheverton Champ* 27-footer may well be the boat for you. Coming from the board of designer David Cheverton this glassfibre motor-cruiser is a boat of real versatility. As the photograph shows, she is a rugged little vessel. The hull is a one-piece moulding in GRP and her

66

upperworks are of marine ply on African mahogany framing. Trimming is also in mahogany. Accommodation consists of, from forward: forepeak, cabin with two 6 ft 6 ins settee berths, wheelhouse (glazed windows on three sides) large open cockpit and after-peak. Her ample power comes from one 115 hp. Perkins Diesel. Smaller (cheaper) engines are available. Coming from a firm called David Cheverton Workboats, one would expect this vessel to be designed for either pleasure or commercial use. Reliability is therefore a strong feature. She must be able to take the weather as it comes and to maintain a good speed. Her 9-ft (2·74 m) beam ensures a roomy saloon, well lighted by windows as can be seen (Plate 23). Her maximum draft of 2 ft 9 ins (0·84 m) removes problems about operating in relatively shallow water.

You don't have to have the largest engine, as a range of alternative power installations are available should you have other preferences. The builders clearly have a high regard for the Perkins, however, as they specify them. Similarly, a variety of layouts below decks are available. At a price of from £3,520 upwards, all this would seem by any standards, to add up to a bargain!

Coronet 24

This is one of the well-known *Coronet* range; every one of which is a winner. Combined in the *Dell Quay* series, they start with the day cruiser, the *21*, and progress through the *24* and the 19 ft 7 ins *J.20*. (a 'flybridge' cruiser for fishing), the 27-foot *Dell Quay Ranger* (a fast, five-berth offshore cruiser) – to the *32* known as the *Oceanfarer* (an all-round family cruiser). Prices range from around £3,500 for the *21* (less if only single engine) to about £11,500 for the *Oceanfarer*. The one shown in the photograph (Plate 24) is the *24* and it is fairly typical of the range. This is a four-berth fast family cruiser; built like her sisters in GRP. Dimensions are LOA 24 ft 2 ins (7.81 m); beam 8 ft (2.43 m); draft: engine units up, 1 ft 7 ins (0.482 m); draft: units lowered, 2 ft 3 ins (0.685 m). The units are twin 130/250 Volvo Penta aquamatics. All these *Coronet* craft are beautifully designed and fitted, great attention being paid to layout below decks. This should not blind one to the fact that they are real sea-going cruisers with a very handy turn of speed. The *Oceanfarer* cuts powerfully through the water at a maximum speed of over 27 knots, while her sporty sister, the *24*, reaches over 36 knots. They are Scandinavian in origin and in Britain a letter or visit to Dell Quay Sales, Itchenor Shipyard, Chichester, Sussex, will soon bring results, the most probable being that you will acquire one!

Oceanic

Here is a beautiful ketch-rigged 'cat' designed by Bill O'Brien, and built by the South Coast Catamaran Company, at Southampton, England. O'Brien, a very experienced designer has paid great attention to strength and seaworthiness. The two robust hulls attached to a strong rigid unit, keep the centre of gravity as low as possible. Fuel tanks, galley, WC, water tanks and all heavy equipment are placed as low in the hulls and as far outboard as possible. Dimensions are as follows: LOA 30 ft (9·144 m); LWL 28 ft 2 ins (8·58 m); beam 14 ft (4·267 m); draft 2 ft (0·610 m); sail area 700 sq ft (65·03 sq m); displacement 3·7 tons (3,403 kg). Yacht measurement tonnage is 9 tons (9,144 kg); headroom is 6 ft 6 ins (1·981 m) and there are berths for seven. The engines usually supplied are two Volvo Penta diesels. Basic price (without sails and engines) is around £4,750. This is a beautifully designed vessel built in GRP. She can be moored in a creek that dries out and she can be sailed across oceans (and several have been).

Many owners of O'Brien-designed cruising 'cats' keep in regular touch with him, sending regular accounts of their voyages, the weather encountered, etc; all of which, quite apart from the interest factor, bears eloquent witness to the sea-worthiness of these boats, and the great satisfaction they give their owners.

Ranger

This is a series (27-foot, 31-foot and 45-foot) of 'cats' by Prout. Let us take the smallest, the 27-foot LOA as our first example. Built in GRP this is a thoroughly seaworthy yet moderately priced vessel, working out at about £3,000 basic (less sails and engine). Dimensions are as follows: LOA 27 ft (8·23 m); beam 12 ft 6 ins (3·81 m); draft 1 ft 10 ins (0·558 m). She is sloop rigged. Mainsail area is 186 sq ft (17·18 sq m); she carries working headsail of 129 sq ft (11·98 sq m); Genoa of 176 sq ft (16·35 sq m) and a smaller headsail (for use when the main is well reefed) of 64 sq ft (5·94 sq m). Mast and boom are aluminium. For mechanical power any suitable outboard will fill the bill. Accommodation can be arranged to provide berths from four to six as desired. The photograph (Plate 26) illustrates the 27-foot *Ranger*.

Now let us take what Prout call their *Ocean Ranger*, a 45-footer of impressive appearance. This is the latest design (at time of writing) in the Prout range and lives up to its name. Accommodation here offers no less than five separate sleeping cabins, two wash and shower rooms; large saloon and galley. From the saloon in the centre of the bridge a direct passage runs to either hull, so pampered guests or crew can reach any part of the accommodation without going on deck. There is an inside wheel in the saloon so that the *Ocean Ranger* can be steered in shelter and, if all this sounds as if this vessel has only an appeal for foppish yachtsmen, let me add that this is a really sea-keeping vessel, capable of being driven hard in rough weather. In light airs she reaches speeds of from 10 to 12 knots and in favourable conditions speeds of 20 are easily attainable. For auxiliary power either outboard or inboard are specified and, to reach 8 knots, 50 hp is recommended by the builders without specifying any particular make. However, with the vast range attainable (see the section of chapter one on engines) that presents no problem at all.

Triune 30

We now come to our trimaran, *Triune 30* designed by P. R. Chaworth-Musters and built by Musters Marine. This hull, in GRP is moulded by Con Cargo Ltd, to Lloyds + 100 A1 specification. Decks and coachroof are in marine ply on pine beams, and the whole exterior is sheathed in GRP. Sails are: mainsail 205 sq ft (19 sq m); Genoa 305 sq ft (28 sq m); working headsail 190 sq ft (18 sq m); storm jib 75 sq ft (7 sq m); spitfire jib 55 sq ft (5 sq m) and spinnaker 700 sq ft (65 sq m). Bruce Banks sails in Terylene are standard specification.

Triune 30 is rigged as a sloop with single headsail and high aspect ratio mainsail. She is a good-looking vessel as a glance at

the photographs of her interior (Plate 28) and her sister ship
Nozomi (Plate 27) will show. She has the roomy accommodation we have learned to expect in these multihull yachts, well-
planned and thought out to give really comfortable living
aboard both at sea and in harbour. For motor power the
standard engine specified is the Watermota Sea Wolf four
cylinder 29 bhp. If diesel is preferred, the builders specify the
Watermota two-cylinder 15-bhp engine. Again if an outboard is
desired the two-stroke Johnson 9½ bhp is recommended. It
mounts on a slide in the stern locker (a normal arrangement).
Dimensions of *Triune 30* are: LOA 30 ft (9·2 m); LWL 28 ft
6 ins (8·7 m); beam 18 ft (5·5 m); draft (board up) 2 ft (0·60 m);
(board down) 5 ft 6 ins (1·67 m) and her displacement tonnage
is 2 (2,000 kg). Basic price, without sails or engine is £3,950.

Here I want to say a word about prices. First of all it must be
realised that the basic prices shown will increase quite a lot by
the time you have bought the engine – or engines and sails, and
other extras you may very well want. Of course the prices I have
quoted in this book are, in the main, *basic* prices. This has to be
so. Sails in a sailing yacht are an essential but not everybody
wants engines and the amount of extras varies from person to
person. In some instances sails are included in the price and
where they are I have said so; the same applies to engines. In
the case of these multihulls, the three prices quoted are basic;
but, even if you add all the extras, the prices are not unreasonable.
Let us take *Triune 30* as an example. Basic cost of vessel £3,950;
now we add the following: mainsail £75, Genoa £52, working
jib £45, storm jib £22, spinnaker £65, spinnaker boom and
gear £35 and for engine let us say the Watermota 29-bhp
inboard (installed) £478, an additional £772 which brings our
price up to £4,722. You can, incidentally, buy this vessel in
various stages of building and finish off the job yourself which
cuts the basic price right down to below £1,000 – but costs a
good deal in time, experience, some knowledge and of course
cost of materials. It is always difficult writing about *prices* of
yachts. They vary (usually increasing!) from year to year and it
is difficult to make comparisons on purely price terms. For
example the *Nicholson 32* costs around £7,000. She is a 32-foot
overall 9½-ton yacht built to a very high specification. She
clearly costs more than the *Triune 30* and the 30-ft *Oceanic*. But
you cannot make a comparison based on price. So many other

things enter into the matter. Again, the 32-ft 9-ton *Hillyard* costs £4,100; less than *Triune 30*, less than *Oceanic*, and a good deal less than the *Nicholson 32*. There is of course a difference in specification. I have put these prices in as a rough guide. If you are in the £4,000 spending bracket you will probably be looking at my examples in that bracket. If £1,000 is your mark, then the £4,000 boats won't interest you and neither will these cruising multihulls. The multihulls in short are not cheap – but my goodness they can give you a lot of fun if you can find the money! As to the question of 'multi' versus 'mono' – that I have already touched on in chapter one.

CHAPTER THREE

Buying the Boat and where to keep her

(1) Buying the Boat

The inspecting and buying of a second-hand yacht provides as many hazards for the unwary as is proverbially found in the world of the horse coper. So let's look at the problem from the start. You want to buy a small second-hand cruising boat. As we saw in chapter one, with very small cruisers, there is not *all* that much difference between a new boat and a two- to three-year-old boat. However, new boats must be *built*. Maybe you don't want to wait. Maybe the particular boat you have decided upon is advertised second-hand while the waiting list for new boats is immense. But, quite likely, you have no idea what you want – so – you probably buy one of the many yachting magazines on the market and start reading the 'Boats for Sale' section. Let us then explore this whole question from there, because we can learn a lot in doing so.

It will immediately become apparent that advertisements for second-hand yachts follow almost as rigid a pattern or formula as the announcement of an engagement to be married. First of all there is a reference to the size. In British waters this is frequently given in tons – 'a 4-tonner'; 'a 6-tonner'. This refers to the Thames Measurement or 'Yacht measurement' tonnage and has nothing whatever to do with the weight of the vessel. It does give an idea of the boat's size. The formula is: Yacht Measurement Tonnage $= \dfrac{(L - B) \times B \times \frac{1}{2}B}{94}$: L = the length of the boat measured on deck from the foreside of the stern to the afterside of the stern post, and B = the extreme beam (widest part of the vessel). This yacht measurement or Thames Tonnage derives from a formula for measurement adopted in 1854 by the Royal Thames Yacht Club of London. It will be seen that it makes use of only two measurements, the length of the vessel and her beam. In bygone days, when yachts had straight sterns, short counters, deep draught and narrow beam, the Thames Tonnage approximated to the displacement tonnage. However, a glace at figure 15 will show that the Thames Tonnage formula length, as shown by the two vertical lines, is not the true length. It is less than the true length for a vessel with a counter stern. A '4-tonner' by Thames formula can in fact have a variety of different beams and lengths. (A boat of 22-foot length and 7-foot beam is just as much a '4-tonner' as a boat with a 25-foot length and 6·5 beam or a 28-foot length and 6-foot beam, but since we normally reckon about 3 beams to length the first of these is what we picture.)

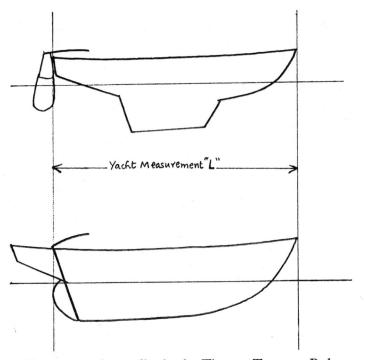

Figure 15. Anomalies in the Thames Tonnage Rule

The expression of '4-tonner' conveys only a rough idea of the boat's accommodation, since the formula does not include depth of hull. However, the Thames or Yacht Measurement Tonnage is still widely used. It is hallowed by tradition and it does have its uses.

A more international method of measurement is that of stating the water-line length (usually written LWL) the first L standing for Load; the overall length (LOA) the beam and the draft (the immersed depth of the hull at its deepest point). There may be a reference to the Net Registered Tonnage. This is of significance in so far as upon it things like harbour dues are calculated. Briefly, it is obtained by a surveyor calculating the cubical contents (by a method known as Simpson's Rules) of the below deck space. This is then divided by 100 (100 cubic feet being taken to represent one ton) to give the gross tonnage, next the space occupied by the engine, fuel tanks, stores, space for navigation, space for crew accommodation are calculated for cubical contents. The figure obtained is then subtracted from the gross to give the net registered tonnage.

This word ton descends to us from 'tun'. In bygone days, ships were measured for dues on the number of tuns they carried; a tun being a wine measure of 252 gallons. Nowadays, when small cruisers are often trailed or shipped all over the place, it is useful to know the displacement tonnage (this being simply the weight of the water displaced by the immersed hull) and this is frequently given. Generally speaking though, all that you will see in the advertisement will be the LOA, LWL, beam and draught and possibly a reference to the Yacht Measurement Tonnage. The sail area in square feet or square metres will be shown too and probably the number of sails, ie mainsail, jib, Genoa and spinnaker; and (sometimes) the age of the sails, the sailmaker's name, and the material of which the sails are made (Terylene, for example). Not all advertisements are so explicit – some such phrases as 'full inventory of sails and gear' being used to cover a multitude of (regrettably often) sins.

The advertisement will (or should!) give the name of the designer, or class of the builder, date of building and a brief description of the materials used: ie 'pitch pine on oak, copper fastened; chine built marine ply resorcinal glued', or 'GRP (glassfibre-reinforced plastic) hull'; and whether the spars are of wood or metal. If there is an engine the type, make and age should be stated, the number of sea miles to the gallon; the speed in moderately smooth water (often shamelessly exaggerated).

Yacht owners are notoriously inclined to neglect the engine and many a prospective purchaser experiences a nasty shock when, after inspecting a well kept, shiny hull and gear, a hatch below is lifted to reveal a rusty piece of ironmongery cringing in a dark, evil-smelling recess beneath the cockpit!

Another important point that should be mentioned is whether the boat has a centreboard, fixed deep keel or twin bilge keels (this will be reflected of course in the description of 'draft'). Further, you will be told the rig – sloop, cutter, gunter lugsail, ketch, etc. Nowadays most boats' mainsails are triangular, the four-sided gaffsail being not nearly as popular as it was. The triangular sail is called in Britain *Bermudan* (said to originate in the island of that name). In the USA it is often called *Marconi* rig, after the complex rigging of the original Bermudan masts. Sometimes too, it is referred to unflatteringly as a 'leg o' mutton' mainsail. You will furthermore be told where the vessel is lying and if she is afloat or hauled out.

The price may or may not be shown. It frequently is and is often followed by the letters 'ONO', meaning 'or near offer'; an encouraging indication of willingness to bargain; although with less happy undertones of desperation for reasons which occur to the experienced buyer after a second thought or two!

(2) Inspection and Survey

The whole advertisement may be under the name of a yacht broker or it may be put in by a private individual. Let us assume you have found one that appears to be what you are looking for. The worst thing you can now do is to make an arrangement to go down and look at the boat because, unless you are experienced, you will fall hopelessly in love with her, and like all lovers become at once blind to any defects, however bad, and you won't be able to make her yours fast enough! This is where you need either a knowledgeable friend or a surveyor. You are going to need a surveyor anyway later but, in the case of a *preliminary* inspection, a knowledgeable and experienced friend would be able to tell you whether the boat is worth the cost of a survey. Surveys, while being in no way excessive, are not cheap because a lot of work is involved. So there is no point in sending your surveyor to boat after boat when a preliminary viewing would in each case have saved you pounds, dollars, francs or what-have-you.

It is a good plan to choose your own surveyor and here again your experienced 'sailing friend' can help you, but if he can't you can get all the assistance you need from the Yacht Brokers, Designers and Surveyor's Association and the Ship and Boat Builders' Federation. They can supply you with a list of qualified surveyors from which you can choose one who lives in the locality of your chosen boat (less travelling expenses to pay). Lloyds' register of yachts also helps as there are a number of qualified surveyors who work for Lloyds. When your surveyor has made his report you can approach the owner of the vessel and, if the surveyor has unearthed (as he probably will!) certain faults, and suggest that the former meets you either in a reduced price or in having the faults put right. For example, the hull may be sound but all the standing rigging on its last legs. Complete renewal of standing rigging will be *essential* for your safety and it can also be quite surprisingly expensive – depending of course on the size of the yacht. Again all may be well – (even the engine!) but the working sails (mainsail and working headsail) old, and so pulled out of shape as to be almost useless. Once again your surveyor will, in bringing this to your notice, stop you not only from 'buying a pup' but could be (for example in conditions of trying to 'claw off a lee shore in bad weather') saving your life! So it will be clear that a survey is a must.

If you have no knowledgeable sailing friend who can make the preliminary inspection of the boat of your choice, you can always ask the surveyor to do it. His fee for this will be much less than a complete survey, and he will tell you whether it is worth proceeding. Now some of my readers may well have messed about in small boats and feel that a preliminary inspection is not beyond their capability. This is of course up to them, but as a guide or perhaps as a reminder, may I list the sort of things you should look for in such an inspection.

We have taken the train or our car to where the boat is lying. We are in luck because it being very early in the season, our boat is hauled out and is under a winter cover and we can get at all points of her with reasonable ease.

We will have brought with us a rule or tape-measure, a pricker, a light hammer, a knife, a screwdriver and a good powerful torch. Let us assume we are examining two boats, the first hull being wooden, of planked carvel construction on wooden frames; the second of glassfibre-reinforced plastic. We start with the first hull, lightly using our hammer on the planking. Any dull reverberation will put us on the alert for rot beneath all that shiny paint! We must look to see whether the planking has moved away from the frames anywhere. If so the copper rivets will need hardening. Not many yachts are iron fastened these days but if you meet one, watch out for the rusty stains that spell 'nail sickness'. If you notice that, look closely at the frames inside – there could be real trouble here! We must also test the planking with our pricker, especially along the water-line planking and below including the garboards. There is no need to drive the pricker in miles and risk damaging the hull. All you want to test is whether the planking is firm to the touch. If it is not there may be rot below the surface.

An enemy of wooden vessels is the gribble (*Limnovia lignorum*), a small crustacean (about 5 mm long) which burrows into any handy submerged timber. When exposed the gribble rolls itself up like a ball somewhat like a woodlouse. Another enemy of the wooden ship is the common shipworm (*Teredo navalis*). These bore into the woodwork of ships, doing considerable damage. The Teredo's common name is 'shipworm' and it looks like a worm. There are theories that it is only found in the warmer seas of the world. This is not so. Teredo can and will dine happily off your hull (if unprotected) in the Atlantic Ocean and the Baltic Sea as much as in the Mediterranean. So we must look out for the little holes that give away the shipworm's presence.

If the planking is seen to be badly attacked by worms all wood at the area will need renewal; an expensive business! When (and if) you come to have the boat properly surveyed, your surveyor will undoubtedly want to examine the keel carefully and, if the vessel has a deep ballast keel, he will certainly have a bolt or two drawn for examination.

Don't forget to examine the decking carefully. It may be of laid planking, of tongued and grooved planks covered with a canvas (in an older boat) or some artificial (but excellent) deck covering like *Trakmark*; or it may be of marine plywood. If the decks are of laid planking (a rarity in small boats these days) look carefully to see the condition of the caulking between the planks. A complete recaulking takes time and costs money!

Check the decking for any soft wood with your pricker, especially from *below* decks. Go carefully all round coamings, king posts and hatches. Examine all shelves and beams. The ends of the latter are especially suspicious places. Examine too, hanging and lodging knees and look closely at the chain plates and any metal strengthening members. Where iron plates are secured with copper fastenings look out for signs of electrolytic action. Take up all bottom boards and poke your nose (and your torch) into the bilges. Have a good sniff. The bilges should smell dry and sweet. Some people say they can smell rot easily. Personally I find this difficult – there are often petrol fumes and other smells which mask anything else. Maybe there *shouldn't* be – but there often are! Examine the floors. If you find any sign of rot here you can bet a dollar or two that the planking attached to them is affected as well. Look at the engine. If the boat is afloat start it up. If ashore, give a turn or two, and look at the general appearance.

But let us now go to the other boat we have come to see. This hull is of resin glass-reinforced plastic. Most of such hulls are made from polyester resins, reinforced with glassfibres. They are generally moulded by contact or by a hand lay up process. Some are moulded by vacuum and pressure bag. We must examine this hull for any damage, for distortion, cracks, discoloration, stains (rust), wet patches. Examine too the interior of the hull carefully, or at least as much of it as we can get at. If we can find no obvious defects in the hull, it is probable that the surveyor's fee is not going to be wasted.

When you have examined the hull of the boats as described, you should then pass to the mast (or masts) and spars. Metal masts, unless obviously strained and distorted, must be left to the all-seeing eye of the professional surveyor. With wooden masts look for shakes (cracks) if these run along the mast, don't worry; if these are spiral – aha! watch out.

Take a look at the standing rigging. Bend it and see if any odd strands stick out. If they do and the rigging is rusty – your surveyor will probably advise renewal.

It goes without saying that sails matter in a sailing boat, and remember sails are quite an expensive item, so look carefully at these and check for signs that they are past their day. It is a good idea to lay a sail flat on the ground and pull the head and clew taut. This forms a line between these two corners of the sail. It should form a gentle curve. Do the same with all three sides of the sail. These curves, called roaches, are carefully built into the sail to give it its wing-like curvature when hoisted. If the leech only is stretched this does not matter as much as the luff or foot. An old sail which has stretched out of shape will not give a satisfactory performance and your surveyor would undoubtedly comment on this and, as with any other faulty parts he may find, suggest that you bargain accordingly with the owner. Do not ever get so carried away that you dispense with the services of the professional surveyor. Never buy a second-hand boat without a survey!

In conclusion to this section I should like to emphasise that nowadays the buying of a boat does not need a vast number of notes in the bank or in a sack under the floor-boards, for you can buy out of income, by making use of hire-purchase, credit sale or marine mortgages. There are a number of finance houses who are specialists in this field. Probably the best thing to do is to consult your bank manager.

The difference between hire-purchase and credit sale is that with the former the finance house is the owner of the boat until you have paid the last instalment, whereas with the latter you, the purchaser, own the boat once you have made the initial payment and the finance house has agreed the transaction. Your bank manager will be able to explain the advantage of a credit sale agreement with tax relief. This enables you to buy the boat and repay only the capital sum which has been advanced plus the net charges after first deducting tax at the standard rate.

If you are over eighteen, you can qualify for a marine mortgage. In everybody's interest the finance house will want to make sure that the monthly repayments of capital and interest can be made out of your income without running you into difficulties. The advantages of a marine mortgage are the favourable interest rates and the fact that repayments of capital and interest can be extended to periods of four to five years; thus easing the pain a bit! At the time of writing certainly the interest you pay qualifies again for tax relief. I have to say 'at time of writing' because, as we all know, the finance laws can move pretty fast nowadays. Marine mortgages can only be written for a registered vessel (see section 4 of this chapter). This section will point out that for vessels under 15 tons registration is not necessary, and I should add here that for boats of under 15 tons it is not worth registration just to get a mortgage, as the relatively high cost of registering will offset the savings obtainable through a marine mortgage on any craft costing less than £1,000.

(3) Localities, Moorings, Marinas, Yacht Yards, etc

Once you have bought a boat the vexed question of where you are going to keep her arises. This can be quite a problem and the larger your boat, the greater the problem! With bilge-keel craft that can dry out, it is obviously less tricky than with a keel boat, for a keel boat needs a mooring. In the far-off days when cruising meant proceeding grandly from place to place in a large vessel, professionally manned and maintained like a royal yacht, the problem of moorings did not arise. True there were a number of eccentrics like R. T. McMullen who cruised (and pretty extensively too) in small boats, but for them too the mooring problem hardly existed. Even in more recent days, it was simple enough to arrange with the local harbour-master to have a mooring laid (or you could lay it yourself without too much strain). Nowadays, the picture is very different. Harbours are getting very crowded indeed. In keen anticipation of the day when there just won't be any more room in the harbours, many local authorities and yacht yards have built, are building or have arranged to have built, 'marinas'. This Spanish-sounding word simply means a virtually enclosed (apart from an entry/exit channel) area of water, with pontoons or quays built out parallel with each other and to which vessels may lie alongside or stern to quay. The yachts are afloat at all stages of the tide, and in the smarter marinas, water, petrol and even a telephone, can be laid on per berth. All this costs money and the price of a marina berth is not cheap. There are however advantages to a marina which provides, all at once, berths where vessels lie alongside or stern-to pontoons, car parking space, lavatories, showers or baths, or both; chandlery, fresh water, fuel and quite often electricity and a telephone connection. The cost varies in the British Isles between £5 to £7 per foot of overall length per year. If this seems expensive remember that with a marina a yacht can lay up afloat for the winter using a tough winter cover supported on a deck framework. This of course represents a saving in terms of 'garaging' space ashore; but the yacht will have to be slipped for fitting out, so the saving, while useful, is not so great as all that. What does save money is the fact that the handiness and proximity of water and electricity enables the yacht owner to do a lot more of his own fitting-out than he would have done laid up in the far corner of a pitch dark shed!

Again for those hardy folk to whom winter weekends on board are attractive, the advantages of the marina berths will be obvious. At the time of writing it is the south coast yards that have shown most interest in marinas; but my guess is that the fashion will spread as the sailing population round our coasts continues to grow.

Let us now consider the question of finding an ordinary mooring. Depending upon the sailing population factor in your area (or where you intend to keep your boat) this difficulty of finding a mooring varies greatly. Only local inquiry will reveal the position, which brings me to the question of where one makes such inquiries. The local harbour-master is the obvious choice, but sometimes moorings are owned by local yacht builders who can be approached. If you rent one of their moorings you will be expected (understandably) to let the yard do such seasonal work on your boat as needs to be done.

The local yacht yard comes very much into consideration when winter arrives. They will have the means of housing your precious vessel under cover should you require it. This is the most expensive method of winter storage. The next (going down the scale) is to lay-up out in the open but under waterproof cover. Thirdly, you (or rather your boat) can lie in a mud berth, which means lying in a tidal berth, your vessel being afloat about half the time and the other half on the mud. Finally you can leave her afloat all winter, with preferably all spars and rigging under cover (either below decks or ashore). Local conditions coupled with the ever-present consideration of finance will help to decide the fate of your vessel in winter. Prices vary greatly. As a general rule the nearer the sun and the more populous the sailing fraternity, the more you will have to pay. So if you like frozen rain and complete solitude your sailing

will cost you a lot less than it will cost the man who likes lots of
other boats within sight and hailing distance, and the women to
whom a bikini is a more desirable sailing rig than oilskins and a
plastic sou'wester!

(4) Yacht's 'Papers' and Registration

You may spend most of your life cruising about in a yacht
without ever having to produce your ship's papers. That is,
you cruise in home waters. Nowadays, however, there is an
ever-increasing tendency to 'go foreign' and, when you do that,
your ship will need her papers just as much as you will need
your passport. For practical purposes a yacht's papers can
really be boiled down to the certificate of registry plus any
foreign certificate (like the French 'Permis de Navigation' for
French inland waterways). In the old days of paid crews, a
yacht's papers would have included a crew agreement or
'articles'; and if the vessel was on charter the 'charter party'.
Today, a Bill of Health can still be requested and, if you fly a
special ensign, your ship's papers should include the warrant
(in Great Britain from the Admiralty) that entitles your yacht
(not you) to fly that ensign when you are on board. So let's
look at the Certificate of Registry. This sets out the yacht's name
and her registered number and certain particulars. If she is a
registered vessel, and bears upon her the official number as well
as the registered tonnage, these details will be in her certificate
which then acts as a document of identity and passport combined. On the certificate will be the name of her present and
her previous owner (only the latest owner), so that the certificate
is also evidence of your ownership. Should you lose your
certificate, the Registrar of Shipping will let you have a
provisional certificate or if you cannot get to him, your nearest
consul. Registration, under Part 1 of the Merchant Shipping
Act 1844 will cost you about £35. It is not compulsory under
15 tons gross, provided she sails within British territorial waters;
so for most of the small vessels discussed in this book, registration
is not compulsory. It is on the other hand very useful should you
envisage much foreign passage-making. If you are unwilling
to make that small effort then the Bill of Sale from the last
owner to you together with your passport and a certain amount
of self-confidence or tact or natural charm should get you by in

most countries. Personally speaking I have played safe and the ability to shove a certificate of registry under the nose of a dispeptic douanier has on more than one occasion proved my salvation. I know of others who have made out all right with the Bill of Sale; but don't say I didn't warn you!

The Bill of Health is a document few yachtsmen bother about today, but it can save trouble abroad on occasion. It is simply evidence at the port of issue of the state of health of the ship's company. It is obtainable free in British waters.

Many British and US yacht clubs enjoy reciprocal advantages with foreign yacht clubs and a certificate or letter carried on board can often prove of great value in the game of cruising yachtmanship, especially if it bears upon it a large red seal!

Last, but by no means least, if you are sailing to a foreign port you will need a customs clearance from your last port; easy to obtain from the custom's officials who are helpful to yacht owners, if treated with common politeness, and essential to have.

(5) Yacht Clubs

Wherever sailing people congregate, you will find clubs. Although to some people the idea of a yacht club may conjure up discouraging pictures of Victorian pomposity, yet a club can be of great advantage. Take, for example, the fact that many clubs have children members, like the Corinthian 'Otters' – junior branch of the world famous Royal Corinthian Yacht Club of Burnham-on-Crouch in Essex, England. For a small sailing family this has obvious attractions. But perhaps the most useful function of the yacht club to the cruising man is that quite apart from having a 'local' club, where information can be exchanged and all sorts of help given, yacht clubs almost always extend a welcome and temporary membership to the itinerant yacht owner and his crew.

To discover the locality of yacht clubs is not difficult. Most countries today have a national (or regional) body which, apart from looking after the interests of yachtsmen generally, provide a list of registered clubs, with (usually) the name and address of the club secretary. In the British Isles we are fortunate in possessing a national body, the Royal Yachting Association, familiarly and internationally known as the RYA, in whose handbook are to be found a vast amount of information concerning racing rules, the international rules for prevention of collision at sea, schools where one can learn to sail, and among other useful data, a long list of clubs. These are shown in two lists. The first is an alphabetical list of the name of each club and the second (also alphabetical) is in section of countries, and within those sections, towns and villages. Membership of the RYA entitles one to receive the handbooks, as revised, each year, but non-members can buy one or all of them. But it is a good idea to join the RYA, and support it in its very real and dedicated work in the service of yachting people. So I can't do better than give you the address, which is 5 Buckingham Gate, London SW1.

CHAPTER FOUR

Where you can go

It has always been possible for those with the time and the knowledge to sail great distances in small boats. Captain Joshua Slocum, sailed the sloop yacht *Spray* all round the world in 1895–98. He was the first man ever to do this. More recently the two yachting knights, Sir Francis Chichester and Sir Alec Rose (both of them seamen/navigators of the first order) sailed, not only round the world single-handed, but with only one stop *en route* (in Chichester's case; Rose had to put into Bluff in New Zealand for repairs). Clearly more people will follow in their wake. Although cruising pioneers like E. F. Knight (who cruised to the Baltic in *Falcon*, a converted lifeboat) and R. T. McMullen (a Victorian stockbroker and tireless cruising exponent) paved the way in the last century, they were regarded more as eccentrics than anything else. In those days, yacht cruising meant passage-making with a crew and probably a skipper. With the excellent books of Dr Claud Worth and the writings of other notable sailor/authors – (for example, Alain Gerbault of France) the period between the two world wars saw a new awareness of the possibilities of cruising in small yachts, an awareness that was to develop into the cruising scene of today – hundreds of yachts manned by men and women, single-handed or with friends, often with their families, sail in almost every quarter of the sea-covered part of the globe. The distance to the fabled Polynesian Islands is still just as immense as it was to the American William Albert Robinson (who wrote some fine books) but there *is* a difference. The aeroplane, television, satellite communication; in fact the speed and facility of all communication and travel now has drawn the far corners of the world together as a seine net draws in to gather its fish. It is not so much that it is less of an undertaking sailing from say Ireland to the West Indies via the trade wind route, as that it *seems* less. Lots of people have done it, and without mishap.

For every yacht that crosses the Atlantic or Pacific there are thousands who give their owners equal pleasure by making cruises of three or four hundred miles, with probably various stops *en route*.

Today the scope is almost limitless. Take a man with a 4-ton sloop who lives in London and keeps his boat in, say, Dover. He may decide to try the Mediterranean for a change one year. He can sail there through the French rivers and canals. He can trail his boat behind his car. He can ship her abroad a freighter. He can leave her on moorings and charter a boat in the Mediterranean and fly, board a train, motor or hike to join her. Take this situation on a world-wide scale; the Bostonian who wants to cruise the Bahamas and West Indies; the Virginian, who is intrigued by Cape Cod and Nova Scotia; the Hungarian who feels a yen to cruise the Aegean Seas, and you will begin to see what I mean. It *is* possible in a 4-tonner, to sail on lakes, rivers, canals, estuaries, inland seas and on the open sea to a degree limited only by your time (most of us are tied by our jobs), and your skill and toughness.

Never underestimate the necessity for the latter. The apparent ease with which Eric and Susan Hiscock twice circumnavigated the world is dangerously misleading. It is necessary to read between the modest lines of his excellent books on his round-world cruises, to realise the knowledge and skill they both possessed and used. You need guts too, sometimes even a very short passage needs guts, if you are caught in a force 7 wind rising to a gale with a weather-going tide and night falling. To run for shelter can at times be as dangerous as it is tempting and it takes guts to do this right and seamanlike thing; keep well offshore and 'see it out'.

I have tried in the chapter on types of craft to give an idea of the great variety now available from small craft suitable (for *most* of us) for short passage-making, to larger sisters who can take us across oceans.

One of the great charms of cruising is the freedom of choice.

In an age where the liberty of the individual is restricted by laws which, though designed for the benefit of the community, inevitably produce sentiments of frustration – the ability of the yachtsman to sail where and when he likes is to many a strong attraction. Of course, the yachtsman must come to terms with the weather, but there is a world of difference between having to anchor in a calm to avoid being taken astern by a strong tide and having to park a motor-car three miles from your destination in a city because of 'no parking' rules. It can be argued that the reason for the latter, over-crowding, applies already to many of the harbours of this world and that the problem will increase. Already, indeed, many a delightful old natural anchorage or harbour has been replaced by a marina designed to pack in as many craft as possible and no doubt, in populous areas the situation will get worse (or better if you *like* crowds). But this book is being written here and now when there are still places where the cruising yacht can moor or anchor in comfort. All the havens of the cruising world have different 'facilities' (a very popular word) to offer – depending on whether facility means to you a ready supply of water, food, petrol, oil and fellow yachtsmen or the company of sea-birds, rushes and the chuckling sound of an evening ebb-tide. Most people enjoy a mixture of the two, with a bias one way or the other. So let us have a look at some of the cruising grounds of the world to whet our appetites.

This chapter is not intended to do anything other than to stimulate the imagination. It could not possibly be comprehensive, but by taking one or two areas, I hope I can show newcomers to cruising the possibilities open to them and may even, with luck, start some of those already experienced in passagemaking, thinking about planning cruises on possibly more adventurous lines than hitherto.

Planning cruises is a wonderful pastime during the winter months. Another delight is reading really good descriptive accounts of cruises and nowadays there is a good choice.

(1) Cruising possibilities

There is, as we saw in chapter two, a wonderful variety of craft (both sail and power) available today. In some you can cruise the world, in others, coastal cruising is more sensible. Since a good many of my readers will be British, let us start by considering the cruising possibilities in the British Isles. I will not dwell on this subject in detail, but the points I want to make apply to any cruising area, so the fact that I am talking about my own home waters does not particularly matter to an American or Australian reader. The principle is the same and it is this. Where you cruise is a question of time. Most of us have a limited time for our holidays and really extensive cruising is difficult if not impossible. Nevertheless with the advent of the small cruiser and the trailer, considerable variety can be experienced in a three weeks' holiday. With larger craft, too big for trailing, rail or car, communication is of importance. But there is another way of cruising, which I will call weekend cruising. Take a look at figure 16. A yacht sailing from Dover to Boulogne can remain in Boulogne while the owner and crew return by packet-steamer. The following weekend they go back on the packet to Boulogne and continue their cruise to, say, Ostend, returning from there in similar fashion. Next weekend they pick up the yacht at Ostend and sail to Ramsgate. The weekend after they sail from Ramsgate to, say, the Blackwater, Burnham-on-Crouch or perhaps Pin Mill. The following weekend finds them back in Dover, their home port. Now they have in fact sailed from Dover to Boulogne to Ostend to Ramsgate, to Pin Mill to Dover. An enjoyable interesting (partly foreign) cruise. Moreover, under normal circumstances, by no means a difficult cruise. It has taken them say, five weekends, but, and this is the point, not a single day of their annual holiday. That is still to come; having cruised the 'East' perhaps the delights of the West Country will claim them – a good idea in August as you nearly always have a south-westerly wind then and you will have to 'beat' against it but can 'run' all the way back. And this is still an advantage to power-boaters too! Unless you have a very high speed (fuel consuming) power yacht, a foul tide is still a foul tide and a good fair spring tide is still a help. I would suggest that, working on the principle of figure 16, you sit down before a map of the British Isles and mark on it the towns and harbours (showing various distances) which are relevant to where you live and where your boat is kept. Now mark in some specimen courses showing distances, also prevailing winds during the summer season. Note those harbours which have a regular railway service linking them with other useful towns and the road networks that do the same. A good long look at

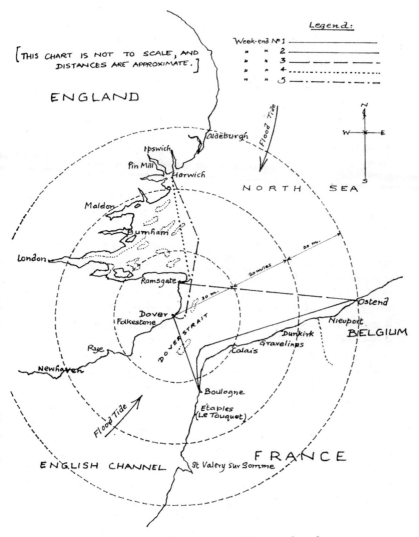

Figure 16.   Weekend cruising – chartlet

your map, at the coastline and the distances should be enough to start you thinking about the possibilities. All you need, in whatever country you live, is to get a map and apply the same principles. If you live in Budapest, and you are used to sailing your *Magyar* on the great Hungarian lake, get a map and work out how easy it is to trail her to Trieste and the blue Aegean Sea. (I know that Homer says it is 'wine-dark' but I have observed it closely and it is blue!)

In chapter five we are going to make a passage along an imaginary coast. The situations we meet with, the changing conditions, will be fairly typical of many a cruising ground. They may vary in degree but the basic problems of wind and weather; of gale, calm, fog and the day-to-day problems of navigation in pilotage waters differ but little no matter where you are.

I say 'navigation in pilotage' waters because, navigation proper means using the heavenly bodies to plot your position when you are well offshore; and the sun and stars are your signposts using a sextant to measure the angles. I have not dealt with navigation as such in this book. The reason is that it is not a subject that can be skimped. It is not particularly difficult to learn. Any reasonably intelligent person can learn to take very accurate 'sights', as they are called, indeed. But it must be learned properly, and to teach the basic principles takes more space than I have allotted myself in this book. Furthermore, this book is mainly for beginners in cruising; and beginners are unlikely to start straightaway sailing hundreds of miles offshore. Those who wish to become deep-water navigators will find that there are plenty of excellent books on astro-navigation. A good second-hand (guaranteed) sextant is not too difficult to come by either from any marine instrument makers and most yacht chandlers of any size. To those who are disappointed I'm sorry but there it is. I am not prepared to give you a short-cut navigational method without explaining what it is you are doing and that would put us several thousand words over and you'd have to pay more for the book! What I am trying to help you do here is to become a proficient seaman; to know your boat and acquire the confidence that will enable you to take bad weather in your stride, and to become very familiar with many things, from the odd habits of tidal streams to the quick tying of a knot.

Having stated that most readers will be unlikely to go blue water ocean cruising straight off, I see no reason, however, why we should not consider the possibilities of extended cruising. For one thing you don't need to cross the Atlantic in a yacht to sail in the West Indies. You can fly there or take a ship there and charter. You don't need to sail to the Algarve in southern Portugal or the Aegean Sea to cruise there. You can trail your boat there (if she is of a trailable size). Later on, when your ambition to cross the Atlantic will no longer be denied, you must buy that sextant and become proficient at navigation. But by then I hope you will have done enough coastal cruising to have experienced some bad weather and acquired the necessary confidence in coping with it. For if you sail right offshore you will eventually run into gale weather as sure as gulls' eggs are eggs.

It is really remarkable how many people sail today, and what long distances they sail. But they are still in a minority. The major part of cruising yachtsmen sail from port to port along their own coasts; and there is nothing whatever amiss with that; you can have endless fun. But just for a few paragraphs, let us take a look at the sort of thing we could do if so inclined (and if given the chance). The cruising areas that follow are chosen at random. They are just a very few (among so many – reasons of space again) to whet your appetite.

Let us begin with (for a Britisher) a cruising ground reasonably near home – the Baltic Sea. The accepted pioneers of cruising in the lovely fjords of the Western Baltic are E. F. Knight and Erskine Childers (who many yachtsmen will know from his classic sea-spy novel *The Riddle of the Sands*). Let us therefore follow in the footsteps of Knight and of Erskine Childers's 'Davies', hero of his novel and sail from England to the Baltic via the Friesian Islands – the location of Childers's mysterious sands.

A glance at figure 17 will be enough to show that there are a good many routes to the Baltic Sea. You can sail the shortest crossing from Dover to Calais up the French and Belgian coast into the Belgian and Dutch inland waterway scheme, and then cross the Zuider Zee, inland again via Mappel and Gröningen back into the North Sea passing the Friesian Islands and so to Brünsbuttel and the Kiel Canal which leads us to the Baltic and the wonderful cruising ground of the Danish fjords. And then, of course, you can sail across the North Sea direct if you are so

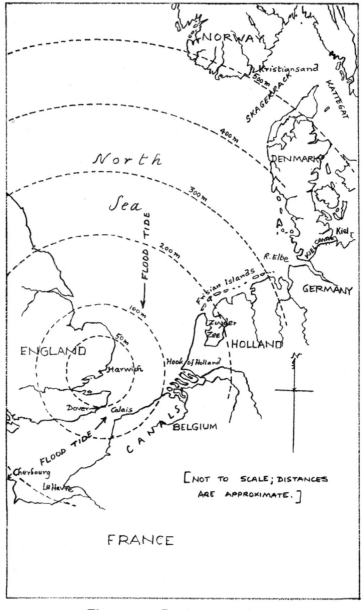

Figure 17.   Routes to the Baltic

minded; or alternatively make the passage out direct and return via the inland waterways. Finally, for those to whom a longer passage at sea is the attraction, you can sail direct to the Skaggerrak, perhaps to Kristiansund (a fine port in southern Norway) and then round the northern tip of Denmark to the Kattegat and from there you can choose once again your own particular cruising ground. E. F. Knight, of course, sailed before the building of the Kiel Canal and so he had to reach Kiel in the Baltic by way of Tonning, the Eider river and the Schleswig-Holstein Canal. Knight made this passage in the jubilee year of 1887. By the time that Erskine Childers made his passage in 1898 the canal was open. Childers wrote an account of this passage which was published in the *Yachting Monthly* magazine under the title *How we drifted to the Baltic in a seven-tonner*. It was this cruise that formed the basis for his great story *The Riddle of the Sands*. There are excellent books on the waterways, rivers and canals which are such a feature of France, Belgium and Holland and they contain all the information you need. Once again time may limit you, but if you can get into the cool, fresh, tideless Baltic Seas you will never regret it, even if it means a hard slog across the North Sea, of which it has been written that it is not even blue in the summer. But it is also a fact that to many people the somewhat austere conditions of the Friesian Islands has an irresistible appeal. To Davies, hero of *The Riddle* and I quote: '. . . the dull, hard sky, the wind moaning in the rigging as though crying in despair for a prey that had escaped it, made the whole scene inexpressibly forlorn . . .', and he loved it! I recently compiled two anthologies; the first, called *The Sea Gets Bluer* catered for those whose wanderlust was for sun, and blue sea, trade winds and palm-fringed shores. The sequel, *The Sea Gets Greyer* catered for those to whom the grey northern seas had an equally potent appeal, and it would appear from the sales that the two types of cruising man (although it is a foolishly arbitrary division – many people like both) are about in equal numbers. And even if the North Sea treats you a little rough on the way across, the summer season in the Baltic will be a revelation.

Let us turn now to another cruising ground, following our idea of examining briefly a few of the available areas in order to whet the appetite, stimulate the imagination once the possibilities have been appreciated.

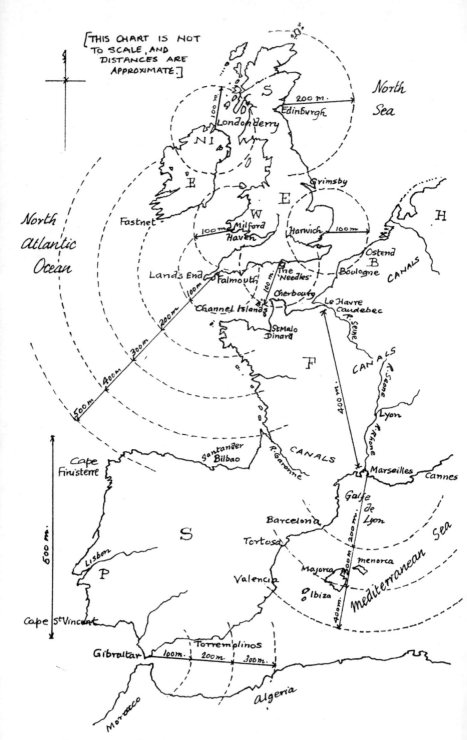

Figure 18.   The Bay of Biscay and the Western Mediterranean

Look now at figure 18 which shows the Bay of Biscay and the western Mediterranean. If one is sailing from an English port, the Bay of Biscay is entered at Ushant, approaching probably through the Chenal du Four. Look now at figure 18 (*a*). From now on wonderful cruising grounds succeed one another. First, as we pass between Ile de Beniguet and the mainland, leaving Pointe de St Mathieu to port we come to the Rade de Brest. This is followed, as we sail southwards by the Baie de Douarnenez. We now pass through the Raz de Sein. Like the Chenal du Four, the Raz de Sein is noted for its fast-running tidal streams. Now as we round the Pointe de Penmarch, comes the Bay of Biscay itself. Once in the Bay we find weaker tidal streams. As we coast down east-south-easterly we come upon a series of granite islands, Ile de Groix, Belle Ile and Ile d'Yeu. Since each has a harbour and anchorages sheltered from various winds, they provide the additional attraction of that indefinable

THE CRUISING AREA OF BRITTANY
[see Figure 18]

Figure 18 (*a*). The Brittany Coast

95

atmosphere which seems peculiar to islands, but which all who have cruised among islands know. Meanwhile the coast to the east provides as wonderful a variety of harbours and anchorages as you could wish for; fishing harbours, holiday resorts, anchorages in deep or shallow water where you can lie in complete quiet, large busy ports, and the great attraction of the Breton himself. The Bretons are a tough race of sailormen, and they are both friendly and helpful.

In the 'Bay', of which so may lurid accounts of gales are told, winds need not worry you too much. In the spring, early summer and late autumn you will often get winds between north and east. In midsummer, or July and August, westerly winds predominate. In spite of its bad reputation the Bay produces on the average only one day in twenty-five from May to September when winds of force 7 or over are recorded.

One is sometimes asked what sort of boat is suitable for cruising in the Bay. The answer is any seaworthy yacht, but, since many of the harbours are shallow, a boat of shallow draft is best for exploring. Several of the yachts discussed in chapter one would be suitable. What you want is a shallow-draft vessel with, say, a centreboard, that can sail pretty well anywhere, even at spring tides. Alternatively, fit your boat with 'legs', in the manner of the local French fishing vessel. With legs securely bolted each side amidships a yacht can safely dry out anywhere, provided there is shelter. Rocky coasts frequently have rocks in their approaches and the Brittany coast is no exception. Such anchorages should only be approached by the beginner in settled weather with good visibility.

As one proceeds southward through the Bay the weather becomes noticeably warmer. Half-way down the coastline lies the harbour of La Rochelle (see figure 18), a very convenient port of call for yachts bound for Spain To the south of the Charente river and the Gironde (leading to Bordeaux) are last outposts of civilisation before the Pyrenees, since from the Gironde southwards the coast is flat, featureless and harbourless, with the exception of Arcachon and that has a difficult entrance, and is at times inaccessible (in a strong onshore wind for example). So La Rochelle is in a very strategic position for yachtsmen and it also has the advantage of being well provided with yacht chandlers, stores, etc

Having got this far you may well be saying to yourself why

not visit Spain, put in at Santander, with its hospitable yacht club, take in a bull fight or two and sail back in a straight line for Ushant! As I have repeatedly said it's a question of time mostly, plus some confidence in yourself and your boat of course The distance involved you can work out from the chart and so get a rough idea of the time necessary for a cruising holiday in the Bay, but only a rough idea You may (with an iron will) be able to restrict the time you spend in the harbours and anchorages but you cannot control the weather!

So far we have had to look at cruising in the home waters of the British Isles, then we have gone somewhat further afield to the Baltic to the north-east and the Bay of Biscay to the south-west. Let us now look further afield and south and west across the Atlantic to the West Indies and the Bahamas.

Just after the last war a number of enterprising yachting people took the trade wind route to the West Indies. Some may have intended to continue their cruises, others eventually to return to England via Bermuda and to pick up the westerlies; but many stayed. Contrary to the opinion of some people, not all yachtsmen are millionaires. Many of the vessels that sailed from England to the sun were modest in size and, when they got there, they found that in order to make a bit of money they were able to charter. With more yachts the charter business grew until we got today's situation of hundreds of families chartering, especially during the winter months. In the yachts that make up the charter fleet (or fleets) you will find a great diversity both of craft and of owner. It is as well to go to a reputable charter firm if you want to make sure of a good, well-found yacht.

A look at the chart in figure 19 will show that this is a cruising paradise, whether you sail your own boat there or fly or take a ship and then charter. You will, as in any area where you plan to sail, need to provide yourself with adequate charts and sailing directions. You will notice that while the islands provide sheltered anchorages, especially on the lee side, the channels between them are open to the force of the trade winds, which have travelled some 3,000 miles across the Atlantic. Sailing between the islands can in consequence be tough going, but few of the channels are more than thirty miles wide and one is seldom exposed to these strong winds for longer than a few hours. In the winter winds blow almost always from north-east to south-east, so it means a lively passage either to windward or on

Figure 19. The West Indies

a broad reach for a few hours. In this way you can sail in a day
from island to island as it takes your fancy. The islands between
Bequia and Antigua are mountainous and their lee side not only
provides shelter but can in fact produce conditions of very light
airs, often head-winds, which can make sailing their lee quite
difficult. By and large though, this is not a difficult area to
cruise in, and for those with the time and the opportunity
provide a wonderful cruising ground. The islands are divided
into the Greater Antilles and the Lesser Antilles. The Greater
Antilles group consists of Cuba, Jamaica, Hispaniola and
Puerto Rico. The Lesser Antilles group is again divided into

the Windward Islands (Grenada and Martinique) and the Leeward Islands (islands north of Martinique). It is well to remember always when cruising in foreign waters, that the local rules concerning customs clearance must be observed. Different countries of course vary. The *laissez-faire* attitude of France, for example, must not blind one to the fact that in the Lesser Antilles you will need to enter and clear your yacht with the authorities at each island, regardless of nationality. Between Puerto Rico and St Martin and Anguilla (the most northerly of the Leeward Islands) lies the archipelago of the Virgin Islands (British and American) a wonderful cruising ground, containing many sheltered anchorages, some of them being in uninhabited islands.

Marinas are of course to be found if not in profusion in the West Indies, in a fair supply, each one similarly packed mostly with high-speed craft fitted out for big game fishing. All marinas supply pretty well every normal want of the cruising yachtsman, whether sail or power.

If cruising the West Indies presents no great problems; the story is quite different when we come to the Bahamas. There is an excellent yachtsman's guide to the Bahamas (an official publication of the Ministry of Tourism in Nassau) which was originally compiled by British yachtsman Harry Etheridge. Etheridge sailed to the West Indies in a *Grebe*, a Norwegian lifeboat (Colin Archer) type yacht and settled there with his family. An able artist, his delightful pen drawings are an attractive feature of the guide. He died unfortunately in 1957 and a talented yachting draughtsman was lost to the world. The present excellent edition is edited by Harry Kline. Figure 20 shows the Bahama Islands. The reason why I said it is not so straightforward as the cruising we have just been discussing is that in the Bahamas much of the sailing is done in shallow water. Enormous banks extend for hundreds of square miles, on which coral is often near the surface. The moral here is to take a pilot. It takes months of study and practice to navigate these waters confidently and safely. Shallow-draft boats that can take the ground have some advantage but even so, the wind can freshen suddenly, short steep seas will get up and you can be in a dangerous situation. Another difficulty in sailing about in the Bahamas is the shortage of lights. Various friends of the author also support the theory that there are inaccuracies in the chart.

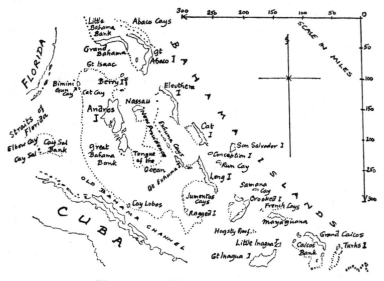

Figure 20.   The Bahama Islands

But all agree that the *Yachtsman's Guide* is unassailable; so if you go there, get a copy.

Before concluding this section I would again emphasise that it is just to start you thinking. It is no purpose of mine to extend this chapter into a yachtsman's Baedekker! And to those whose favourite cruising ground has been omitted I apologise. There are far too many. The beauties of the west coasts of Ireland, Scotland and the Norwegian fjords, the boisterous Grecian Islands, the wonderful coasts of Massachusetts – Buzzards Bay, Martha's Vineyard, Nantucket Sound and further north by Princetown across Cape Cod Bay to Plymouth, Boston and so to Gloucester are all worth visiting. The very names are of the history of sail. Massachusetts has wonderful bays and so good shelter and it is often called the 'Bay' state. Then there are the Great Lakes – but that brings me to the next section!

(2) Lake Sailing

Quite a lot of misunderstanding exists about lake sailing. Most people are aware that yachts are sailed on huge lakes like Michigan, or any of the Great Lakes in the north-western hemisphere, but I have frequently observed that it surprises sailing people when you tell them that for example in Lake Constance, there are on the German side no less than ten yacht clubs; on the Swiss side there are seven and on the Austrian side, four. Furthermore, there are seven sailing schools on this thirty-nine-mile long stretch of water which lies about thirty miles east of the southern end of the Black Forest. Again it is to their surprise to be told that in the regattas held in this lake (which are many, from April to September) the regularly competing classes include 5·5-metre *Dragons, Stars, Finns* and *Moths* in the international classes as well as many national classes, like the *Lacustre, Korsar, Vaurien* and 30-sq m *Schärenkreuzer*; and the friends you tell stare their surprise at you. They had no idea!

It hardly needs reiterating that in a book of this size it would be ridiculous to try and do more than give the reader an idea of the many new and varied forms of cruising that exist. For example, there are navigable lakes all over the world. However, if we turn our attention for a moment to the lake systems of Switzerland and eastern Austria and southern Germany; we build up a picture and see something of the possibilities offered by lake cruising, wherever it may happen to be.

I said that Lake Constance (called in Germany, Bodensee) was thirty-nine miles long. This may not sound much, but in fact it covers an area of 208 square miles and it is a very varied cruising ground. However, if you will look now at figure 21 you will see that if you think in terms of trailing you have almost endless possibilities. You will see that the two larger lakes Geneva (Leman) and Constance (Bodensee) lie, the first at the eastern end; the second in the centre of a system of lakes in a plain north of the mountain systems from the Bernese Alps to the Bavarian Alps. There are over thirty lakes in fact to choose from. Of course the larger the lake, the more reliable the wind system and the better scope for cruising, and while on the subject of wind I should mention that, while aware that lake sailing exists, many people dismiss it as being too easy and providing no challenge for the sailing man. Let me assure both sail and power cruising enthusiasts that this is far from being the case. When you get proximity to mountains you can get unreliable and at times dangerous weather conditions. (Those who know the fjords of Scandinavia and the west coast of

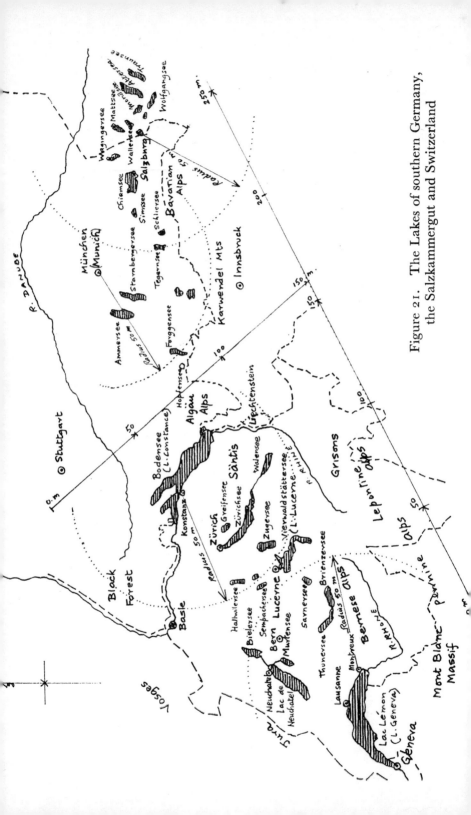

Figure 21. The Lakes of southern Germany, the Salzkammergut and Switzerland

Scotland will be well aware of this.) Lakes Geneva, Constance and the Zürichsee for example suffer from a wind called the Föhn. Having made this point let me assure the reader that the locals are ready and most willing to provide weather information and this coupled with the local forecasts enables one to plan one's passages and take any necessary precautions. I only wish to make the point that sailing on these lakes is not a tame affair.

For those who do not wish to trail a craft to such a cruising ground there are innumerable opportunities on the larger lake to hire; and the charges are moderate. But I would personally recommend trailing your boat if she is suitable, and if she is not you won't be considering this sort of cruising anyway. A few years back I trailed a small boat to the Mediterranean, cruised there a while; trailed from Genoa to Venice, cruised the north Adriatic; trailed to the Dolomites and sailed on the Italian Lakes, from there, over the Alps to Lake Geneva where I also sailed a while, and so back to the Channel ports to finish the round trip. It was a novel and fascinating experience and I would never have compassed so many quite different places and countries or covered such distances within the space of my holiday if I had had to sail the whole way. Furthermore, without trailing I would not have been able to sail my boat on the Italian Lakes. It made a change from, say, cruising from the Solent to France and Spain, or the North Sea foreign ports, and I recommend it.

Look now at figure 21a. Let us take Lake Geneva as an example of what you will find on a large lake of this sort. First of all, scenery. Behind the Geneva basin rise the Jura mountains to heights of 5,500 feet. Near the lake the shore is flat but as you go eastward the mountains approach the water so that at some places the vineyards on their lower slopes touch the lake. These vineyards continue along the northern shore until we reach fashionable Montreux where the shore bends round to where the Alps begin, and the Rhône valley winds away to the southeast flanked by the Dents du Midi and the Grand Muveran, great ridges that rise to over 10,000 feet. The southern shore of the lake is quite different. Meadows and farmland predominate here, in the distance can be seen the Haute Savoie, in which range Mont Blanc, Europe's highest mountain, towers to 15,786 feet.

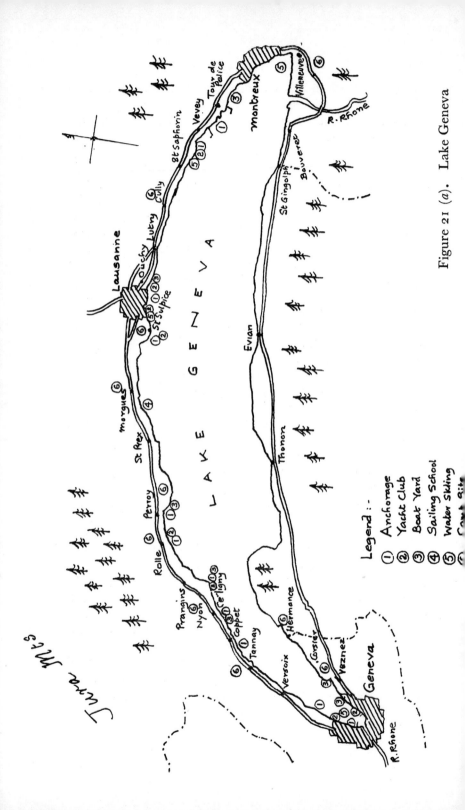

Figure 21 (a). Lake Geneva

Next size. Lake Geneva is 50 miles long and 8½ miles across at its widest point. It covers 224 square miles and its greatest depth is 1,017 feet. It is 1,230 feet above sea-level; which brings me to its climate. The best months are March, April and May because then you can rely on good fresh winds as opposed to the light airs of the later summer months. There are two principle winds; the vent du sud-ouest (south-westerly) and the bise (north-easterly). As a general rule, the former means bad weather and the latter, fine weather. The bise in the spring can reach force 7 or 8.

In considering the weather of Geneva it is necessary to divide it into two. The first part, the 'Petit-lac' from Geneva to Nyon and the second part, the 'Haut-lac', which is the main part. The wind pattern in these two halves differs fundamentally and it is this sort of thing that gives lake sailing such interest. The Föhn, for example, which blows from the Alps along the Rhône valley towards Lausanne at forces of between 3 and 6, seldom extends into the Petit-lac, where the winds are more predictable, although here local winds can blow up to force 5 from the south-west at times when the eastern Haut-lac is reflecting its wonderful coast-line in a flat calm.

There are to my knowledge at least seven boat-builders round the lake and about the same number of yacht chandlers.

To continue about Lake Geneva will still further upset a balance which even now is in danger; so I will end this section by emphasising that whatever the country and the lake or lakes, there will be regulations concerning the use of pleasure craft, and you must get hold of these and comply with them. For example, all Swiss craft must obtain a licence from their cantonal Schiffinspektorat and are issued then with a number. Foreign boats, as long as they obey regulations, may be used on the lakes for one month without having to take out a licence.

Drivers of motor vessels (except outboard dinghies with a maximum speed of 15 km/h) and all helmsmen of sailing craft with a sail area exceeding 15 sq m (162 sq ft) must have a cantonal certificate of competency. Now it is practically impossible to acquire this in a short time, so visitors to the lakes are restricted to outboard dinghies not exceeding a speed of 15 km/h or sailing dinghies whose sail area does not exceed 15 sq m.

Now if you have the time and facilities to acquire the

necessary certificate all well and good; otherwise this lake cruising is going to be restricted as far as you are concerned to a dinghy of one sort or another. It is not only feasable to cruise in a dinghy, it is fun, and in chapter seven we shall discuss it.

(3) Trailing

This would seem as good a place as any to comment on trailing. We have mentioned trailing as a means of conveying craft, ranging from dinghies to small cruisers, over considerable distances. The advantages will be obvious. To take a very simple example. To trail a 3½-ton yacht to the Mediterranean is simple and quick. To motor through the canals is entertaining, but takes a good month before you emerge in the 'Med'. To sail there via the Bay of Biscay, the Strait of Gibraltar and the Gulf of Lions will need a very much longer holiday than most of us get; and anyway, being caught off Cape Finisterre in a force 8 in a 3½-tonner isn't everybody's idea of sailing bliss; so here are a few words on the subject.

The essence of a good trailer is that it should combine lightness with strength. Independent suspension is a good idea. Wheel bearings should be waterproof. In loading a boat and securing her on your trailer take good care that she is correctly balanced. This is really a matter of common sense – not too far forward as this puts a strain on the tow-bar, and in particular makes the trailer difficult to manhandle when detached from the car. The boat should rest on her keel on the trailer; the weight being taken there, and not by the planking or skin of the hull. The chocks on a trailer are there to hold the vessel in position, not to take the weight. Some trailers make use of battens across the top of the boat secured to brackets on the trailer. These battens are called strong backs. They are often secured by long rods with screw ends. Straps are also often used. A lot depends on the size and shape of the boat. Stowing the mast and spars can be a problem in the case of a sailing boat. Shrouds and stays should be very firmly lashed and the mast secured fore and aft above the deck. Some trailers have special fittings to carry the mast. An outboard engine can be towed in its usual position but 'cocked up'. It depends on the length of the journey as to whether you like this idea; but it is difficult to find other suitable places to stow an outboard. To stow it securely in the hull is not at all easy and you don't particularly want it in the car with you! On the stern, with good protective cover and well secured is as good a place as any I know. Remember, when lashing your boat to a trailer that all towed boats tend to creep ahead on the trailer going downhill and vice versa. So get out from time to time and have a look, and if necessary tighten the lashings or screws.

What about rules? As far as the British Isles go they are laid down in the latest 'Statutory Instrument' made under the Traffic Acts. This can be obtained from HM Stationery Office and is cheap. Make sure that your car policy covers your trailer, by the way. There are scores of trailers on the market nowadays – ranging from, say, a trailer suitable for towing a 12-foot dinghy (250 lb) to one that will carry a 4-tonner and larger still. To quote a couple of examples, for your (250 lb) 12-foot dinghy a 9 ft 3 ins × 5 ft trailer such as the *Tom Smart* trailer will cost you about £30. For a heavy dinghy of that length weighing, say, 800 lb, James Trailers make a 12 ft × 5 ft 9 ins model called the *Delta 12*. This costs anything from £49 to £59. For larger craft, you can, for example, carry a boat of 4 tons weight on a *Star* (Marine) 30-ft HC 80·00 *Tornado*, dimensions 24 ft × 7 ft 3 ins and this will set you back £335. For a 2-ton weight cruiser the 19 ft × 7 ft 2 ins *Delta* by James Trailers will cost you about £150. This is for a boat of about 19 feet in length. I am assuming that the 4-ton boat would be about 30 feet in length. I should point out that these tonnages are weights and not the yacht measurement formula. For a boat of, say, 18 feet in length – for example, the *Alacrity Mk II*, Bramber Engineering make a 16 ft 3 ins × 6 ft 4 ins trailer called the TRB 1250/19 which costs £112. This is a tough braked model. Small Boats Supplies make a trailer called the *Clubman 10*, size 14 ft 6 ins × 5 ft 6 ins (a bit smaller, but still all right for a 19-foot overall length boat) for £58.

I hope this has given you some ideas; which indeed this whole chapter is designed to do. Now it is time to get down to brass tacks and sail somewhere. The following chapter deals with an imaginary passage at sea. We have discussed types of craft, moorings and cruising grounds. Now, at last, we can do some sailing!

CHAPTER FIVE

On Passage – from Start to Finish

It has been said (repeatedly) that one of the charms of sailing is
that one is always faced with a novel situation, nothing is the
same as before. This is undoubtedly true and while I am well
aware of the stimulating nature of new situations while actually
afloat (caused by a hitherto unexperienced combination of a
number of individually well-known factors), it is difficult for
the writer on sailing to arrange his facts and figures in a
sufficiently new way to stimulate the reader and still provide
instruction in sailing that is coherent. For the complete novice;
the facts of themselves will probably stimulate without any
garnish, in fact the less garnish the better; but since many of my
readers will, I suspect, have sailed dinghies and small boats, they
will already know quite a bit about the game. It is therefore my
problem to cater for them while serving up sufficient data to the
newcomer at least to get him or her from A to B in safety. The
following chapter is in the form of an imaginary passage, made
in a motor-sailer (or 50/50) (since this book caters for power
cruisers as well as sail, a 50/50 was the obvious meeting-point).
In this chapter I hope you will find all that is necessary to make
a passage in safety under normal conditions of weather; and if
by the end of it you don't feel confident enough to go out and
buy a brass-bound jacket right away, it's your fault – or at
least I like to think so. It is a good sail, the one on which we are
to embark and if you enjoy reading it as much as I enjoyed
writing it, I shall be well satisfied, because what we enjoy
reading, we remember. Those who have not sailed before

should read chapter six, 'How to Sail', which sets out the basic techniques of sailing and of manoeuvring under power; with a section on temperamental engines.

(1) The boat . . . checking gear on board – preparation for the passage – aneroid barometer – weather-forecasts

This imaginary passage is being made in a sailing yacht with a large diesel engine; a type that is at home either under power or sail. Some people call such vessels motor-sailers; other call them 50/50s, but those who are familiar with them often call them the best of both worlds. Is there such a thing? Well this passage will help to go some way to answering that. She is of no particular class vessel, but fairly typical of the species we considered in chapter one, for example, the *Spey* or the *Nicholson 38*, but smaller.

The essential difference between a motor-sailer and a motor-cruiser with sails is that the motor-sailer is really a sailing vessel, while the other is a motor vessel with a small sail area, only really of use for steadying purposes. The line of demarcation is fine. There are many auxiliary cruising yachts around our coasts that might better be described as motor-sailers (even though their owners might take offence at such a description). In the case of our boat here, her engine is powerful enough to drive her at the speed she sails in a good whole sail breeze; and in her case that is about 7 knots.

Now who is going to make this passage with us? Let us take an owner who is a naturally cautious person, more than a bit put off by the mystique of sailing and worried by horrific stories. I know him well – don't you? So let us see what we can do to give him the confidence that will enable him to get the best in every way out of his sailing. I am going to assume some knowledge on the part of our yachtsman friend. He knows port from starboard and how to steer on all points of sailing among other elementary things. He has just not had much experience of passage-making.

The first thing to do, on arriving on board before a passage, is to check gear – your own and the ship's.

Is there fresh water on board? Diesel oil (or petrol)? Is there oil in the engine sump? Paraffin (for the spare lights in case the electrics fail)? Matches (*plenty* of these!)? First-aid gear?

Brandy? Sugar? Coffee? Tea? etc. (Everything should be in air-tight jars or tins *and* labelled.) Life-jackets? Fenders? Anchors? Make sure the cable is secured below? Warps? Heaving lines? Spare rope? All the sails? In this case the mainsail is bent (attached) to the boom and there are a working jib, a No. 2 jib (for when the mainsail is reefed) and a spinnaker. Yes, a spinnaker! Why should racing yachts have all the fun? Then what about charts? The compass? Is it corrected? Have you a deviation table to correct courses, etc by? Navigational books and instruments? Nautical almanack? Tide tables? Light lists? Pilots? Patent log? Lead-line? Anchor light? Distress flares? Binoculars? In short you must check that the cook and the navigator have done their stuff – for when you're becalmed in the middle of a large bay, with say another twenty-five odd miles to go, is no time to run out of fuel and fresh water on a scorching day! You should also check your clothes. Oilskins? Sea-boots? Sou'wester? Adequate sweaters and change of trousers, socks and shirts? There's no point in prolonging the list, for it's all really common sense, but it does need attention before departure. If the boat is registered (you will remember we discussed registration in chapter three), you can, with permission of your local customs officer, buy spirits at duty-free prices – but *ONLY* if you are going abroad on a bona fide foreign cruise. In this case we are not; so the question does not arise.

The next thing is preparation and as far as the navigator is concerned this consists of two main things – studying the passage in terms of tides, distances, headlands, etc, and, as far as possible, in terms of weather. Let us start with the latter; it is obviously of importance, and take a look at the local conditions. A lot can be done in local weather-forecasting by the combination of barometer readings, the wind's direction and the appearance of the sky. In fact, an absolutely essential piece of gear on board is the aneroid barometer. There are certain basic rules which help in interpreting its readings. For example, an approaching gale will be given away by a fall of the barometer combined with a backing (anti-clockwise) of the wind. The duration of such warning varies, however. It can be anything from ten hours to two hours. If the barometer stops falling and no gale has arrived, don't heave a sigh of relief too soon for this can be dangerous unless you are on your guard! Many a gale comes not only when the barometer has stopped falling, but when it has started to rise. Remember, too, that it is not only a falling barometer that heralds bad weather; a rapidly rising glass can also forecast an approaching gale; often of a more squally nature. The point is; watch for rapid *movement* of the glass.

It is not necessary to have a fluid or mercury barometer, which though more reliable than the aneroid, is more complex and has to be corrected for temperature, for height above sea-level and for latitude. The ordinary aneroid barometer is quite accurate enough for the yachtsman; but get a good make and treat it well. Screw it to a bulkhead where you won't bump into it, but where it can be easily read.

Next we must look at the sky. Clouds can tell us a lot. Most people know the cumulus cloud; the fine-weather, billowing cloud that forms over the land after sunrise and disappears at sunset. However, if such clouds are sharply defined, showers and squalls can be expected. But this is not the place to embark further on this subject. We will consider it in more detail in chapter nine. But I would remind you here that we can get great help from the radio weather-forecasts; they are a most important safety-factor for coasting yachtsmen. Whatever some wise-acres may tell you over a beer in the yacht club bar, the wireless reports are very helpful. They cover about twelve hours. Remember that they are only general and may be late in fast-moving weather. For the British yachtsman, the BBC shipping forecasts prepared by the Meteorological Office give the position of weather systems and their intensity. They give the fronts and an idea of their expected positions some hours later. They give wind directions and speeds and barometric pressure. From the 'Met' office (Met Office, 1 London Road, Bracknell) you can get a leaflet (No. 3) which sets out full details of special services which are available in addition to the normal broadcast schedules.

At sea, you should watch the weather continuously, as well as study it while preparing for a passage. The times and wave-lengths of weather-forecasts can be easily found for example, in a good nautical almanack (an essential part of the navigator's equipment). This brings us to the latter's duties regarding preparation for our passage, a fascinating and vitally important subject.

(2) Basic navigational equipment – why and how a compass works – variation – deviation – making a deviation graph – charts and projections – preparation by navigator – planning the passage – various checks (engine, etc) before departure

Although no one would want to take away from the navigator his title; yet on a passage of this nature, when we are unlikely to be out of sight of land for very long we are going to be concerned not so much with *navigation* as with *pilotage*. Now although, in theory, pilotage requires little more than some charts and an elementary knowledge of geometry, in practice piloting a yacht efficiently requires a certain skill, and to do it properly we need to prepare carefully. Let us take the essentials first, a compass (with a deviation card), a chart (or charts) and a nautical almanack, a pair of parallel rules, a protractor, a pair of dividers and at least one sharp pencil. Also essential is a lead-line for measuring the depth of water and a patent log for recording the distance run through the water. Not *essential* are such things as a calculator for working out variation and deviation when plotting courses, a hand-bearing compass (unless you can't take bearings from the steering compass, when it does become essential), an echo-sounder, a sextant and a radio-direction-finder; also such things as a pilot, tidal atlas, star atlas, etc, and there are other refinements like a distance and speed indicator, steering indicator and a wind direction and speed indicator – all electronic navigational aids – not essential, but they *can* be invaluable. However, we won't need them this time. A good compass *is* very important. The compass is in fact so important a piece of navigational equipment that we should examine how and why it works, and this seems to be the ideal place to do so.

A man out of sight of land at sea in a boat will quickly become lost without a compass. At night, a knowledge of even such a simple fact as where to look for and find the Pole (or North) star gives some guide to direction; and by day the combination of the time of day and the position of the sun (if you can see it!) will also serve as a guide. But clouds can hide the Pole Star and the sun all too often and at best they give only an approximation. With a reliable compass, we are half-way home; and with a chart on which to plot our course we're home, at least in theory!

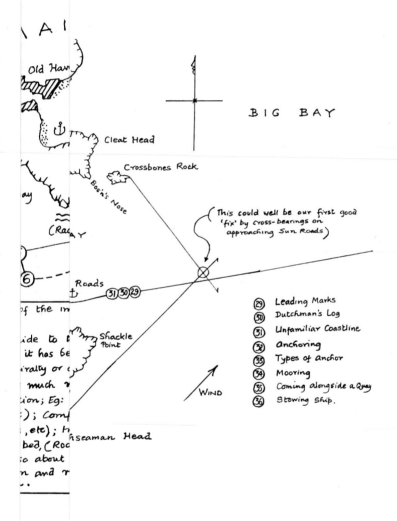

Imaginary passage in chapter five

So the cruising yachtsman needs charts and a reliable compass. The compass we use in small boats makes use of the principle of magnetism, of magnetic poles attracting and repelling each other. You can make a simple magnet by rubbing an iron bar with another magnet. Hammering it in a magnetic field or passing an electric current through it will achieve the same result. Take this small artificially induced magnet, suspend it or balance it so that it is free to revolve in a more or less horizontal position. One end of your magnet will always point north. Place a card beneath it with the points of the compass marked on it and you have your compass.

The north to which the compass needle points is not true north but magnetic north, a point situated somewhere to the north-west of Hudson's Bay. This point is located deep down in the earth, consequently as you approach it from the Equator, the compass needle is attracted slowly downwards. This downward deflection of the needle is called 'dip'. It will be clear therefore that in areas near the Pole, the magnetic compass becomes less reliable, but this fact, interesting enough in theory, is unlikely to worry most cruising yachtsmen. So far we have talked of North, but as most people know, there is a south-seeking end of the compass needle as well. The north-seeking end is called the red end; and the south-seeking end, the blue. Now not only is the north-seeking end of the needle attracted to the north it is repelled by the South Pole (the other magnetic pole, situated deep down in the northern part of South Victoria Land). This attracting and repelling is the result of the fundamental law of magnetism: like poles repel, unlike poles attract. If you were to take a magnet and place it near the compass needle the *blue* pole of that magnet would attract the *red* end of the compass needle. The earth can be likened to a huge magnet, with a *blue* end at the North Pole and a *red* end at the South. So we see that the needle of a compass points to the North Magnetic Pole with its red end and vice versa.

Of course, as in many things in life, nothing is quite as simple as it at first appears and the magnetic poles have their own little game with us by shifting their position by a few miles every year. This fact is noted on the chart. If your charts are new you need not worry. If they are very old a correction (again indicated on the chart) will have to be made; but more of that later. What is more important is to realise that magnetic north being located north-west of Hudson's Bay, means that a line drawn to that point from a point south of it – say from the Fastnet Rock off southern Ireland – will vary slightly from a line drawn from the same point to true north. Furthermore, it will also be clear that a line drawn from the Fastnet will differ in its relationship to north from a line drawn from Montauk Point on the eastern seaboard of North America or from Norderney Lighthouse in the Friesian Islands. This difference between true and magnetic north is called variation and as we shall see later it plays its part in navigation; a small part probably as far as the average cruising yachtsman is concerned, but you never know. After three years of pottering about the Irish Sea, you might find yourself next year bound down the trade wind route to the Leeward Islands on the other side of the 'Pond'. Variation also exists between the true and magnetic South Poles; a fact that Aussies, Kiwis and other southern hemisphere yachtsmen must fully understand before they start calling themselves navigators! As far as the annual change in variation is concerned, you can forget it. For example, the variation change is shown on the east–west axis of any compass 'rose' printed on a chart. Now supposing this reads as follows 'variation 10° (degrees) west decreasing 5' (minutes) annually'. Even if your chart were ten years old, the variation would have altered by less than a degree.

If you now think that that concludes the problems connected with compass needles you are wrong. A compass whose needle points accurately enough when bought may cease to do so when placed on board your boat. This is distinctly upsetting but fortunately the malady is easily diagnosed. It is suffering from deviation, and the cause lies in the magnetic field of the boat or more likely of iron objects in that boat. To complicate matters a bit more, the extent of the deviation varies according to the direction in which your ship's head is pointing. For example, when steering east there may be no deviation, but as soon as she swings to sail south you may get a deviation of 3 degrees.

This tendency of the compass needle to deviate may be compensated for by small bar magnets placed under the compass by a gentleman known as a compass adjuster. However, in practice, very little if anything, in the way of compensating magnets is needed in the average wood or glass-reinforced plastic hull. In a metal hull it can be a different story. In the average boat such deviation as may appear will most likely be caused by the engine and its fittings or by metal stanchions. These relatively small degrees of deviation can however affect navigation very considerably and the deviation on each course of the yacht must be allowed for in the navigator's calculations. To know how much to allow, a deviation card (or graph) must be made and I will describe a little later how you do this – it is quite simple.

To sum up. The compass needle of a magnetic compass does not point to true north and, on certain courses, its own idea of magnetic north may not coincide with magnetic north as shown on the compass rose on the chart. Variation is the amount by which north on the compass varies from true north and deviation is the amount by which north on the compass deviates from magnetic north due to magnetic influences on board.

To put it another way: variation is the difference between a true and a magnetic bearing, and deviation is the difference between a magnetic bearing and a compass bearing.

When, therefore, we have obtained from the chart a given course, the necessary corrections (probably nothing for variation but quite likely something for deviation) must be applied. We now have a new course, known as the course to steer. The course on the chart is called the course to make good. If variation and deviation are applied correctly the course steered by compass should result in 'making good' the desired course on the chart. (If I hear a small voice saying: 'what about the effect of the tide?' I can only say at this point patience, PLEASE!)

There are scores of makes of compasses in the world's markets. Take advice and don't economise! A reliable compass is of paramount importance. The size and type will depend on the size of your boat. A boat of, say, 20 feet on the water-line and above will have the compass bowl fitted in a small binnacle with a gimbal ring so that the compass can remain horizontal regardless of pitching and rolling. It is advisable to have some form of illumination for night sailing. The compass should be placed so that it can easily be seen by the man at the wheel or tiller. It should ideally also be located so that you can take bearings from it. If this is not practicable, a second small hand-bearing compass should be carried on board. When using the latter, care must be taken that you do not hold it close to wire rigging or other metal fittings or you will come up against deviation once again.

Now deviation does not matter as long as you *know* what it is, and can apply the correction. For this purpose you will need a deviation card or graph and there are several ways of doing it. Here is one easy way. Beg or borrow another compass (which is accurate), line it up with the fore-and-aft line of the yacht in such a position that it is a good 6 feet away from the nearest iron or steel. Take the yacht round in a circle, row her round her anchor, or warp her round, the object being to steady her on the successive magnetic points (cardinal and inter-cardinal), and note the difference between the correct compass and the steering compass (affected by deviation). If you can't acquire that other (correct) compass, find any two objects on the harbour plan of where you are lying which when brought into line give you a fixed, known bearing. Now row, or turn the yacht slowly round with the engine, or warp her round as before and steady her on the successive magnetic points and note the difference between the reading of the bearing of the two marks in line on your boat's compass and the correct magnetic reading. Once again note any differences (eg 1 degree or $2\frac{1}{2}$ degrees, etc, east or west) and make your deviation card. These may now be plotted on graph paper. Compass points on the vertical scale and deviation degrees along the horizontal. With your deviation graph you can see at a glance what the deviation is by running your eye down from the horizontal scale along the top for any given course. While a table will only show you the deviation east and west for cardinal and inter-cardinal points, with the deviation graph you can quickly find that deviation for any intermediate direction of that ship's head. Figure 22 will give you the idea. Incidentally, in small boats a compass card marked in points, like fishermen have used since it was first invented, is quite sufficiently accurate for navigating. It is very difficult, in a seaway, to steer to 'a degree'. However, the many people who prefer using degrees rather than points will not agree with me.

Now we have got a deviation graph, let's turn to charts. The British Admiralty charts like all official 'Navy' charts, are excellent. They are clear and full of information. They are, however, often rather large and there are a number of very good smaller-sized charts on the market, but whatever make of chart

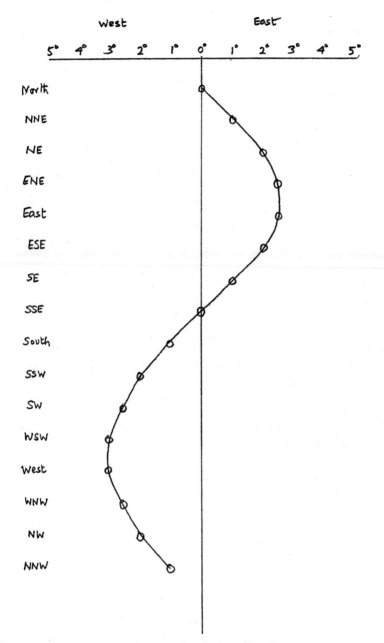

Figure 22. Deviation Graph

you get – get *enough* of them. There are, basically, three main types of chart. Passage – on which the whole of our voyage may be shown; coastal – on a larger scale – and harbour plans. As a basic rule, get one small-scale passage chart, then a set of coastal charts to cover the area, each one overlapping the other slightly; and a set of harbour plans of the harbours that you *may* visit, *not only* from inclination but from *necessity* in bad weather! It is also important to see that your charts extend beyond your destination in case you have to run for it.

It is wise to select your charts with care. They are admittedly quite expensive and although you should always err on the side of having too many rather than too few, you can save yourself money by a judicious choice. With the Admiralty charts you can consult their annual catalogue, which shows the areas covered by each chart and from which you can get a good idea of the scale and appearance of each. At the foot of each chart is the date and there are references to that date and to the source of any corrections which have been made since the chart was published. When you buy a new chart it will (or should) be corrected and up to date. Each chart has a number and a 'title'. The latter gives not only the descriptive name of the chart, but a few of the abbreviations and conventional signs used in it, and other relevant notices. It also tells you whether the soundings showing the depths of water are in feet or fathoms, a most important bit of information. Admiralty charts are on the large side, which for a very small cruiser presents a space problem. Such vessels may well be better off with charts of the folding up variety, like the *Stanford* charts. As I said, a visit to a chandlers or a good shop where they sell charts will soon show that there is quite a range to choose from.

Most charts are drawn on what is called Mercator's projection. Without going into too much detail, the effect of this projection is that the Equator is shown as a straight line and the meridians of longitude are parallel to each other running from north to south. The parallels of latitude are also all parallel to the Equator. And any course between two places will appear as a straight line. Distance on a *Mercator* chart is measured along the *vertical* edges, taking care to use that part which is as nearly as possible opposite (same latitude) as the part of the chart on which you are working. On a *Mercator* chart the latitude scale is not uniform but increases north and south as you approach the poles.

It will be clear enough that for working on a chart it is a great advantage to deal with straight lines. Now the shortest distance between two places on earth is an arc of the circle (the earth is round, remember?) passing through those places. On a *Mercator* chart this would appear as a curved line. A straight line drawn on a *Mercator* chart (called a rhumb-line) is therefore not the *shortest* distance between two points. For distances of three or four hundred miles, however, the difference between the two is very slight and when you are planning your world cruise, you will need to use another type of projection called *Gnomonic* on which great circle courses appear as straight lines. But we are not really considering lengthy passages in this book and so the usual *Mercator* projection will serve us very well.

We shall also need some tide tables which we can find in our *Nautical Almanack*, to look up the time of high water at various places (the use of these will be elaborated on later). Parallel rules, and dividers for measuring, will also be needed. If you cannot find any parallel rules you can use transparent set-squares. A transparent protractor is useful for measuring angles when working on a small-scale chart. Make sure your dividers work easily (not *too* easily) and to your pencils (hard ones), add a knife or sharpener and a rubber. Nautical almanacks are mines of information. The one I personally use is Reeds, published by Thomas Reed and Co Ltd and edited by Captain O. M. Watts, FRAS, ALINA, MIN of London, one of those legendary figures, like Olin or Rod Stephens, or Jock Sturrock, John Illingworth, Alec Rose or Uffa Fox – choose your own favourites – that all yachtsmen have heard of, if not met. Captain Watts has done a fine job here and this almanack contains not only tidal information, but such things as a list of lights, buoys, fog signals, etc, distance tables, radio beacons, star charts, bearings of the sun at sunrise and sunset and gale warning signals – surely that's enough to show that even if you don't use it *all* (and we won't) there is enough reading in it to while away a dog-watch or two, and you'll be surprised how much you learn!

Having seen that he and the ship are properly equipped, the navigator gets out the passage chart and plans when to leave so as to take full advantage of the tide (and the weather). For example, round a headland the tide always runs faster; indeed round some, races can form which can be at best tiresome and at worst, dangerous – such a race lies on our projected passage. Let us have a look at this passage now, as illustrated in chart 1 (between pages 112 and 113).

You will see that from the 'Bell Buoy' there is (dotted) a more or less south-westerly course to the 'Fairway Buoy' between the shallow ground to the west of the 'Isle of Wrecks' and the mainland and this course alters but little so as to leave 'Smugglers' Head' to starboard. Now this is all very fine if the wind is free, or if we are motoring (the amount of motoring we do will depend on conditions, but let us assume that we want to enjoy as much sailing as we can).

If the wind is south-westerly, and we have to tack it is a different matter. Now here is where the navigator, having observed the sky and barometer and heard the latest weather information can use this information to plan the passage. For example, if he thinks the wind will back or in any way come 'free' in time, he may deem it wise to start with a fair tide to help him to windward while tacking. But the tides themselves are a vital consideration too. Look at chart 1. The stream runs strongly through 'Rum Narrows' down between the mainland and 'Jack A'shore Rocks', and the wise navigator makes certain he has this part with a fair tide. On the other hand, there are tidal races off 'Smugglers' Head' and, particularly so off 'Black Point' within a quarter of a mile of the shore in from 18 to 30 feet of water, otherwise, the race must be given a wide berth. Our imaginary race is at its worst with an easterly gale and a strong east-going stream; with southerly winds the race seldom exceeds more than half a mile offshore. We will examine it more closely when we get there! The point I am making is that the navigator, by looking carefully at the passage chart, noting the times when the tidal streams change direction and when they are at their fastest rate; and noting headlands, races and bays (where the stream sets 'in' with the tide and 'out' the far side) can plan his passage to take such advantage as he can. At worst he can minimise delays, at best he can make the whole passage easier and pleasanter. It is foolish to generalise, but as a very broad rule it is wiser to *start* with a fair tide, since it is a good plan to make as much headway as possible in the first five or six hours of a cruise. In the case of our cruise here, however, we want to sail at such a time as to take the maximum tide advantage through 'Rum Narrows' and this will involve starting with a *foul* tide. The degree of 'earlyness' depending on the yacht's average speed and, of course, local conditions. It pays to study carefully on the chart, and also on the excellent tidal chartlets in the almanack, the times when the tide will change over the passage. Chart 1 is, of course, greatly simplified. On a proper chart you will find all the data we have been discussing.

While the navigator has been busy, the member of the crew who holds himself responsible for the engine will have checked that all is well; fuel tanks full, lubricating oil level OK, the engine starting and running smoothly, cooling water running freely, ammeter and oil gauge registering correctly, and the ahead and astern gear operating properly. All is now prepared for our departure save for hoisting sail and slipping our moorings.

(3) The dinghy – hoisting it aboard – stowage – getting underway – rule of the road at sea – watches and crew's duties – meals – on starting

The weather looks favourable. A light south-westerly is blowing. This means we can sail free from the mouth of the 'River Thin', down 'Broad River', to the two buoys at the mouth of that river (see chart 1). Once there, it will be tacking unless we choose to use the engine (as I said before, a matter of individual choice). At all events we have working sails, that is, mainsail and jib, ready for hoisting. However, before we can actually slip our moorings there is one job to do, hoist the dinghy. Impatient as we are to get underway, this is a good a moment as any for a few words on the subject of dinghies.

Dinghies come nowadays in four basic forms: (1) the traditional type with stem and square stern; (2) the collapsible dinghy; (3) the pram (which is similar to the traditional type but is 'square' at the bows as well as the stern, the 'square' part being raised above water-level); and (4) the inflatable dinghy. They can be constructed of wood, either planking or marine ply or of glassfibre-reinforced plastic. The latter have the advantage of being light to handle. The argument for the collapsible dinghy centres on stowage; they are of course easy to stow. But they are in my opinion somewhat fragile for use as a ship's lifeboat in an emergency – especially those that make use of canvas or folding plastics. So we are left with (1) or (3).

Whatever make you choose, make sure it is a good shape with reasonably flat bilges and reasonable beam – in other words don't get a sawn in half barrel, they have no stability in a seaway. Also make sure you have a fender all round the gunwhale, otherwise your top-sides will soon show signs of ravage – no matter how careful you think you are being with those fenders. It need not be expensive, a length of 3-inch coir will do quite well. (It is better if you cover it.) Or again, a strip of rubber screwed down at intervals of about a foot is excellent. It is also a good idea to fit buoyancy tanks or bags (from the lifeboat point of view).

Inflatable dinghies nowadays are very sophisticated by comparison with those of fifteen years ago. They come in sizes ranging from 6 feet to 12 feet. They are very tough yet can fold up into a surprisingly small and stowable article. They can be inflated by foot pump, bellows or CO_2 bottle gas. They are designed for use with paddles, sails and/or outboard engines. The price varies from £7 for a 6-foot *Campari K* dinghy, foot pump inflated and using paddles, to £65 for an 8-foot *Avon Redstart*, using oars or an outboard. Remember, though, that a yacht's dinghy is also her lifeboat and don't compromise. Get a good tough one, and have a good look round before you make your final choice as they vary surprisingly. Having said which; for a yacht's tender (*and* lifeboat) in my opinion you cannot beat a wooden or GRP dinghy of traditional shape. But that's just the writer's opinion. Many people use inflatables nowadays.

Now the question of stowage. Let me say straight out that it is downright silly to tow dinghies on passage. They cause a slight loss of speed certainly, but the real reason is that in bad weather they are an appalling nuisance. If you *have* to tow, tow close to the stern unless you are running when it is better to tow on a long line to prevent the dinghy running up on the following seas and bumping you where you least want to be bumped. In such a situation remember to use *two* painters, in case one parts. Dinghies in small craft are best stowed on the cabin top. Larger sisters can often find room forward of the mainmast on deck.

Now, hoisting. This can be done simply by hauling the dinghy over the transom, over the bows or over the side, but it can be a tedious business if the boat is sizeable or or just plain heavy! The best thing is to bend the painter to a hallyard (the main hallyard will do) bring the hallyard to a mast winch and hoist away. As the dinghy comes level with the deck, members of the crew can keep it off the side and away from guard-rails, stanchions, etc. When she is high enough she can be swung inboard, positioned and carefully lowered. It is a matter of seconds rather than minutes. Once in position, the dinghy would be secured with ropes diagonally, but far better still, with diagonal bands that can be quickly cast off in an emergency. I have seen some dinghies secured with so many lines and knots on occasion, that I have hoped privately that all members of the crew had sharp knives in case a rapid launching was necessary!

Now we have hoisted our dinghy, we can hoist sail and get under way. As I have already stated, this chapter assumes rudimentary sailing knowledge on the part of the reader. For the novice, the niceties of getting away under sail are discussed in chapter six.

Of course those who like to manoeuvre under sail can get under way without the engine, but if you get away using the engine, hoist sail as well, in case the former should fail, for if that happens you can then at least keep out of trouble. In crowded anchorages it is very important always to have the boat under control. Currents can run fast at times and one can easily be carried on to one or more of the vessels moored on either hand. For our owner (described briefly earlier) it will be advisable to leave under power, with sail hoisted and proceed downstream with caution and which brings me to the important question of rule of the road.

An essential part of your navigational equipment is a copy of the *International Regulations for the Prevention of Collision at Sea*, but there are just a few that must be known so well that one reacts instinctively; these are the 'steering and sailing rules' which may be found in 'Part D' of the printed regulations. Broadly paraphrased, the ones you *must* know are:

(1) If two *sailing* vessels approach one another with the wind on the *same* side, the vessel to *windward* keeps clear (see figure 23).

(2) If two *sailing* vessels approach with the wind on *different* sides the vessel which has the wind on the *port*-hand side keeps clear (see figure 24).

(3) If two *power* vessels (and don't forget that a sailing vessel

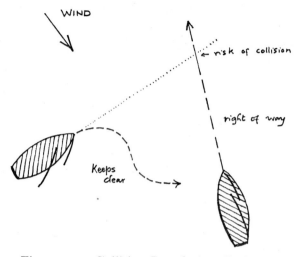

Figure 23. Collision Regulations Rule 17 (i)

using her engine to drive her is a vessel under *power*) are approaching nearly end on, *each* alters to *starboard* (in other words, each passes on the *port*-hand side of the other).

(4) If two *power* vessels are crossing, the vessel which has the *other* on her starboard side keeps clear.

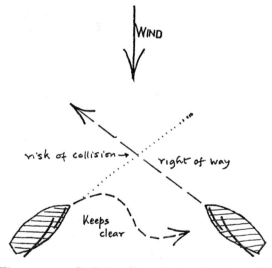

Figure 24. Collision Regulations Rule 17 (ii)

(5) When a *power* vessel is likely to collide with a sailing vessel the *power* vessel keeps clear. This last rule needs to be interpreted with common sense (rules 24 and 26 in the regulations make this clear). Obviously if a sailing vessel meets a large steamer in a narrow fairway she would not only be crazy to steer by the rule, but should an accident occur, she could well be in the wrong. These few rules must be known by heart, but that does not mean that the efficient and wise skipper should not be familiar with *all* the basic rules. A copy must form part of your equipment. Where the rule talks about being 'to windward' it means the side opposite to that on which the mainsail is being carried at the time. Of course these rules are designed to avoid collisions. Risk of collision is usually pretty obvious, but in some cases it is less so and an alteration of course can be made too late. Where there is an uncertainty, watch the compass bearing of the other boat. If it does not appreciably alter as you both approach, then you will not pass ahead or astern of the other craft; you are going to hit her!

It is advisable to give your crew definite jobs; and times to be on and off watch. It is very important to get enough sleep on a long passage and the proper arrangement of watches is essential. The number of people in each watch will depend on how large your crew is. For those who do not know them, the traditional watches are as follows:

am
{
12– 4 Middle watch
4– 8 Morning watch
8–12 Forenoon watch
}

pm
{
12– 4 Afternoon watch
4– 6 First Dog-watch
6– 8 Last Dog-watch (*not* 'second' Dog!)
8–12 First watch
}

Of course this time-honoured system can be altered to suit the requirements of different yachts and different crews. The only important thing is that there is a definite system so that *each person gets enough sleep*. Once you know which your duty watches are you can arrange your sleep accordingly. If you have no system you will find that everybody tends to be on deck at the same time and then when the middle and morning watches arrive everyone is tired; and this can be very dangerous. For most people four hours at the helm is long enough and for many two is quite sufficient; some people lose concentration and tire quicker than others. A boat with a crew of three can use three-hour watches quite conveniently. If there are four or more in the crew the four-hour system is better. Each man can then do two hours at the helm alternatively, his fellow watchkeeper meantime keeping look-out, attending to sheets, sail trim, etc.

Meals at sea are important. If you have an early start get a good breakfast. Nothing is more of a tonic to men getting under way in a cold drizzle at 6 am than the sound and smell of eggs and bacon frying!

There are two types of yacht owner. One holds that meals are of secondary importance to navigation and seamanship, and consigns the galley up forward out of sight and sound. The other maintains that a lot of time is spent eating and drinking and that the cook should be given the place of honour in the centre (and therefore most stable) part of the boat. Number two is right in my view. The cook *must* be able to cook properly not only in harbour, but *underway*. He (or she) must be able to keep himself and his pots and pans upright when the yacht is heeled over. He should have everything to hand and not have to move about once he has 'chocked' himself into his 'operating' position. In chapter eleven we will go into these important questions of sleeping, cooking and other domestic matters more fully.

Before we come to grips with the actual pilotage (courses and tides and all that) a word about starting. Once the time has come to start – do so. If the weather-forecast is very bad and the bottom is falling out of the glass, you may well find it prudent to keep harbour, but unless it is dangerous to start – start. Postponing a start is quite extraordinarily demoralising. It almost always pays at least to go and have a look at it. There may be only a short lived patch of bad weather. The climate is notorious for the way it fools us. It is also often very difficult to judge the strength of the wind in harbour. The wind can be funnelled down between hills and so give a completely false idea of its true direction. What appears to have been going to be a tough 'beat' to windward, can become under the true wind, a pleasant broad reach and no doubt a fast passage. Again in the shelter of a harbour, the *sound* of wind in the ship's rigging can give a false idea of the gale outside! If you can and the forecast and glass deem it safe – make sail and start – you won't regret it – and you won't have lost a day of your holiday cruise.

(4) Underway – the International Buoyage System – pilotage – we run aground – tactics – courses and tides – use of the patent log

We are now underway; and since we shall be meeting, crossing and possibly overtaking other vessels, we must not only be thoroughly familiar with the 'rule of the road at sea', but the buoyage system will need to be known (see figure 25). The 'hatched' buoys are coloured red and the black buoys are black; 'wreck' buoys are green with the word 'wreck' in white letters. If we are entering an estuary or river by night it is important to know the various characteristics of the lights of buoys in the International Buoyage System. They are: starboard-hand marks ... white light: showing 1, 3 or 5 flashes (odd numbers); port-hand marks ... showing white 2, 4 or 6 flashes (even numbers), or red, showing 1, 2, 3 or 4 flashes; and middle-ground marks ... no colours used other than white or red and the rhythm of the flashes will be distinctive. Isolated danger marks are spherical buoys with wide black and red horizontal bands separated by a narrow white band and a round top-mark, the lights if any, will be white or red flashing. Sometimes a landfall marker buoy is used to help the navigator find his exact position especially where the coast-line is not easy to recognise. Such buoys will be in accordance with the normal rules for channel markings, they will be coloured with black and white or red and white vertical stripes. The light, if any, will be flashing. Wreck buoys have green flashing lights any number of times; on that side of the wreck nearest the centre of the channel. In the International Buoyage System, a port-hand buoy is left to port when sailing with the main flood stream and vice versa.

In order to get uniformity, the use of these general shapes, colours and characteristics of lights have been agreed internationally and are used on the coasts of the United Kingdom. While this international agreement does produce a buoyage system of similar basic shapes in most countries, there are a

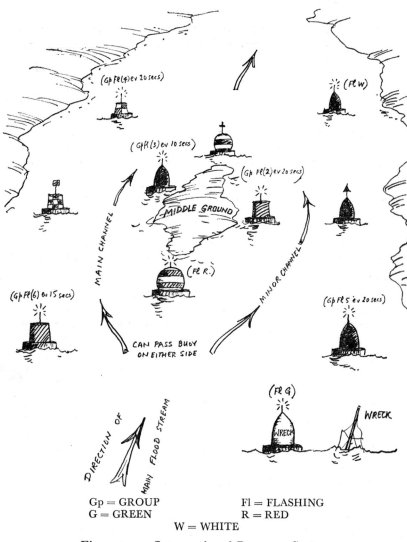

Gp = GROUP   Fl = FLASHING
G = GREEN   R = RED
          W = WHITE

Figure 25.   International Buoyage System

Plate 10   *Contest 25*

Plate 11   *Folkboat*

Plate 12   *Merle of Malham*

Plate 13   *Nicholson 26*

Plate 14 *Hillyard 9-tonner*

Plate 15 *Apache 37*

Plate 16 *Spey 35*

Plate 17   *Nicholson 38* (*a*)

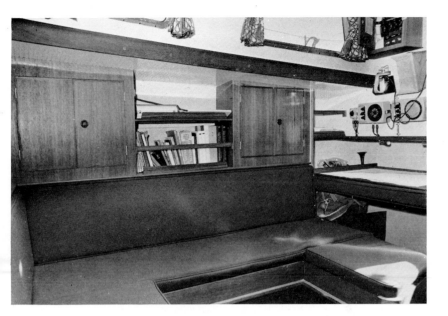

Nicholson 38 (*b*) and (*c*)

Plate 18 *Gipsy II*

number of variations to be found. For British yachtsmen the variations for France, Holland, Germany and Denmark are to be found in the *Nautical Almanack*. For yachtsmen cruising in other waters detailed information about the local buoyage system are usually easily obtained at chandlers, shipping agents, etc; but the basic shapes, if interpreted imaginatively will usually see you through!

The essence of pilotage (navigation in pilotage waters) is to know where you are, and know it all the time. This involves fixing the position of the boat at fairly frequent intervals and plotting these positions on the chart. Look again at chart 1. On leaving the 'River Thin', the course to the open sea (via the 'Fairway Buoy') is not one which presents much difficulty in the way of pilotage. The channel is well marked and the chart is not difficult to read, so that provided we don't run aground we should be all right. But, let us suppose that our skipper friend, in his eagerness to reach the open sea, does run aground, perhaps on the mud-flats that flank the mouth of the 'River Trick'. In such a case certain basic rules are worth remembering. The first essential is speed. Grounding at this point with a south-westerly wind is running aground on a lee-shore; and the sails must be lowered quickly to stop her driving further on. (If you run aground on a weather shore you can leave sails hoisted and sheet them in to give the vessel a list.) With the powerful engine of a motor-sailer we can probably get her off stern first; trying correctly, to get her off reversing the way she came on. If this does not work we can in this case afford to be patient because we started with a foul (in this case flood) tide and we should therefore float off as the last of the tide makes. But we do not want to waste time if the tide is falling. If the engine fails to move her, we must quickly lay out a kedge anchor in the dinghy. The direction in which we lay it will be decided by the nature of the shore-line at the point where we have run on, the angle to the shore-line of the yacht, and the underwater shape of the yacht. As a general rule a yacht will come off best 'the way she went on'. Certainly this is likely to be true of our motor-sailer with her relatively moderate depth of keel aft and fairly full sections forward. In the case of a very deep-draughted boat aft, and with very fine bows and shallow forward, it will often pay to try and slew her round to point her bows to the deeper water.

I think by now we can assume that the engine, perhaps helped by a little tough kedge hauling, has got our 50/50 back in deep water and we are proceeding as before towards the open sea.

Mention of the tide has been timely because it is going to play a big part in our passage. The navigator must make continual allowance for the effect of the tidal stream in estimating his position and in plotting the course to give to the helmsman to steer. There is, too, another factor to be allowed for, and that is leeway, by which is meant the amount a vessel is set off her course to leeward by the effect of the wind. In the case of a motor-sailer under power this is probably negligible, but under sail it can become a factor to be reckoned with. Leeway can be expressed as a line deviating to leeward from the course to steer line. It can be compensated by steering the same amount up to windward. Modern yachts make but little leeway, but in bad weather the amount increases. The leeway that any vessel makes will vary and can only be learnt by experience with her, but if you look over the stern you can estimate the angle your wake is making with the course steered; and this is a useful guide.

In rivers, estuaries and narrow stretches of water the tidal stream will tend to move one way or the other; we either have it with us or agin' us. In more open water, however, we can get it across us and this complicates matters. Obviously if it is dead against us it will slow us down by the amount of its rate. (By the way with tidal streams it is 'rate' and not 'speed'.) Again, if the stream is with us, it will simply help us along by the amount of its rate – ie if we are sailing at 7 knots and the tide rate is 3 knots, we shall cover ten sea miles in one hour.

If the stream is across your course, however, you can find yourself in trouble if you don't allow for it. Let us assume now that, having caught the fair tide through 'Rum Narrows' we have laid off a course to leave 'Smugglers' Head' two miles to starboard (see chart 1). You will notice that the coast-line forms three bays: two small bays, 'Haven Bay' and 'Catspaw Bay' and a larger bay called 'Big Bay', from 'Black Point' to 'Southseaman Head'. There is a strong tendency for the ebb-tide to sweep into the eastward of these bays, and then out again the westward side.

With the wind at south-west we can probably lay 'Smugglers' Head' especially if we make use of the engine, and the tide sweeping out of 'Haven Bay' will help us. In these circumstances we are as glad to have the outward (or southerly) sweep of the tide as much as we would dislike the inward (or northerly) one, which would force us to make an unnecessary tack. So we will use the engine to get in a good position to weather 'Smugglers' Head' still sailing on the port tack. (By using the engine we can sail much closer to the wind.) Now the tidal stream is going (as we planned) to help us very considerably on this stage of the passage. Should we have to tack, however, and sail east of south to get out to seaward the tide again will be helping us because it will be pushing us to windward (the way we want to go) – a procedure known as 'lee-bowing', for obvious reasons. The *amount* it pushes us up is clearly of importance and the wise navigator will plot this effect of the tidal stream on the chart, so as to be certain of his position.

Now supposing the current was across our plotted course on the chart and we wanted to allow for it in our course to steer, so as to cancel it out; how would we set about it?

We need three bits of information; the direction of the tidal stream, its rate and our yacht's speed (through the water). From our *Nautical Almanack* (or from the chart) we can get the first two; the latter we get by using a device known as a patent log, which measures the distance run through the water. On the end of a 75-foot (22·86 m) line a metal fin rotator is towed. At the inboard end of this line is a flywheel and a dial graded in nautical miles and an indicator needle. To find your speed you take one reading of the log and then a second reading, say quarter of an hour later. Multiply the distance run by 4 and you have got your knots (nautical miles per hour). With our data we now do the following simple calculation. Look at figure 26. *XY* represents the course. We take point *C* at any place along it and lay off a line in the opposite direction to the direction of the tidal stream. We take an hour's worth of tide and with this on our dividers and with centre *C* cut off a point *B*. With centre *B*, and with our ship's speed on our dividers we now cut off *A* along *XY*. Join *AB*, and that is our course to steer to allow for the tidal stream. It is very simple. Notice these points however and look again at figure 25. *AB* is shorter than *AC*, the tide is in fact helping us. It is setting us a little on our way. In the drawing can be seen the hull of yacht. Notice that it is pointing, not along *AC*, but along *AB*. Since *AB* is the course steered, this

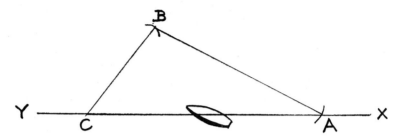

Figure 26. Laying off a course, allowing for tidal stream

may seem childishly obvious, but the point I want to make is that the yacht's course *over the ground* (*AC*) is a crab movement, at any point in time while the yacht is sailing between *A* and *C* she will be along the line *AC* and nowhere else (provided the helmsman has steered a steady course and that leeway has been correctly estimated or is negligible). *AB* is the course and also the *distance sailed* through the water; but *AC* is the course and also the distance sailed over the ground.

The distance over the ground (in figure 26) is greater than the distance through the water; a practical geometrical illustration of the advantage of a fair (or relatively fair) tidal stream. Practise at this simple calculation enables a navigator to find the course to give the helmsman to steer to allow for tide, and conversely to plot, with reasonable accuracy, the position of the vessel on the chart.

(5) Bad weather – reefing; 'roller' and 'point' – tactics in bad weather

Our motor-sailer, having weathered 'Smugglers' Head', has now to cross 'Catspaw Bay'. The wind continuing south-westerly means we must tack. By using the engine we can sail much closer to the wind and so reduce our tacks but, even so, we shall have to tack unless we sail under power alone. This in a motor-sailer we can perfectly well do, but the boat will be very much more comfortable under sail, and not 'plugging straight into it'; and in the long run, will get there just as quickly. (Were we in a motor-cruiser of modest size it would still pay us to sail at a slight angle to the wind and waves and not into them. The motion will be easier and we will make better speed.) Let us assume that while doing this, the wind is steadily increasing in force. The barometer and weather signs leave little doubt that we are in for a hard blow, and the skipper orders a reef in the mainsail.

There are two methods of reefing a yacht's mainsail. You either roll the foot of the sail into a sausage and secure it with short lines called reef points (or with a long line running through eyelets in the sail) or you can roll the sail up round the boom by revolving it. Generally speaking you would find the former method used in very small boats and the latter in larger ones.

Look now at figures 27 and 28. We are here concerned with reefing at sea. Let us assume our motor-sailer has point reefing. Although roller reefing is very commonly found nowadays there are still a lot of people who prefer point reefing, holding that the sail when reefed, sets better; and as it is slightly more complicated than roller reefing let us assume our motor-sailer has point reefing. (Figure 28 shows the principle of point reefing and figure 27, that of roller.) Now it is perfectly possible, if time is of little consideration, to heave-to (back the jib with the weather sheet) and tuck in the reef in comfort. But as often

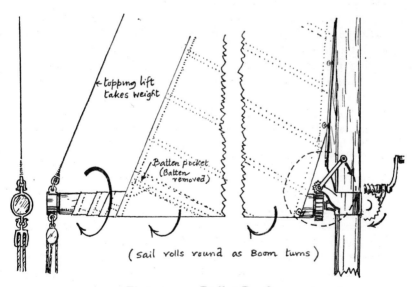

Figure 27. Roller Reefing

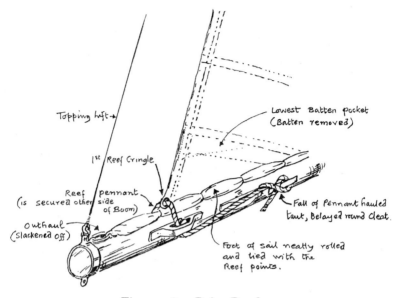

Topping lift→

Lowest Batten pocket
(Batten removed)

1st Reef Cringle

Reef pennant
(is secured other side
of Boom)

Fall of Pennant hauled
taut, belayed round cleat.

Outhaul
(Slackened off)

Foot of sail neatly rolled
and tied with the
Reef points.

Figure 28.   Point Reefing

as not, time is important, for example, to make the most of a
fair tide. It is therefore essential to be able to reef efficiently and
quickly under way. This can be done by keeping the boat going
under headsail (and engine) if the boat is close-hauled. If she
is running you stand a risk, when lowering the mainsail, of
tearing it on spreaders, shrouds, etc, and in that case you should
turn into wind. Should the wind be on the beam, luff into the
wind sufficiently to get the boom well in. It is a great advantage
if your boat is fitted with a strong boom gallows. Ideally there
should be three positions for the boom on the gallows and you
use the leeward one for reefing. The weight of the boom is first
taken by the topping lift, thus spilling the wind out of the sail.
At the same time the mainsheet is hauled on to control the
boom and when it is in the desired position over the leeward
slot, the topping lift is eased a little, the boom lowered into the
slot, and the mainsheet hauled taut and made fast. As in
figure 28 the standing end of the reef pennant is fast to the boom
leading up through the cringle in the leech of the sail, and so
down to the sheave on the other side of the boom. The drawing
shows how the sail is then neatly furled and the points tied

(appropriately with reef knots). When all points are tied the sail can be rehoisted, the mainsheet trimmed once more and off we go. The more you have to do it, the quicker you will get! If a second reef is required the process is repeated but will this time involve a change of headsail as well.

The smaller headsail will be taken forward and the snap hooks on its luff should be clipped to the forestay underneath the lowest hook of the existing headsail. If you cannot do this, unshackle the lowest hook to make more room on the stay. Now unshackle the tack and substitute the tack of the small headsail. One of the crew now lowers the sail while another gathers it in as it comes down and at the same time unshackling the clips. When all clips are off, the new headsail is shackled on to the stay, while a second member of the crew transfers the sheets to the new sail. The small headsail is now ready for hoisting.

Now let us suppose that the freshening wind shows every sign of turning into a gale; we are faced with a decision – to run for shelter, or see it out. Here there are fortunately some basic rules for our guidance.

(1) If the nearest harbour has deep water and can be entered at any state of the tide – fair enough.

(2) If there is a bar to cross at the harbour mouth – don't try it.

(3) Avoid entering against an ebb-tide and . . .

(4) If you have a sound ship and plenty of sea room, you may not be particularly comfortable riding it out, but you will be safe.

If you decide to stay out at sea you will probably heave-to, but if the wind increases to the point when you cannot do so in safety, you will have to choose between lying a-hull, riding to a sea anchor or running before the gale.

I do not want to spend more time here on this question of dealing with bad weather at sea, so I have devoted a later chapter (nine) to it.

To return to our passage across 'Catspaw Bay' (look at chart 1). If the wind increased very strongly from the south-west we might consider it advisable to retrace our course round 'Smugglers' Head' and take temporary shelter in 'Haven Bay' (the bay north of 'St Anne's Point' outside the entrance to 'Old Haven' harbour). This has good holding ground and is well protected from the south-west. We might however decide to press on to make 'Scupperton'. It would depend on prevailing conditions. An important point worth making here is that it is always a temptation to run for shelter when the weather deteriorates, but one must remember that the conditions have to be right. More craft are lost trying to make harbour in bad weather than in any other way. Near a harbour mouth the sea becomes confused and treacherous, due to shallow patches, etc. Again, running for shelter, although it may seem a welcome relief at the time has a demoralising effect. Once snug in harbour there always seems to be delay in leaving and precious time for the projected cruise is lost, and maybe favourable winds missed. In this case, however, the relief afforded by the sheltered anchorage behind 'St Anne's Point' could allow the weather to moderate, and could be a wise move. If you anchor in a sheltered bay (as in the example on our cruise here) you should take into consideration possible shifts of wind. This involves setting an anchor watch at night, having sails ready for instant hoisting (in case of engine failure) so that you can get out of it if the wind shifts and you suddenly find yourself on a lee-shore. However, if we *can* make 'Scupperton' it will be to our advantage to do so (see chart) as we shall be that much further on our way. Furthermore, we can, by leaving 'Scupperton' at the appropriate time (the next day, or whenever the weather moderates) probably take the inshore passage between 'Black Point' and the race off that point, thus saving ourselves a lot of time. Assuming that the strong wind remains in the south-west, the chart shows that we can sail on the port reech the whole way and that, as we near 'Scupperton', we shall come under the lee of 'Bald Point' and the approach to the harbour will be sheltered. It is, however, dangerous to find oneself on a lee-shore in a bay in bad weather. Under the conditions in this case, the yacht will make a lot of leeway. However, we have in our 50/50 a good strong engine to hold us to our course to 'Scupperton', yet another example of the usefulness of this excellent type of craft.

(6) Using the spinnaker – navigation – fixing the ship's position – allowing for effect of tide in calculations – on further navigational instruction – schools

One of the attractions of sailing is the problem continually posed by weather conditions. Storms are fortunately often short-lived; they not only test us, they add to our appreciation of fair weather. On most cruises the bad weather one meets is compensated by a period of the kind of sunny, sparkling conditions that brochures advertising yachting holidays portray. And so it is only fair that the bad weather of section 5 should be followed by what the French aptly term an 'amelioration'. Let us assume that the wind, having headed us for most of the passage so far, has backed to south-east, and we are able to free sheets and run effortlessly before it.

Section 5 found us faced with the alternatives of taking shelter in 'Haven Bay' or of going into 'Scupperton' harbour. It is very possible that we chose the latter, and were able to leave the next day, when the weather had moderated. And so now, carefully choosing our time of departure, we have been able to take the inshore passage round 'Black Point' and between the point and the race.

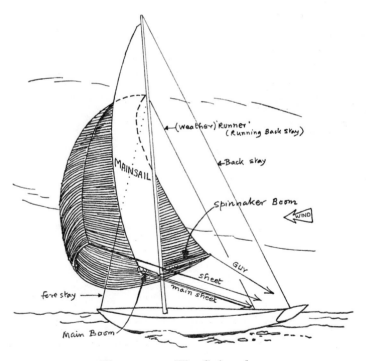

Figure 29. The Spinnaker

This will have saved us a lot of time and we are now in 'Big Bay' with some forty miles to sail to 'Sun Bay'. We are 'running' and this is the time to get a bit more speed (as well as fun) by hoisting our spinnaker.

Most readers will be familiar with the baggy, triangular, nylon sail that is a spinnaker. It is set flying, that is, secured only at three corners. Look now at figure 29. You will see that the tack is made fast to the end of the spinnaker boom. The latter is controlled by the boom guy. The clew is attached to the sheet. Both guy and sheet lead aft to the cockpit. To hoist the sail, shackle the head to the halyard; having first made sure there are no twists in the sail. The tack is made fast to the boom and the sheet to the clew. A member of the crew now passes the boom guy round outside the weather shrouds, back to the cockpit where it is belayed (temporarily) round a cleat.

The spinnaker can now be hoisted by hauling on the halyard. As the member of the crew responsible for this hoists, he pushes

1 Helmsman
2 Spinnaker sheet hand
3 Spinnaker guy hand
4 Main sheet
5 Spinnaker sheet
6 Spinnaker boom
7 Spinnaker boom guy
8 Spinnaker boom topping lift
9 Spinnaker downhaul
10 Fore guy

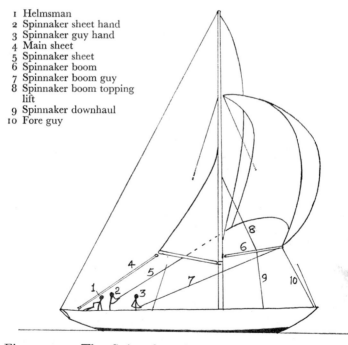

Figure 30. The Spinnaker; its gear and crew's duties

the boom out over the bows and out to the weather side. Another member of the crew, whose duty is to control the boom guy, hauls aft on it until the boom is roughly at right-angles to the centre line of the boat. He then belays the guy (again, temporarily) round a cleat. It now becomes the job of the crew member controlling the sheet to keep the sail full of wind by hauling or easing on the sheet. Figure 30 illustrates the various lines and their functions.

There is an art in keeping a spinnaker full of wind. Watch the luff of the sail. At the slightest sign of collapse, haul in on the sheet until the sail fills again. The crew member on the guy should work in conjunction with the sheet hand. He does not just belay the guy and light a pipe (or go below!). If the sheet hand has to haul in hard the guy must be eased. It may be that the helmsman has, on the advice of the navigator, altered course and brought the wind more on the beam. This means that the boom will be well forward from its original position. Figure 31 shows the effect of this from a gull's-eye view.

AS A GULL SEES IT —

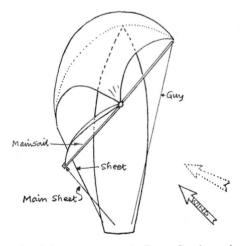

As wind comes more on the Beam, Guy is eased and sheet hauled in to keep the spinnaker full and drawing.

Figure 31.   Gull's-eye view of Spinnaker with beam wind

139

The helmsman has a part to play too, in keeping the spinnaker full and drawing. He too should carefully watch the luff and can help to prevent a collapse by small alterations of course. Ideally the helmsman and the guy and sheet hands should all work together. Of course, if the helmsman is sailing a course set by the navigator his first responsibility is to sail that course. If he is sailing for a mark or a buoy easily visible he can manoeuvre in the way described to help keep the sail full; but if he is, as we are, in the open sea with nothing to guide him but his compass, he must sail the course and leave the crew to keep the spinnaker full. Should the wind back or veer and make it impossible to carry the spinnaker, it must be handed (taken in).

Handing a spinnaker is not difficult, in fact you just reverse the order of the stages of setting it. First ease off the guy, allowing the boom to go forward, so that the sail is blanketed by the mainsail and collapses. The spinnaker boom can now be unshipped and brought inboard. Next unhook the clew and tack, and gather in the foot of the sail, continuing to gather in as the sail is lowered in the lee of the mainsail. Take another look at figure 30. I have put in a topping lift and a down-haul on the spinnaker boom. As will easily be seen from the drawing, these two items of gear help to control the boom; and although not essential are worth the trouble of rigging. Another item shown in figure 30 is a forward guy; this again, while not essential, is very useful in controlling the spinnaker when the boom is well forward of amidships. It is usually led through a block just abaft the stem-head and so aft to the cockpit. It is hauled on or slackened in conjunction with the after boom guy.

With the long crossing of 'Big Bay' before us, the navigator must fix the ship carefully while the coast is still in sight, and this 'fixing' of the ship's position can be done in a number of ways; let us have a look at three of them.

The simplest is a fix by cross bearings – look at figure 32. This shows a stretch of coast-line, on which two easily identified objects, a tall mast X and a water-tower Y can be seen. We are sailing from east, westwards, and we will call our course line AB. As our ship comes abeam of X we take a bearing of the tower Y (probably with our hand-bearing compass) and plot the bearing as a 'position line' on the chart. Notice that at the seaward end of the position line I have marked the time (10.00) when the bearing was taken. However, before we plot this on the chart (we just make a quick note of the bearing and time). We take a second bearing, this time of the mast *X*. The two position lines plotted are shown in figure 32. Where they cross is our position at the time of the second bearing. It is called a fix and is 'ringed round' to indicate it. When taking bearings take that of the object most abeam *last* because its bearings will alter much faster than a distant object as you sail past. Notice

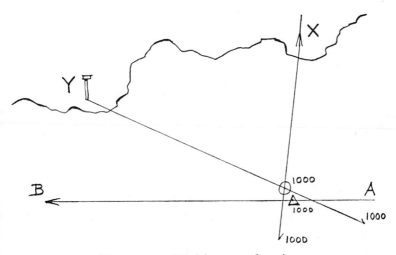

Figure 32.   'Fix' by cross-bearings

in the figure that there is another point with a triangle round it, on the course line. This is where we had estimated our position (EP) to be. Now that we have our 'fix' we can start again. The difference in the two positions at 10.00 hours shows how far the effect of the tide or perhaps leeway has differed from our estimation of it. You can see, therefore, what a useful safety-factor this checking your position by cross bearings is. An even more certain check can be had from three position lines. It is very unlikely that the three lines will meet; there will be a little triangular space in the centre. This is called by navigators a 'cocked hat'. Look at figure 33. Notice that the fix has been put nearest to danger (in this case, rocks). If there is no danger near, put the fix in the centre of your cocked hat.

Now look at figure 34. This shows how we can get a fix although there is only one suitable object on shore (*C*) to be seen. If you were just to take a bearing of *C*, you would know

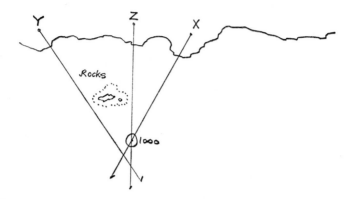

Figure 33.   'Fix' by three cross-bearings, showing 'cocked hat'

that at the time of taking it, your ship was somewhere *on* that line; but not *where*. This method, known as the 'four-point bearing' gets round that difficulty. For this we need to make use of the patent log mentioned earlier – a device for measuring our distance run through the water. At *A* at 10.00 hours we take a bearing of *C*. We continue our course and speed and at *B*, we

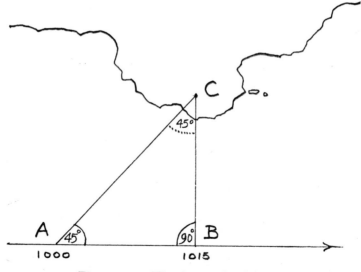

Figure 34.   The four-point bearing

take another bearing. Now the whole essence of this method is that at A, C should bear 45° from the ship's course; and at B, C should be 90°. Note the times of the two bearings and the distance run on the log. The difference between the two log readings at A and B give this; and this distance will be the distance from C (along CB). When C was abeam (at 90°), once again you can compare your 'fix' with our estimated position.

There is a useful development of the four-point bearing known as 'doubling the angle on the bow'. This is shown in figure 35; the principle is the same. Instead, however, of using

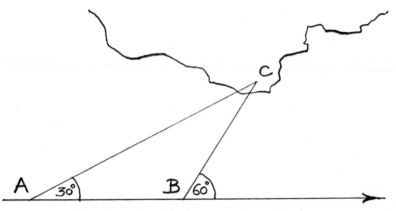

Figure 35.   Doubling the angle on the bow

45° and 90° we take a bearing, say, when C is 30° and carry on our course and speed until it is 60°. We note the times and the log readings; obtain the distance run between the two bearings and this gives us our distance from the object on shore at the time of the second bearing.

But I am wondering now if I can hear a voice asking whether the tide makes any difference? Indeed it does! With the two methods of fixing described you must work from the course made good (as described in section 4). There we saw that the *course made good* is by no means necessarily the course steered through the water. Suppose your course to make good was west on the chart, and suppose the tidal stream was setting you a bit to the south; you would steer an equal amount to the north to compensate for it. You would then sail west with your bows pointing in a north-westerly direction. Your course steered will differ, in fact, from your course made good; and it is from the course made good that we work on the chart when fixing our position. Similarly, you should calculate your distance run from the speed you have made over the ground (*the speed made good*) and not just through the water, because once again, the tide may have affected it.

The method we used in section 4 must be used to get this distance run. As I said earlier, once you have got your fix, it is a useful check on how correctly you have assessed the effect of the tide on your course. If you allowed too little to the north, for example, this would be indicated by the fix being somewhat to the south of your estimated position.

We have been talking of course in terms of our motor-sailer, with her speed of about 7 knots. Were we in a motor-cruiser capable of maintaining higher average speeds, say 15 knots or so, the effect of the tidal stream would clearly be less. It will be equally obvious though, that the tide cannot be left out of calculations. It can still help or hinder you, or set you off your course to make good. Conversely, a sailing yacht with only a very small auxiliary engine, can find, on occasions, especially in conditions of spring tides and light airs, that the tide is more than somewhat of a headache. But it teaches one to be both philosophical and ingenious!

To conclude this section. While the simple navigational evolutions in this chapter will be normally quite sufficient for a cruise such as the one we are taking now, many cruising yachtsmen, once they have got their teeth into passage-making, will doubtless wish to enlarge their repertoire, culminating in learning to fix their position by using a sextant to measure the angles of the sun and stars. There are a number of excellent textbooks on navigation on the market to help them acquire this knowledge. There are also, as advertised in the yachting press, a number of navigation schools where personal tuition will help the keen navigator to become really proficient. It is a large subject (indeed whole books are devoted to it) and we cannot do more here than learn some basic methods. When you want to go into navigation more thoroughly as your cruises become longer and further offshore you will find it pays to take the trouble to learn this fascinating subject 'from the bottom'. But for the beginner, there is quite enough here to keep you happily on course on many a passage.

(7) Continuing the navigation – fog – the lead-line – using a line of soundings – radio aids to navigation

While crossing 'Big Bay' we have managed to get in some practice at simple navigation. We fixed the yacht's position by using bearings in various ways. Still (metaphorically at least), on the same tack, let us have a look at two other methods of obtaining our position. The first is known as a 'running fix'. It is useful in conditions where you can see one object on shore only (easily identified on the chart). You take a bearing of this and as before, note the time and the distance reading on the patent log. You maintain your course and after, say, fifteen minutes, take a second bearing of the object, again noting time and distance. Figure 36 will make things clearer. Position *A* at

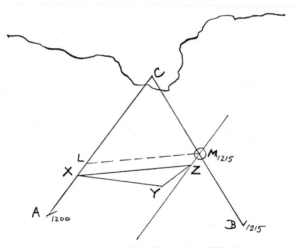

Figure 36. The Running 'Fix'

12.00 hours tells us that, at that time we were somewhere along the position line *AC*, and the second position line (*BC*) tells us we were somewhere along that at 12.15. The two log readings will give us our speed and distance. The object now is to produce a line of the same length as the distance made good in the same direction exactly as our course made good, and where this line meets the two position lines *AC* and *BC* will give us our exact position at 12.15. Now we must remember that by distance and course made good we mean our course *over the ground* which will include any effect of the tidal stream.

Look again at figure 36. We take a point X on AC and draw from it a line to represent our course through the water (the course steered by compass). Call this XY. We will have looked up the tidal stream on the chart or from a tidal atlas or almanack for the time, the day, and the area in which we are sailing. Let us say it is north-easterly 2 knots. From Y we lay this off to give us fifteen minutes of tide, so with our dividers we measure off half a mile along the tide-line and call it Z. We join XZ which gives us our course and distance made good. Now put the parallel rules on AC and run it across until it touches point Z. Where this new line cuts BC, gives us our fix M at 12.15. As a check, run a line parallel to XZ up, so that it touches CB. This new line (LM in figure 36), will be equal and parallel to XZ; and M will be our fix at 12.15

The second method of fixing is called the transferred position line. Look at figure 37. The line PQ represents a bearing taken at 10.00 hours. Now let us suppose that we run into fog and it is two hours before we get another sight of the coast and can identify a landmark, W. We take a bearing shown in the figure as WV. Let us assume that between these times we have maintained a steady course and speed. In this instance the tidal stream is exactly with us, so while there is no appreciable

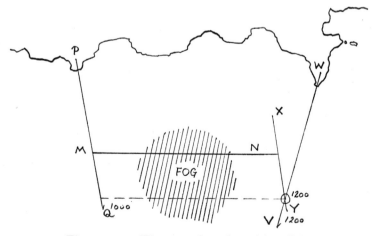

Figure 37.   The transferred position line

difference between the course through the water and the course made good, the speed (and/or distance) has been increased by the amount of tide in the two hours which have elapsed. Let MN equal this course and distance made good. Once again we take our parallel rules and putting the edge along PQ run it over until it touches N, and draw in this line, shown as XY in the figure. Where XY cuts WV gives us our position at 12.00 hours. It is not a completely certain fix, relying as it does on an accurate working out of the course made good between 10.00 hours and 12.00 hours; but it will be near enough in all probability. This, as I have said, is very useful when the shore is temporarily obscured and it brings me to the important subject of – Fog!

If you run into fog check your position on the chart at once. If you are in a shipping lane get out of it. To do this you will have to proceed very carefully, sailing on dead-reckoning from your last fixed position and taking careful soundings either with echo-sounder or lead-line (or both). Thirdly, obey the sound signals for fog laid down in rule 15 of the *International Regulations for the Prevention of Collision at Sea*. In the case of our motor-sailer here we may be under sail, or under power (if under sail *and* power it ranks as power). If under way under power we must 'sound, at intervals of not more than 2 minutes a prolonged blast' (this means of course on a fog-horn). If under sail alone, we must 'sound, at intervals of not more than one minute, when on the starboard tack one blast, when on the port tack two blasts in succession, and when with the wind abaft the beam three blasts in succession'.

If we have been sailing under power in fog and have stopped, say to check our position, and are making no way through the water, we must 'sound at intervals of not more than two minutes two prolonged blasts with an interval of about one second between them' and if we then decide to anchor, we must obey paragraph (iv) of section (*b*) of rule 15, which says that we must 'at intervals of not more than 1 minute ring a bell rapidly for about 5 seconds'. The same paragraph states that 'every vessel at anchor may in addition, in accordance with rule 12' (the rule re attracting attention to oneself) 'sound three blasts in succession namely, one short, one prolonged, and one short blast (the letter 'R' in morse) to give warning of her position and of the possibility of collision to an approaching vessel'.

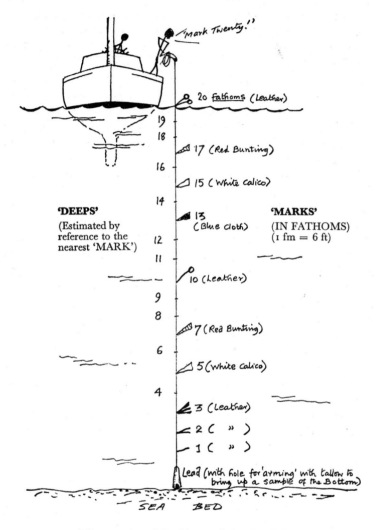

Figure 38. Markings of the lead-line

I must emphasise that these are just extracts, and by no means the whole of rule 15, just to show the basic idea of identifying oneself and other vessels in fog. If you go to sea you must have a copy of the collision regulations on board.

I mentioned earlier taking soundings with lead-line or echo-sounder. The lead-line is simply a length of line marked as shown in figure 38. Its use is self-evident to any intelligent person. It should be made of plaited line that does not twist. A cheap substitute is window-sash cord. An echo-sounder will cost you a good deal more than a lead-line but it is a very useful piece of equipment. It works on the principle of the sending of an impulse by a transmitter in the hull and the receipt of the impulse on rebound from the bottom by a receiver; the depth of water being shown on a scale, frequently in the form of a clockface presentation for small yachts. Other types make use of a moving paper so that a continuous picture of the bottom may be obtained.

In fog and thick weather a yacht will of necessity navigate by dead-reckoning. Under these circumstances some form of sounder (echo-sounder or lead-line), if the yacht is in waters where soundings can be taken, becomes of paramount importance.

If the bottom is such that the contours follow fairly definite outlines and the depths vary enough to enable you to distinguish one part of the sea from another, a line of soundings can often tell you the ship's position with considerable accuracy. The method is as follows: you take soundings at regular intervals by time and distance, noting the log and carefully watching the course steered. You will have to apply to this the effect of any tidal stream so as to get your course made good. Take a piece of tracing-paper and rule on it a number of parallel lines to represent true meridians on the chart. Across these meridians rule a line so that the angle at which it cuts them is equal to the course made good (see figure 39).

The scale of the chart at roughly the parallel of latitude where the yacht is thought to be, must now be used to mark along the course made good the successive positions at which the soundings were taken. You must be careful to make the distance between the marks equal to the distances between the soundings. Against these you now write in the corresponding depths (reduced to the mean level of chart datum, so as to be the same

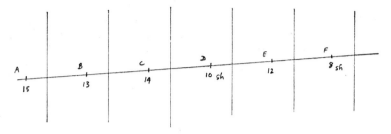

Figure 39.   Line of soundings

as the chart) and if you have been able to tell whether the bottom was shingle, or mud or blue clay, etc, mark that in too. (The 'lead' on the lead-line has a hollow in it for arming with tallow to bring up a sample of the bottom.)

You now place the tracing on the chart, with the meridians parallel with the meridians on the chart. Move the paper about near the supposed position of the yacht until you find the line along with the soundings agree. When they do, the yacht's position at the time of the last sounding is known. Easy!

Always proceed with caution in fog. Sound is very deceptive. A fog signal close by may not be heard at all whereas some miles off it will be audible. There are undoubtedly patches in some fog through which sound cannot pass. The direction of sound in fog is also very deceptive and the sound will often seem to come from a place quite different from the ship's actual position. Remember, whenever you are in soundings in fog, use the lead-line or the echo-sounder. As rules go, that one is of pure gold!

Before leaving this section I should I think mention the various radio aids which are today available to the navigator. These, it must be emphasised are aids and do not take the place of the time-honoured methods of finding the ship's position by bearings, soundings and sights. Of course they improve in efficiency each year, but they still have their limitations and also most of them require practice to get good results. They are as follows:

(*a*) *Radio-direction Finding*. This is the oldest of the radio aids and depends on communication by stations onshore equipped with apparatus that enables them to find the bearing of another station or ship. For a vessel it necessitates special apparatus and an operator to work it.

(b) *Radio Beacons.* These are a logical development of RDF. They send out radio signals which can be picked up by vessels equipped with a direction-finding (DF) apparatus. Small radio sets are obtainable with such apparatus attached, and this method of finding a yacht's bearing is very suitable for small yachts.

(c) *Position-finding Methods – 'Consul', 'Loran' and 'Decca'*

(i) *'Consul.'* This does not require any special apparatus other than an ordinary radio receiving set. Bearings being sent out from certain shore stations.

(ii) *'Loran.'* Short for Long Range Navigational Aid. Signals sent out from shore stations and picked up on a radio receiving set, but being essentially a long range aid it requires a special radio when used by small yachts unless they indulge in ocean navigation!

(iii) *'Decca.'* This again works from transmitting stations onshore and again requires special receiving equipment. It is undoubtedly a very accurate system but it is also very expensive.

(d) *Radio Direction and Range (Radar).* This wartime invention which enables the operator to see far beyond the range of the eye, whether in fog or at night is of enormous assistance to modern navigators, though once again it is an *aid* and not a substitute. Like Decca, it is a very useful piece of equipment to have, but it too is expensive. Both Decca and Radar are of course frequently found aboard large yachts and in moderate-sized vessels where expense is not a problem.

(e) *Radio Telephony.* This I have dealt with briefly elsewhere in this chapter. I should point out, however, that though special receiving and transmitting sets are required, many makes are not only of a size suitable for small yachts but are moderately priced. To be able to talk to other vessels and shore stations is obviously a useful adjunct to the sophisticated navigator's equipment.

Having surfeited the reader with all these technical aids; what really is likely to be suitable for the ordinary cruising man? The answer is the radio beacon system. Radio beacons are now in operation on nearly every coast-line in the world. In British waters all radio beacons operate on the 285–315 kilocycle band, (roughly speaking 1053–952·4 metres) on the long wave of any radio set. In Europe the beacons are generally distinguished by a call sign of two letters. For example, Start Point in the English Channel has a call sign SP. Your *Nautical Almanack* will contain a full list of radio beacons with call signs and transmitting timing sequences, etc. Since the DF apparatus is not expensive and because of the simplicity of operation allied to a very comprehensive system of beacons – that is the system which I would recommend here.

(8) Sailing at night – navigation lights – international regulations regarding lights – lighting below – go carefully at night – working up the navigational reckoning – effect of leeway – the estimated position at the end of the passage

Most cruises in small boats involve some night sailing. Although to begin with, the idea of sailing at night may seem as repugnant as it did to the foppish 'Carruthers' in Erskine Childers's immortal book *The Riddle of the Sands*, yet, provided the weather behaves reasonably, it has much to recommend it. It is novel and fascinating, at times exciting. It brings with it certain problems that do not arise by day, for example, lights. At sea at night there is always the chance of meeting other ships, particularly fast steamers. An essential safeguard against collision is to carry efficient navigation lights. Again the navigator must have effective lighting and so must the cook, apart from the crew. There are really three ways to light a small boat – electricity, paraffin and candle. At sea, the most reliable is probably paraffin on account of the dangers of damp to electrical systems in small yachts. An efficiently installed system of wiring with good batteries that can be easily charged, removes much of this worry however; and I would always recommend electricity whenever it can be installed, with a few paraffin lamps (and a supply of paraffin) in case of failure. Candles are really a safeguard in case someone has lost or drunk the paraffin (or just forgotten to put it aboard). Electric light of course involves batteries which mean you either use a portable battery which can be taken ashore for charging or you charge your batteries on board by means of a generator on the yacht's engine (much the best idea). Large yachts will often have a small charging engine to avoid using the main engine just for charging, when the yacht is in harbour. One argument which is used against electric lighting is that it creates a guilt complex about wasting the battery. Although I have personal experience of one yacht owner who burnt so many lights simultaneously aboard his luxurious craft that, when the time came to start the engine, there was not enough juice in it, I still think electricity is worth the trouble. I should mention, too, that you can have acetylene lighting; but I have no experience of it, and I would think it is seldom used today. Again, just as one can use bottled gas for cooking, so you can both heat and light a yacht by this means (below decks anyway). Personally, although I favour gas for cooking, the presence of too much bottled gas in devices below would worry me because of the risk of leaks and fire (and explosion), but this is a purely personal viewpoint, with which doubtless, many will disagree.

While on the subject of lights; don't forget to have at least one reliable torch on board, with a spare battery or two; and this brings me to the question of navigation lights. If there is a sea running or a big ground swell or if the yacht is heeled on a windward leg, it is very difficult for a steamer to see the yacht's

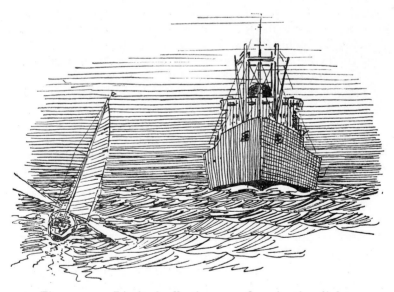

Figure 40.   Limited effectiveness of navigation lights

navigation lights. Figure 40 will explain why. Under these circumstances, a powerful torch that can be shone on the sails is invaluable.

The *International Regulations for the Prevention of Collision at Sea* we mentioned earlier (a copy of which you should have on board) include rules for lights to be carried by vessels. They state the position, colour, height and arc of each light, which normally means (in the case of sailing vessels of less than 40 feet in length and power vessels of less than 65 feet in length) a red port light and a green starboard light (rule 7) (a white forward light [rule 7] in the case of a power vessel only), and a white stern light (rule 10). An anchor light to be shown when the vessel is at anchor is also prescribed (rule 11). Since, as I said, you should certainly possess a copy of the regulations, I will not take up space here by detailing them further.

It is important that the interior lighting of a yacht is so arranged that the chart table light is not only adequate, but that it is shielded, not only from those sleeping in the cabin, but from the eyes of the helmsman when the cabin doors are open. Again, the compass light should be not too bright so as not to dazzle the helmsman. Too bright a light in the binnacle is very tiring to the eyes. Large compasses will often have a secondary lighting method (paraffin) in case the electrics fail. With a small compass a handy torch will do. An illuminated adjustable grid can also be useful. The grid can be set for the course required; and all the helmsman has to do is to keep the illuminated point on the compass between the parallel grid lines.

Finally, those with a taste for interior decoration below decks, should overcome a natural tendency to hide the wiring. Moisture is a deadly enemy of all electrics and dark unventilated spaces assist it with its work, so keep as much of your wiring in the open as you can. As a piece of functional design it is by no means unattractive. Personally, such things as wiring, deck-head compasses, barometers, clocks, chart racks, etc appeal to me very much more than fitted carpeting and velvet cushions delicately embroidered with burgees, rope, anchors, crowns, etc; but this is entirely a matter of personal taste (even of heated argument)!

When sailing at night, it is a good idea to go carefully. It is good seamanship. A cruising yacht seldom carries a large crew, and when in night watches only a small number of people (possibly only one) will be on deck. If you are carrying full sail and it comes on to blow it may be necessary to reef. This means calling out the watch below, robbing them of their proper quota of sleep. So it is best unless the weather is very settled, to carry only working sail after sunset – no spinnakers, big Genoa jibs, etc; remember, too, when working on deck at night, to anchor yourself to the ship. The simplest way is to tie a bowline round your waist and make the standing part of the rope fast to a good strong fitting (see chapter seven on knots).

We have now looked at various ways of fixing the yacht's position by bearings of objects onshore. Now that we are crossing 'Big Bay' it is a good time to consider how to estimate our position by 'working up the reckoning' as it is called. Our object is to achieve a landfall with 'Shackle Point' slightly to port. From there we can take the yacht into 'Sun Harbour' without difficulty (we hope)! We have been sailing for some hours now crossing the Bay and it is quite likely that at the end of our passage the fix that we will obtain from bearings of 'Shackle Point' and 'Crossbones Rock' will put us in a position that differs from our estimated position by a mile or two. This is not a matter for concern, provided you have been able to identify the landmarks and obtain your fix. With practice and experience the eventual fix and your estimated position at the end of a run will get nearer and nearer together! Winds are uncertain things, tides can be erratic in their behaviour (flooding for longer than usual for example), your patent log may be under-registering the distance run, you may not have allowed enough for leeway; or again, a surface drift may have caught you unawares. All these things are there to make the navigator's task not only harder but far more fascinating. Only experience can teach you how to allow for all these things. Again, knowledge of the way your ship reacts is another thing that comes with time; each yacht being quite individual in this respect, indeed that is one of the reasons that those bitten by the sailing bug become so completely absorbed by it. To offer guiding principles on these matters is not easy. Leeway, for example, can (as we saw earlier) be estimated to some extent by judging the yacht's wake astern with the course steered (see figure 41). If you are close-hauled, in a moderate breeze a rough guide to leeway would be $\frac{1}{2}$ to 1 point. But it depends so much on the type of vessel – for example, a deep-keeled vessel will

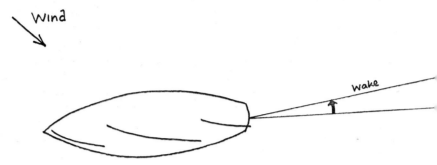

Figure 41. Estimated leeway

make less leeway than a ship of shallow draft. On the other hand, you may well find that leeway has been *more* than compensated for because of the known fact that most helmsmen, when on the wind, tend to steer up to windward of their course. (It is a good plan for the navigator to observe each helmsman for a time while sailing to windward.)

It is unlikely that one will have a fair wind for a whole passage, and almost certainly one will be beating to windward for part of it. It is the navigator's job to note all alterations of course and plot them on the chart. He can then work up his reckoning. The final position he gets is called the 'dead-reckoning position'. This is his *estimated* position. Look now at figure 42. At 09.00 hours we are at position *A*. Whenever there has been an alteration of course the time and course has been noted. The illustration shows how, after making three tacks, two of four miles and one of two miles, we are at position *B* at 11.25 (2½ hours later).

The navigator, wanting to estimate his position at *B* now applies the tidal stream, which in this case is two hours in one direction and half-hour in a slightly different direction. (This information he obtains from the chart or almanack as we saw earlier.) This gives him his dead-reckoning position at 11.25; and which like all estimated positions is marked with a triangle to differentiate it from the *fix* (at 09.00) marked with a circle. Of course, with a motor-sailer if you choose, you can motor most of the time and sail a more direct course into the wind (as with a motor-cruiser) depending on conditions.

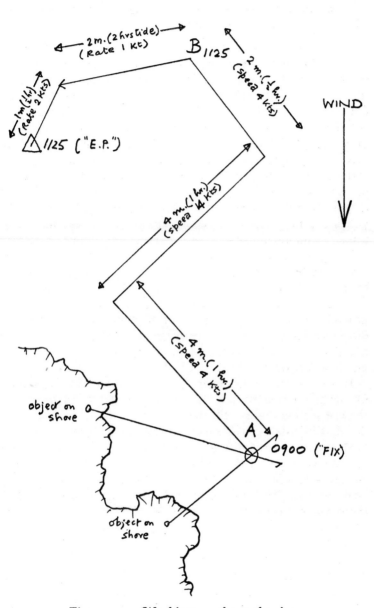

2m.(2 hrs tide)
(Rate 1 kt)

B 1125

2 m.(½ hr.)
(speed 4 kts)

WIND

1m (½ hr)
(Rate 2 kts)

1125 ("E.P.")

4 m.(1 hr.)
(speed 4 kts)

4 m.(1 hr.)
(speed 4 kts)

object on
shore

A

0900 ("FIX)

object on
shore

Figure 42.   Working up the reckoning

157

(9) Approaching harbour – signalling – morse code – use of leading marks – Dutchman's log

We are now approaching the end of the passage in our motor-sailer, and are about to make our landfall. The best time to make a landfall is debatable. If at night, you can fix your position by the various flashing lights, buoys, lights on shore, etc. On the other hand, there are obviously some disadvantages in entering a harbour, particularly a strange one, at night. Personally, I like to make any landfall a little before dawn. You can identify the coast by the lights and then by the time you arrive at the harbour entrance, it will be daylight, and you can see what you are doing. Of course it is not always possible to arrange things this way, but it is usually just a question of when you leave the harbour of your departure. For example a 7-tonner (which will average, say, 5 knots) setting out on a sixty-mile night passage, has only to leave at, say, 6 pm, to arrive ten hours later (having covered fifty miles) ten miles off the coast at 4 am where the lights onshore will give an excellent fix. Two hours later, having completed the sixty miles of the passage, the yacht will be entering harbour at 6 am in broad daylight. She can see her way across the harbour quite easily; and it won't be long before all on board are sitting down to an excellent breakfast!

It is some forty miles from 'Black Point' to 'Shackle Point'. Of course the tidal stream will affect your landfall as we saw in the last section and so will the vagaries of the wind. If it turns out that it is daylight when the coast looms into view, we will have to try and identify it from the chart or handbook. Our dead-reckoning position will be invaluable at this point. Once we have identified two or three shore marks we can get a fix by bearings and check our estimated position. Nobody minds if the navigator (who after all must be allowed to keep some of his mystique), works this one out on his own, unhampered by critical eyes!

It is not all that often that a yachtsman has to signal another vessel by lamp, but it is a useful accomplishment to be able to send and receive morse. It is often very much easier to call up a vessel than to get near her and hail her, unless of course she is a fishing boat relatively stationary. If one is badly lost on an unfamiliar shore, to be able *in extremis* to ask one's position can be very useful. This is nothing to be ashamed of. After a long passage at sea, when contrary and varied winds have made navigation difficult, it is often very hard to identify a piece of coast-line. Again morse is useful in case of accident or illness aboard. Anyone with a little practice can become quite efficient at sending and receiving morse. The type of lamp you use depends on your pocket. A large torch is adequate, but a proper signalling lamp with a key is much better, although more expensive. Figure 43 sets out the basic morse code. Any form of radio telephonic system is of course a great asset (as Sir Alec Rose found when he was able to contact Arawua and Melbourne from distances of over 800 miles). Such equipment, though not cheap, is available to small vessels under licence. In Great Britain at all events it is necessary to pass a simple examination in radio telephony (R/T) to get a Certificate of Competency. Full details of this and a great deal of information concerning radio communications are to be found in Reed's *Nautical Almanack*. This includes the International Maritime

MORSE CODE

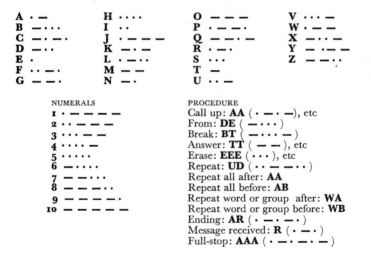

A · —	H · · · ·	O — — —	V · · · —
B — · · ·	I · ·	P · — — ·	W · — —
C — · — ·	J · — — —	Q — — · —	X — · · —
D — · ·	K — · —	R · — ·	Y — · — —
E ·	L · — · ·	S · · ·	Z — — · ·
F · · — ·	M — —	T —	
G — — ·	N — ·	U · · —	

NUMERALS

1	· — — — —
2	· · — — —
3	· · · — —
4	· · · · —
5	· · · · ·
6	— · · · ·
7	— — · · ·
8	— — — · ·
9	— — — — ·
10	— — — — —

PROCEDURE

Call up: **AA** (· — · —), etc
From: **DE** (— · · ·)
Break: **BT** (— · · · —)
Answer: **TT** (— —), etc
Erase: **EEE** (· · ·), etc
Repeat: **UD** (· · — — · ·)
Repeat all after: **AA**
Repeat all before: **AB**
Repeat word or group after: **WA**
Repeat word or group before: **WB**
Ending: **AR** (· — · — ·)
Message received: **R** (· — ·)
Full-stop: **AAA** (· — · — · —)

If you cannot read a sender's message due to bad lighting or his light being badly trained on you; send: **W** (· — —); **C** (— · — ·) means 'You are correct'.
   For convenience there is an international code of group signals and single letter signals; the latter are as follows:

Figure 43.   The Morse Code

INTERNATIONAL CODE OF SIGNALS

The most important code signals of all – the single letter signals – consist of very urgent signals or those in common use, and are the characters representing each letter of the RADIO BEACON Call Sign. For example a Call Sign RYE would use the Morse characters set in front of the letters R, Y and E on this page in this order.

The Morse Code symbols are given before each letter for immediate reference.

A	· —	I am undergoing a speed trial
B	— · · ·	I am taking in or discharging explosives.
C	— · — ·	Yes (affirmative).
D	— · ·	Keep clear of me – I am manoeuvring with difficulty.
E	·	I am directing my course to starboard.
F*	· · — ·	I am disabled. Communicate with me.
G	— — ·	I require a pilot on board.
H	· · · ·	I have a pilot on board.
I	· ·	I am directing my course to port.
J	· — — —	I am going to send a message by Semaphore.
K*	— · —	You should stop your vessel instantly.
L*	· — · ·	You should stop. I have something important to communicate.
M	— —	I have a doctor on board.
N	— ·	No (negative).
O*	— — —	Man overboard.
P*	· — — ·	In Harbour (Blue Peter). All persons are to repair on board vessel is about to proceed to sea. (Note – To be hoisted at foremasthead). At Sea. Your lights are out, or burning badly.
Q	— — · —	My vessel is healthy and I request a free pratique.
R*	· — ·	The way is off my ship; you may feel your way past me.
S	· · ·	My engines are going full speed astern.
T	—	Do not pass ahead of me.
U*	· · —	You are standing into danger.
V*	· · · —	I require assistance.
W*	· — —	I require medical assistance.
X	— · · —	Stop carrying out your intentions and watch for my signals.
Y	— · — —	I am carrying mails.
Z*	— — · ·	To be used to address or call shore stations.

Only those marked with an asterisk (*) should be used by flashing.
These also, with the several others that would be used for the purpose indicated, ie G = I require a Pilot and the 'alter course' signals E, I and S, and others would be given by sound signals (Morse Code) as required (and shown in brackets).

Figure 43. The Morse Code

Mobile R/T Service as well as details of the United Kingdom Coast Station R/T Service.

Chart 2 (between pages 112 and 113), illustrates 'Sun Bay' in more detail, the bay of our destination. While still some distance from the harbour approaches, you should study the harbour plan carefully, noting depths and all relevant details concerning buoys, lights, channels forbidden and permitted and any signals governing entering the harbour. The harbour plan and pilot together will supply this very necessary information. There won't be time to look it all up when you are there.

Sometimes when the entry to a river is both winding and rocky, great use can be made of leading marks; by which I mean simply two prominent landmarks easily seen from seaward, which, when brought into line, give a safe entry into the harbour. Leading marks are often marked on large-scale charts and harbour plans, but even if they are not, you can make your own. Look at the chart and choose two easily identified objects which, by being brought into line and kept there for as long as is necessary, will give you a safe course. Sometimes a second pair of leading marks can be used to turn to a new course and so find your way to a quiet anchorage. Use can also be made of prominent fixed objects. Figure 44 shows this. You can of course use lights in line in the same way, but it is obviously a little harder and you must be very sure of your identification. I once employed a red light and white light in line to approach a certain French harbour by night. It was about two in the morning. Suddenly the red light went out. Fortunately I knew my position and was only using the lights in line as a lazy guide to maintain my course. In the morning, in harbour I found my red light. It was a neon sign over a café at the far side of the harbour. I located it on the large-scale chart and found that a line from it projected through my white light (a landfall buoy) gave a perfect approach; but one might not always be so lucky!

In section 10 we will be entering harbour and mooring (or anchoring). We have come safely from the 'River Thin' to the approaches to 'Sun Bay'. We have experienced a variety of weather conditions and I hope learnt a bit. Every time one makes a passage, such as this, one picks up a bit more of the game. For example we have made good use of our patent log but it might have happened that the log was unsatisfactory; perhaps seriously under- or over-registering. The rotator might

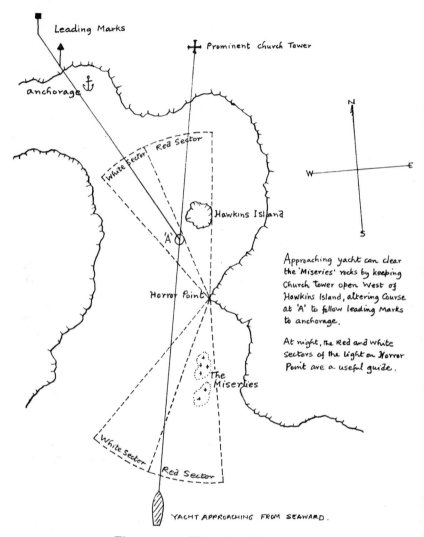

Leading Marks

Prominent church Tower

anchorage

N

W — E

S

Red Sector

White Sector

Hawkins Island

'A'

Horror Point

The Miseries

Approaching yacht can clear the 'Miseries' rocks by keeping Church Tower open West of Hawkins Island, altering Course at 'A' to follow leading Marks to anchorage.

At night, the Red and White sectors of the light on Horror Point are a useful guide.

White Sector

Red Sector

YACHT APPROACHING FROM SEAWARD.

Figure 44. Using Leading marks

have carried away, or the log itself carried away in rough weather. Unlikely occurrences perhaps, but *if* that had happened what would we be able to do about it? The remedy is to make use of the time-honoured 'Dutchman's log'! For this we need to procure several small pieces of wood – anything that floats will do. Select two marks on deck a given distance in feet apart. Station two observers, one forward and one aft at these marks. Now throw the first float overboard clear of the yacht's wash as far out and ahead of the bow as possible. Take the time the float passes at right-angles to the fore-and-aft line of the ship at the stem head (or whatever forward mark you are measuring from). Again note the time that the float passes the stern mark. A good watch, preferably a stop-watch, is needed; the times must be exactly recorded. Now multiply the time that the float has taken to pass between the two marks to find the vessel's speed in knots; remembering that one nautical mile equals 6,080 feet. It is a simple and surprisingly accurate way to find your speed through the water – a method in use from time immemorial.

When approaching an unfamiliar coast-line remember that it is always better to stop or heave-to and study the chart and work things out slowly and carefully. Never allow pride in your navigation to make you carry on if you don't know where you are or you may find yourself subsequently faced with the humiliating task of identifying the ledge on which you have just grounded, and that is a calculated understatement!

(10) Anchoring, mooring – types of anchor – coming to an anchor under sail – mooring with two anchors – entering harbour and mooring alongside – stowing ship and clearing up after passage

We have arrived! It is now open to us to anchor in 'Sun Roads' or enter the harbour or to sail into 'Wrymouth' at the northern end of the bay. We will probably have made our decision long before and will have studied carefully the relevant harbour plan. If we have decided to anchor in 'Sun Roads', we must remember that although there is good shelter generally, it is unwise if the winds are north-easterly or easterly. Let us assume, however, that the wind is south-west and the weather set fair and we have decided to anchor in the 'Roads' and have a meal before entering harbour. This is the first time we have had to anchor on our passage from the 'River Thin' and it will give a good chance to consider some aspects of this simple but important manoeuvre.

A yacht like our motor-sailer will usually carry one main anchor and one lighter, smaller anchor, called a kedge. The anchor must be easily accessible, not lying under a mound of chain or pile of sails. It should always be connected to its cable, and the inboard end of the cable firmly fixed on board. The cable itself should be marked in some way so that you can easily tell how much has been let out. These may seem facts too obvious to mention, but it is surprising how often the cable can take charge and rush over the side. It can be difficult to stop it in such a case, and if it is not firmly secured below, you may well have lost an expensive piece of equipment.

There are a variety of types of anchor available to the yachtsman. Figure 45 shows the traditional *Fisherman* or *Naval pattern* anchor together with the names of the various parts. Figure 46 shows a jointed anchor type, the *Danforth*. Figure 47 illustrates the *CQR* anchor.

Nylon rope is very suitable for the anchor warp. It has elasticity, is light, easy to handle. But remember that there

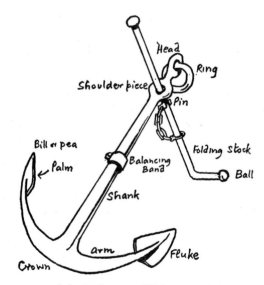

Figure 45.   Admiralty, or 'Fisherman' Anchor

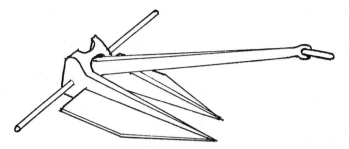

Figure 46.   Danforth Anchor

should be at least three fathoms of chain joining the nylon warp
to the anchor so that it will lie along the sea bed and make
sure that the pull is horizontal.

Now let's come to the business of anchoring. The anchor
must be ready. If it is of the *Fisherman* type, see that the stock is
in place and secured by driving the small pin well home (see
figure 45). Range a fathom or so on deck and make certain that
the cable can run easily through the chain pipe or fairlead. We
will have looked up the depth of water (as we learnt in section 9)
at the place in which we intend to anchor. Let us assume that
there are 3 fathoms (18 ft – 5·48 m) at high water. It is wise to
veer about three times the depth at high water so we will veer
9 fathoms (54 ft – 16·45 m). If it blows hard it may be necessary
to veer more as required to stop the anchor dragging. We will

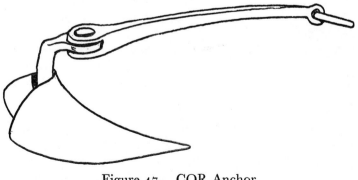

Figure 47.   CQR Anchor

165

have selected a sheltered place reasonably near the shore, and with room to range about and swing as the tide turns without endangering other yachts in the locality. Now unshackle the cable and lead it through the fairlead in the bows and back inboard where it is re-shackled to the anchor ring. We will have observed (and looked up) the direction of the tidal stream. All we now have to do is chuck the anchor over the side and the cable will run out after it. We control it as it runs out and when it gets to 9 fathoms we stop it, make fast and there we are anchored!

Now if (as is likely for it simplifies matters) we are going to use the engine of our motor-sailer, we will have lowered sail and be proceeding to the anchorage under power. We must decide whether the effect of the wind is going to be stronger than that of the tide. If the tide is the stronger, we turn into it. If the wind is the stronger, the anchor must be let go on the weather bow so that the yacht's bows will blow away from the cable. But I cannot emphasise enough that with an auxiliary sailing yacht or a motor-sailer you must know how to anchor under sail alone. Here are some simple rules of thumb for coming to an anchor under sail:

(*a*) If there is no tide: 1. luff head to wind; 2. lower head-sail(s); 3. wait until the yacht gathers sternway; 4. let go the anchor.

(*b*) When wind and tide are in the same direction and yacht is close-hauled – same as for (*a*).

(*c*) When wind and tide are in the same direction (yacht running): 1. lower mainsail and approach under headsail; 2. lower headsail a little way from the selected spot; 3. let go; 4. snub (stop running out) the cable and allow the yacht to swing to the tide. Finally

(*d*) When wind is against tide (yacht is running): 1. lower mainsail and approach under headsail; 2. lower headsail just before reaching anchorage; 3. wait till yacht gathers sternway; 4. let go.

We have now reached the anchorage under power, so we put the engine into neutral and then astern, remembering that with a right-handed screw the bows will go to starboard as the vessel starts to come astern. The initial kick of the bows to starboard will allow the anchor chain to run clear through the port fairlead in the bows, and this way the cable will not fall all over the anchor flukes and foul it. As it runs out the marks are noted and the cable snubbed (made fast) at the appropriate mark. Bearings of three objects onshore should now be taken as a check against the anchor dragging. If the wind increases and a single anchor seems insufficient, the ship can be given a sheer by putting the rudder to starboard (see figure 48). The tide will

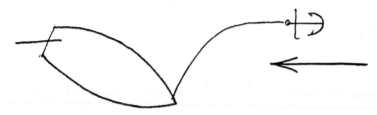

Figure 48.   Giving a sheer with the helm

then bring her bows over to starboard and we can let go a second anchor to starboard, and veer on both cables. Anchoring with more than one anchor is called mooring. It is useful not only in the conditions just described but in harbours where there is not enough room to swing to a single anchor. To moor correctly is somewhat different from the method just described. The latter is a temporary measure, and if you are going to spend any length of time at anchor, it is always wisest to moor, and essential if the vessel is to be left unattended. When mooring with two anchors in tidal waters the anchors should lie in line with the direction of the tide, the heaviest anchor taking the greatest strain (for example, if the ebb runs more strongly than the flood).

Let's now have a look at three ways of mooring with two anchors under sail. To make a standing moor, stem the tide and sail a little past the selected spot and down sail. As the yacht gathers sternway drop one anchor. Let the tide carry her astern and pay out twice the length of anchor warp you will be needing to ride to. Snub until you feel the anchor bite and check that it is holding. Now drop the second anchor. Heave in on the first warp paying out the second until you have 'middled' between them.

To make a running moor you approach the anchor under the

lee-tide. Shortly before reaching the chosen spot, drop one anchor and pay out warp to twice the amount needed (while the vessel continues with the tide). Then snub and let the vessel swing to the anchor. Now drop the second anchor and heave in on the first warp, paying out the second simultaneously until, once again, the vessel is middled.

Sometimes, when there is not much room to manoeuvre, it is better to let go the heavy anchor and snub the warp or cable at the required depth (as if coming to a single anchor), then carry the second (kedge) anchor in the dinghy and drop it where it is wanted. The kedge warp (nylon again) can now be made fast to the cable (or warp) of the main anchor (this is done on board) and then both eased until the join is well below the level of the keel (figure 49 illustrates this). (The knot you use will be a rolling hitch and chapter seven tells you how to tie it, if you don't already know!)

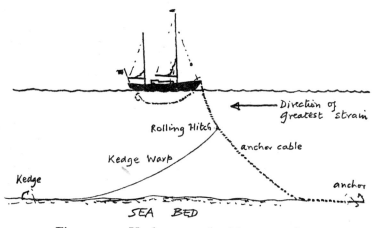

Figure 49.   Yacht moored with two anchors

But now let's assume that we want to enter harbour. This may entail mooring alongside a quay or alongside another vessel. It may involve picking up a vacant mooring buoy, or it may mean securing stern to quay with the bows moored to a buoy or with a single anchor out. Securing stern to quay, formally associated with continental harbours, is now commonly found in yacht marinas. The method adopted in each harbour will be clearly seen on entry if you do not already know it. To secure to a mooring buoy, while quite difficult under sail (or at least requiring practice) should present few problems under power. To pick up a buoy or anchor and come astern to a marina pontoon is also reasonably simple. It is a matter of common sense. Have plenty of fenders out both sides and work out in advance the probable effect of wind and tide. Mooring alongside a pontoon, quay or another vessel is just a matter of putting out enough lines and putting them out correctly. This is very important in places where the current runs strongly. Figure 50 shows these ropes. The 'springs' are well-named; the leverage

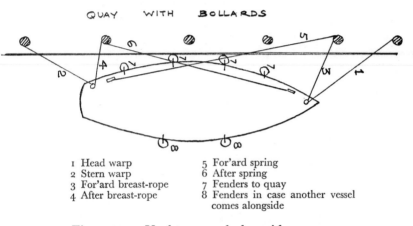

1 Head warp	5 For'ard spring
2 Stern warp	6 After spring
3 For'ard breast-rope	7 Fenders to quay
4 After breast-rope	8 Fenders in case another vessel comes alongside

Figure 50.   Yacht moored alongside a quay

effect is very important as will be seen from the drawing. If there is a strong wind blowing you on to the quay, great care must be exercised in coming alongside. Only experience and practice will teach you the wrinkles. Our motor-sailer, having a single screw, needs a little thought to manoeuvre under power. Motor-cruisers with twin screws will of course be able to turn more sharply and quickly by going ahead on one engine and astern on the other. It will be obvious that twin screws give a wonderful degree of manoeuvrability to a vessel under power.

We are at the end of our passage, but before going below to change into shore-going clothes there are two or three things we must do. First, stow ship. Take battens out of the mainsail, furl it and put on the sail cover. (If it is wet, do not cover, and hoist to dry at the first opportunity.) Unhank headsails, put them in their bags and stow them; unhook sheets, coil and stow them. Give the deck a general clean up (if possible a wash down). Your ship has carried you bravely for so many miles – she deserves to be looked after. It is worth a good tidy up below decks too. After dinner ashore, coming back to a shambles below is depressing. And before going ashore, put a couple of fenders over your outboard side. Other vessels may come alongside you and it is an insurance against scratches on your topsides.

So that's it! I can now, paraphrasing Captain Joshua Slocum's ending to his book *Sailing Alone Around the World*: '. . . moor ship, weather-bitt cables and leave . . . our motor-sailer . . . for the present, safe in port'.

CHAPTER SIX

How to Sail

How to Manoeuvre under Sail and under Power

(1) Sail

Although this book is primarily designed for those who have done a little day sailing and want to cruise, I am aware that the contents may appeal to some people who have never sailed before. There is no reason why a person who takes up sailing should not learn to cruise at an early stage. Once the basic principles are grasped and some degree of confidence acquired, short coastal passages can be attempted. A book can only be a guide. Practical experience afloat has no substitute. The most useful auxiliary is a knowledgeable sailing friend. From him or her, an intelligent person can pick up more in a day than in weeks of reading. Nevertheless the practical instruction of your friend will be translated into competent actions much more quickly if you have first read (and understood) it in a book. So to the tyros among my readers, welcome, and here are the basic methods of – to put it crudely – starting, continuing and stopping. Figure 51 illustrates a small cruising yacht and shows you the main parts and their names. This yacht is rigged as a sloop (mainsail and headsail).

The easiest way to sail is to run before the wind. This is the way the first sailing vessels sailed; the second easiest way is to have the wind on the beam (the side) and the third, and hardest, way is to sail at an angle (about 45°) to it called sailing 'close-hauled'. But first we must start.

Now most small cruisers today have an engine perhaps just an outboard, but enough to get away on so that the boat may be turned head to wind and the sails hoisted easily. If you do not have an engine you should know how to leave your moorings or anchorage under sail. It all depends on the direction of the wind; and if you are in tidal waters, of the tide. Fortunately it can all be compressed into a basic rule. If wind and tide are in the same direction there is no problem about hoisting the mainsail filling on one tack or the other, letting go the mooring (or heaving in the anchor) and sailing away. The same applies if there is no tide. However, if wind and tide are in opposition, and the tide is strong enough to make the boat lie stern to the wind, then you will find hoisting the mainsail is distinctly tiresome. It will wrap itself around stays and spreaders, will jam and may tear. Furthermore the moment you have hoisted it a few feet, the yacht will start to sail. The answer is simple – drop moorings (or weigh anchor), hoist the jib and sail away under it until you have enough sea-room to turn head into wind and hoist the main in comfort.

Before getting under way, have a look around you. Note the positions of other craft and what the tide is doing otherwise you may get carried on to one of them. Plan your getaway before you touch a single rope. If you are lying in a marina, bow or stern to quay or alongside a quay and you have no engine, once again the direction of the wind is of paramount importance, and the same principles apply. If necessary you should lay a small anchor (using your dinghy) a sufficient distance from the quay or jetty to pull your boat away from it so that she lies to the anchor. From then on it should be, literally, plain sailing.

Now let's assume we are under way; the wind is aft and we are running before it. To do this properly pay out the mainsheet until the mainsail (not the boom) is roughly at right-angles to the fore-and-aft line of the boat. The wind should be on one-quarter or the other not *dead* astern, as there then would exist the risk of the wind catching the sail aback and swinging across with a crash – a manoeuvre known as 'gybing all standing' – quite a different matter from a controlled gybe which is when you turn from one course to another with the wind aft. To do this gather in the mainsheet as the boom swings over and ease her gently round. When running, the jib should be trimmed with its sheet so that it too is nearly at right-angles to the fore-and-aft line; both mainsail and jib being on the opposite side to the wind. If your boat has a centreboard, raise it when running. If she yaws (swings) about with the board

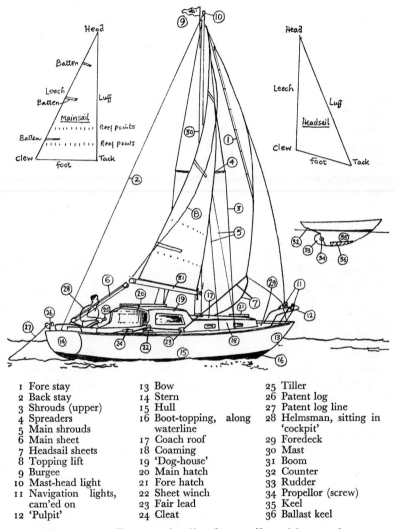

1 Fore stay	13 Bow	25 Tiller
2 Back stay	14 Stern	26 Patent log
3 Shrouds (upper)	15 Hull	27 Patent log line
4 Spreaders	16 Boot-topping, along	28 Helmsman, sitting in
5 Main shrouds	waterline	'cockpit'
6 Main sheet	17 Coach roof	29 Foredeck
7 Headsail sheets	18 Coaming	30 Mast
8 Topping lift	19 'Dog-house'	31 Boom
9 Burgee	20 Main hatch	32 Counter
10 Mast-head light	21 Fore hatch	33 Rudder
11 Navigation lights,	22 Sheet winch	34 Propellor (screw)
cam'ed on	23 Fair lead	35 Keel
12 'Pulpit'	24 Cleat	36 Ballast keel

Figure 51.   Parts and sails of a small cruising yacht

completely raised, then you must lower until she steadies. When running before the wind, watch out for two dangers — rolling excessively and broaching-to, ie: coming up into the wind.

If the boat is rolling a great deal she may get her boom in the water. As soon as this happens the rudder becomes useless. It is sometimes difficult to stop a boat rolling but you should try lowering the centreboard (if she is a centreboarder). Another good tip is to haul in the mainsheet a trifle. If the rolling is severe, top up the mainboom with the topping lift to keep it clear of the water. Broaching-to can be more alarming than rolling. You may be happily running when the boat suddenly begins to come up into the wind with the boom of course, broad off, ie: sticking out at right-angles to the fore-and-aft line of the boat. (Once again there is a danger that it may dip in.) The answer here is alertness. As soon as she starts to broach-to, check her at once with the helm. If the boat is continually tending to broach-to you are carrying too much sail, so heave-to and tuck in a reef (see chapter five for how to do this). When running you can increase your speed (and pleasure) by hoisting a spinnaker and since we have seen how to do this in chapter five, I won't elaborate here.

Now let's assume our course has altered and we are reaching. This is the fastest point of sailing. Trim the sails by easing the sheets so that both mainsail and headsail are making the same angle with the boat's fore-and-aft line. As to how much you should ease sheets, continue until the luffs begin to shake; then haul in slowly until they cease. Provided the wind holds true (and it often doesn't) you are now trimmed correctly for your course. To tell if the wind draws ahead or aft watch the angle of the burgee at the masthead. As you acquire experience other things as well will tell you what the wind is doing; the direction of the waves, the feel of the wind on your head, the boat's movement (she will lose speed or get sluggish) and of course if the wind draws too far ahead, the sails will lift (shake). All these things will tell you that you should retrim sheets.

With a dinghy, changes in wind direction are met by an alteration of helm. Dinghies are very sensitive to sail. With a keel boat it is often easier to adjust sheets. Very small cruisers like some of the small centreboarders or twin keel boats we have discussed in chapter two will often behave like a dinghy.

You will soon get to know your boat and how to get the best

out of her. This is half the fun of owning your own boat; you learn her foibles and her strong points. Sailing to windward is the hardest, but the most exhilarating point of sailing. The hardest because it requires a lot of continuous concentration to do it properly and the most exhilarating because, apart from the pleasure which the efficient practice of any skill brings, you get, with the wind ahead, a wonderful feeling of speed (quite unrelated to your actual sea-miles-per-hour). There is one golden rule in sailing to windward and it consists of four easily remembered words 'Don't starve the boat'. Don't trim the sails so flat in a laudable effort to sail close to the wind. If you do you will slow her up. Most boats sail about 4 'points' (45°) to the wind. Most *will* sail 3 points (33¾°), but they will sail it slowly. If she is sluggish look at the burgee angle, etc; free her, that is sail 45° or more and you will feel her gather speed in response. Sailing a well-balanced boat to windward is like riding a spirited but obedient horse. If you use rein or helm correctly you will get a wonderful response; if you use them unthinkingly, the resultant sluggishness will tell you (and everyone else) that you are not doing it right. All this may sound difficult but it is not. It *is* a matter of experience though. You can't learn to sail a boat to windward from a book. Just as with reaching the various 'signs' mentioned (burgee, wind feel, waves, lifting sails, etc) will tell you whether you are sailing the right angle to the wind. As to trim of the sails a rough guide is, in strong winds, sheet in as flat as you like, but in light airs ease sheets and get more curve in the sails.

When sailing a course to windward it will eventually become necessary to go about on to the other tack. There is no particular magic about this. To reach a given objective dead to windward of you, you must proceed in a series of 45° angles called tacks. When the wind is blowing over the port-hand side of the boat, she is said to be on the port tack and vice versa. The length of each tack will depend on circumstance. Supposing you can make the object ahead (say a buoy) in two tacks, you should continue on the first tack until the object is well on your weather quarter *not* abeam (90°), because although your second tack will *point* approximately 90° from your first tack course, the effect of leeway will surprise you. After you have tacked you should have the object well on the lee bow if you are going to reach it without having to tack again. Leeway, incidentally, is simply the amount a boat is set down to leeward – ie failure to maintain the course through being 'set down' away from the line – by the wind when close-hauled.

The method of going about when tacking is as follows. Have plenty of way on the boat. As you approach the point where you have decided to make another tack, call out 'ready about' to warn those on board of your intention. Call out 'lee oh!' and put the helm down. As the boat turns through the wind's eye the lee jib sheet is let fly and the old weather jib sheet which will now be the new lee jib sheet, is hauled taut. The boom will swing across and the mainsail and jib will fill on the new tack. It is in the timing and co-ordination of helm and sheet movements that makes for the quick, efficient tacking that wins races.

Not many boats have runners or running back-stays nowadays, but if your boat has them remember to ease the new lee runner and set up the new weather runner as the vessel goes about. You should aim to set up the new weather runner before the strain comes on it, otherwise the mast will not be properly stayed against the pull of the sails. Also it is much harder to set up the runner once the strain has come on it. If you are tacking in heavy weather, choose a relatively calm patch (called a smooth) to come about in and it is very important, when seas are steep, to have plenty of way on.

Don't jam the helm down hard but ease her gently round. It is not in the helm movements that speed is required but rather in the handling of the headsail sheets. Once on the new tack sail her a little 'free' so as to get plenty of speed before you ease her back into the close hauled position Figure 52 illustrates the points of sailing we have been discussing.

Sometimes, when tacking, a boat will not go right round and hangs in the middle of the turn, pointing straight into the wind, with sails flapping and drifting astern. An undignified and maddening occurrence. Do not panic! Haul the jib hard to, let us say, the port side. You want the wind to push the bows round to starboard. You are drifting astern so the rudder will work in the opposite way to normal. In other words to turn to starboard put the helm to starboard (which means the rudder to port) and as she drifts astern she will turn to starboard, the wind will catch the jib sheeted to port and push her round to starboard. The mainsail will fill and the jib can now be sheeted to starboard and off you go on the port tack. Just keep

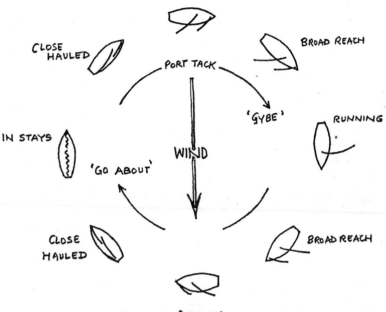

Figure 52. The points of sailing

your head and carry out this simple evolution and all will be well!

If the wind freshens and the boat is heeling so far over that she is dragging her rail through the water, you are losing speed. Tuck in a reef. Boats are designed to sail at a slight angle of heel when sailing on the wind but not too much because then the extra surface friction will slow her down (and make life uncomfortable for those below decks).

If your boat has a centreboard, lower it right down when sailing to windward and when reaching too. It is your safeguard against too much leeway. When your sail is finished and the time has come to anchor, pick up a mooring or come alongside a quay, don't try and do it in a hurry. Know what the tide is doing and relate it to the wind's direction. For example, if you are anchoring against the tide but with the wind (running) turn into the wind and lower mainsail. Now approach the spot

M   177

slowly under headsail. When you reach the spot, lower headsail and as she starts to fall astern on the tide chuck over the anchor (preferably fastened to a rope or chain *and* the end of the rope or chain must be securely made fast below or on deck!). If wind and tide are in the same direction approach to windward and turn into the wind to stop her as you reach the spot, then lower jib and over with the hook as she drifts astern. If you happen to be running and wind and tide are in the same direction, you just lower mainsail (turning temporarily into the wind); approach the anchorage under headsail; lower headsail and let the tide carry you to the chosen spot. Over with the anchor and check the warp or cable and let the yacht swing to the tide.

If there is no tide, come head to wind (this is called 'luffing'), lower headsail wait until she gathers sternway and then over goes the hook.

If there is a buoy to be picked up, this requires quite a little practice to do well (and to do first time), but the principles are easy to understand. A glance at figures 53 and 54 will show you the successive stages in this manoeuvre under two typical conditions of wind and tide.

To moor alongside a quay, first of all put out fenders to protect the hull. Have the necessary ropes coiled and ready with their

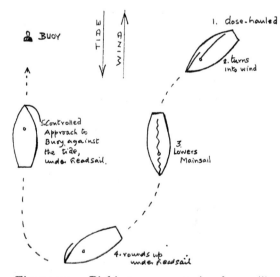

Figure 53. Picking up a mooring buoy (i)

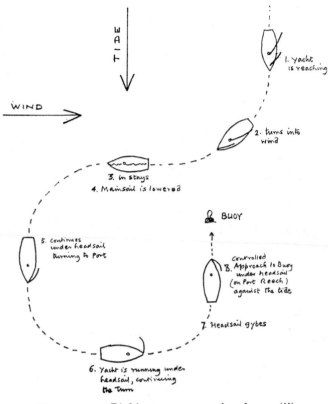

Figure 54. Picking up a mooring buoy (ii)

inboard ends made fast on deck. Whenever possible come alongside against the current, and slowly! Get the bow rope ashore
as soon as you can. Figure 50 (in chapter five) shows how the
well-moored yacht should look. If yours is a sailing vessel with an
auxiliary engine don't always rely on it completely. Modern
engines don't often let you down but even so, faults can occur
and you *must* know how to do it under sail. And when you have
become good at it you will want to do it under sail for the sheer
pleasure and satisfaction of it.

(2) Under Power

I turn now to the question of handling a vessel under power
alone. Just as this book assumes a certain amount of knowledge

on the part of the sailing-boat owner, nevertheless for those with no experience of motor vessels the following will, I hope, come in useful.

Let us assume that your boat has one engine (single screw). The important thing to realise when manoeuvring in crowded anchorages is the effect of that screw when starting, turning (either way) and when stopping. If you have no experience of vessels under power the ensuing paragraphs may surprise you!

As a boat with starboard helm moves ahead water, pressing on the fore-side of the rudder, will push the stern to port. If going astern the water would be pressing on the after-side of the rudder, and consequently when the latter is put to starboard, the stern will be pushed to starboard, not to port as when going ahead. The rudder has less effect when going astern because the force acting on it is that of the water flowing past it, whereas when going ahead water is forced on to it by the propeller.

Most single-screw boats have right-handed propellers but you can have either. Twin-screw boats will tend to have one of each. It is very important to know which your boat has because it will determine the direction the stern (and so the bows) kick when the engine is first put in gear. Let us examine why. Imagine a twin-blade propeller revolving in water. When the blades are vertical, the lower of the two will be in denser (because deeper) water and so has a denser mass against which to push as it turns. Because of this, it is the bottom blade that decides the direction of the initial kick of the stern. Let us imagine we are behind the boat, looking forward, at a single, two-blade right-handed screw. As the engine is put into ahead gear, the lower blade will push the denser water to the left, and so the stern will kick to starboard, and the bows to port. Conversely if the engine were put astern, the bows would move to starboard. This movement to starboard or port happens before the boat gathers way; and it will be obvious that it can be of great assistance in manoeuvring once you have got the knack of using it.

Let us take an example of using this knowledge in a given situation. Imagine we are in a narrow stretch of water, say a river, with a fairly strong current running. We want to turn our boat, with her single right-handed screw, to starboard. We are moored near the left bank bows to current. (The current is the same as an ebb-tide.) We know that with a right-hand screw the stern will kick to port and the bows to starboard when the engine is put into astern gear. So all we have to do is to give her a touch astern to bring our bows out into the centre of the river. In a stretch of water like this, the current will run more strongly in the centre than at the sides, so, by using the engine to put our bow into the stronger current, we are harnessing the latter for our purpose and the initial kick of the bows to starboard will be continued by the force of the current.

Next we must consider the effect of wind. Motor craft, with their relatively shallow draught and high freeboard are very much affected by wind when manoeuvring in rivers, anchorages, etc, the upper structure acts like sails. If, for example, your boat has high bows and a long open cockpit of moderate freeboard the bows will move away from the wind, especially since power craft have less draught forward than aft.

If your boat has twin screws they will probably be arranged so that the two propellers turn outwards, that is to say, the starboard screw will be right-handed, and the port screw, left-handed. When the vessel moves ahead the lower blades of the propellers will be moving towards the centre-line of the ship. It will not require much imagination to see that if you go ahead on the starboard screw (initial kick of the bows to port) and astern on the port screw (also kicks the bows to port) you can turn around in your own length. With twin screws you have more control, more power, and of course the safety-factor of the second engine. But the same principle of understanding the use of the propeller and the varied interaction of wind and current apply. As with everything to do with boats and the sea, once you have grasped the general principles, only experience in carrying out the maneouvres in practice and under many different conditions can give you real confidence in handling your boat whether she be power-boat or sail-boat.

I am well aware that in this short section for the novice to boats there is much that is missing. I have not told you how to row a dinghy for example, but really for all that you must buy another, more elementary book, maybe one of mine? But in any case, remember the sea itself is the best teacher!

(3) The Engine (Starting Troubles, Overheating, etc)

You do not have to be an expert mechanic to keep a yacht engine running at sea. Often an engine fault may be due to a very slight defect. If this defect is not attended to promptly, trouble can follow, but the remedy will more often than not be quite simple and will require only a slight knowledge. The most likely troubles are: (*a*) difficulty in starting; (*b*) engine stopping suddenly; (*c*) engine 'spitting' and then stopping; (*d*) engine firing erratically; (*e*) engine will only run fast; (*f*) engine will only run slowly. These are the most common faults in a four-stroke petrol engine, so let us take them in that order. Two-stroke engines and diesel engines I will deal with later.

(*a*) If the engine is hard to start, it may be due to the following:

    (i) dirty sparking-plugs. Remedy – remove plugs, take to pieces, clean and dry;

  (ii) valve clearance not big enough. Remedy – adjust the tappets accordingly;

(iii) the jet is choked. Remedy – remove jet, and clean carefully. The fault could be in the magneto and this would involve stripping the latter; a simple enough function to those with expert knowledge but tricky for the newcomer – let's just hope it isn't that!

(*b*) Maybe the engine starts all right but stops suddenly. This could be either a broken timing chain – in which case you must fit the spare chain (a good idea to carry one), but if the engine has coil ignition it is more likely to be a broken earth wire. Remedy – examine and, if necessary, replace.

(*c*) If the engine is running well and then starts spitting and finally stops (how familiar that sounds) this could be (i) water in the carburettor, which means of course a clean out of the latter or (ii) dirty jets. Remedy – clean or again, (iii) a blockage in the petrol pipe or possibly filters. Remedy – unscrew pipe at carburettor to see if petrol is running through; if not, blow hard up pipe to try and clear. Cleaning the filters may be the answer. (iv) you may have a broken cylinder-head gasket. Remedy – simple, remove and fit spare gasket.

(*d*) The engine is firing erratically. This is very likely to be due to a dirty distributor, so take off the distributor cover and give the distributor a clean.

(*e*) If your engine will only run fast you may have burnt magneto points that need filing smooth again.

(*f*) If, on the other hand, your engine will only run slowly it may well be that the mixture is too weak. Remedy – adjust air valve. It could be that the timing is too retarded and needs advancing or it could be that the main jet is choked, in which case you have no alternative but to remove it and clean it!

You should of course check your oil pressure gauge from time to time and, if this registers loss of oil pressure, stop the engine at once. The following may be the cause of the trouble: (i) dirty sump. Remedy – drain out, clean sump and refill with oil; (ii) choked-up oil filters. Remedy – remove and clean; (iii) diluted oil. This may be due to the mixture being too rich or to a broken cylinder-head gasket – the remedies for which are obvious. A good temporary remedy for diluted oil is to drain out and refill with fresh oil.

Now let's take a look at what can go wrong with two-stroke engines. With a two-stroke engine the lubricating oil is mixed with the petrol in the tank; there are no valves and the explosion happens once in each revolution. How often has one seen some unfortunate boat owner pulling away at a lanyard while his outboard engine stubbornly refuses to start! So the first on our list of troubles is:

(*a*) Difficulty in starting. The first thing to try is to remove the sparking-plug, take it to pieces, clean and dry. If this is not the answer the trouble may be a choked-up carburettor. Remedy – remove jet and clean. If still no response, clean the magneto points with a file. It could, however, be that the magneto has become damp. Outboard engines are of course more exposed (unless they are of the now popular inboard/ outboard or sterndrive variety) and dampness is quite a possibility. Remedy – remove magneto and dry. This is easier said than done; but no doubt your own ingenuity will come to your rescue.

If, of course, while vainly trying to get your two-stroke to start you find the carburettor will not flood, your answer is staring you in the face. Remedy – clean the filters, and as with the four-stroke engine blow hard up the petrol pipe having unscrewed the union at the carburettor.

(*b*) If your two-stroke runs for a bit and then stops and who hasn't experienced that one, it may be due to two things:

(i) overheating – in which case clean filters and valves on water pump or (ii) the petrol system has got itself blocked whereupon you act as described above to remedy carburettor not flooding.

(c) Sometimes a two-stroke loses power mysteriously. This can result from too much oil. You must follow the instructions very carefully in regard to the proportion of oil to petrol. The remedy in this case is to add more petrol; but prevention is much better than cure! Loss of power might however be cured by adjusting the carburettor air valve as the mixture might be too rich.

(d) With diesel engines their great reliability is to some extent counterbalanced by the fact that if something goes wrong with a diesel, a certain amount of expert knowledge is required to remedy it. For this reason many makers of diesel engines run a short course of instruction, which, if you can spare the time is well worth taking. To give an example, a fault which can cause a diesel to 'miss' on one or more cylinders is that the sprayers are blocked. This necessitates removing them and cleaning; not too difficult a task I agree, but it helps to know exactly what you are doing and why. There is however one thing you can do if your diesel won't start. It is most likely to be due to an air lock in the fuel lines and is the most common diesel ailment. To remedy – test your pumps, clean the filter and draw out the air. Most other minor diesel troubles can be cured by removing and cleaning the sprayers, so if you learn to do that quickly and thoroughly you should feel pretty confident about keeping the power unit of your boat turning over happily.

CHAPTER SEVEN

Cruising in a Dinghy

Although in this book I have been writing for either the new-comer, or the dinghy man who wants a bigger boat to go cruising in, I must in all fairness include this short section on cruising in a dinghy. It is idle to pretend that a dinghy as a cruiser offers as much as a little cruising yacht of 2 or 3 tons, say, nevertheless it is fun cruising in a dinghy, and surprising how far you can get. It is a challenge too and it is cheap!

The basic idea of all cruising is self-sufficiency or, if you prefer it independence of the shore. Even Carruthers (in Erskine Childers's *Riddle of the Sands*) became a rapid convert to the cruising way of life. While still the foppish young man in the Foreign Office, 'Independence of the shore . . . the very thought made one shudder!' was his initial reaction to the suggestion, but before many chapters we find him frying eggs, and generally attacking the domestic as well as the seamanship side of cruising with all the fervour of the newly-converted. Cruising in a dinghy poses its own problems of course. For example, sleeping – on board or ashore under canvas? There is not too much doubt that the latter is more comfortable, but it is far less convenient. Each night (not spent under way) a suitable site must be found near a safe anchorage with reason-ably good facilities for getting ashore (or, of course, hauling up a suitable beach). It is surprising how infrequently these requisites come together! This method also needs time. Time to find the place, get camping gear ashore, pitch the tent and the converse applies in the morning. For a combined camping/sail-ing holiday, where several people are involved, where it is not

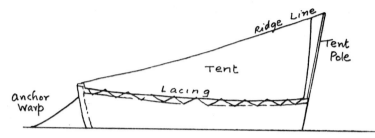

Figure 55.   Tent rigged for dinghy with lowered mast

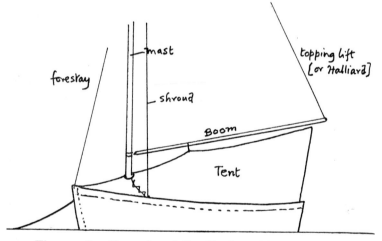

Figure 56.   Tent rigged for dinghy with mast raised

intended to cover much distance, a tent is the best answer. But for the serious dinghy cruise by, say, two people, the ease with which one can anchor (maybe just for a tide), and get under way again enables one to cover far greater distances. So if you are of the latter fraternity – sleep on board.

Sleeping on board means you need a tent. Tents can easily be rigged on small boats. It is largely a matter of commonsense. Figure 55 shows a tent for any lugsail dinghy whose mast can be easily lowered and stowed. The 'ridge' line of the tent is secured to the stem head by its fore-end while its after-end is made fast to a pole. This pole can fit into sockets on the fore-side of the transom. Use a good strong pole, say 1 inch diameter at least, so that you can set up the ridge line good and hard; for this is how you get your headroom. Lace the edges down through hooks fitted to the underside of the rubbing strake (see drawing), the lacing running through eyelets in the sides of the tent. An elastic line running round the hull under the rubbing strake can take the place of hooks in a glass-reinforced hull (or any other similar method that commonsense – or genius – suggests to you).

Look now at figure 56. Here we have a mast to contend with; a mast not easily lowered or stowed. A slot is cut in one side of the tent so that it can pass round the mast. This slot must be able to be tightly closed by a lacing. A reliable zip-fastener will do the job too. The tent is shown in the drawing as being supported midway along its length by a line a third of the way along the boom from forward. Once again, this increases headroom.

The arrangement in figure 57 differs in that here we have a boat with a foredeck that comes abaft the mast. Her tent has no need to be split. In this drawing the mainsail has been left rigged and is shown furled on the boom — a perfectly reasonable method. This question of whether to leave the mainsail rigged or not is a matter of personal preference. (How much room below you have to stow it is of importance!) If you unrig it, you can pass the tent *over* the boom, a good idea since you get still more headroom and more rigidity of the tent; but as I say, you need room to stow the sail (which may be wringing wet).

If you are really headroom minded, figure 58 may be your ideal but here you need a boom with jaw and not a goose-neck fitting. Figure 59 shows how to achieve something of the same

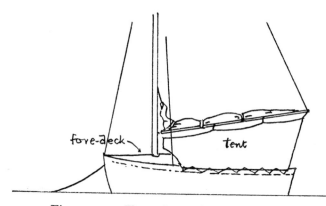

Figure 57. Tent rigged for dinghy with a fore-deck

effect if your boom does have a goose-neck fitting; but it is slightly unsatisfactory because of the boom running up the centre of your otherwise capacious sleeping cabin. Other changes can be rung but that should be enough to show that rigging a tent on a small open boat is not only easy, but entertaining.

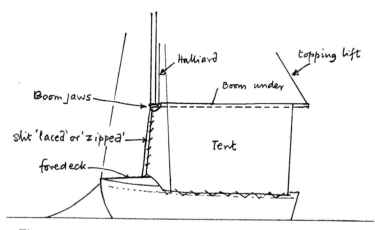

Figure 58. Tent rigged for dinghy using boom with jaws

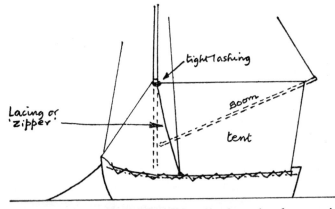

Figure 59.   Tent rigged for dinghy using boom with
'goose-neck'

What about the domestic problems? Cooking, for example,
and clothes. The modern dinghy-cruiser has a great choice
nowadays. To take clothes first. The advent of man-made
fibre has produced a wonderful range of gear for the sailor.
From anoraks and all kinds of waterproof clothing to sleeping-
bags the choice is wide and exciting. There are innumerable
excellent sleeping-bags on the market today. Made in nylon
filled with down or Dacron, the prices range from about £5 to
£10 and over. (Get one with a good heavy-duty zip-fastener.)
A visit to any shop catering for such demands is all you need
(except of course a little money). As for cooking equipment,
again a good choice. As a guide I would suggest, more as a
stimulus than a dogmatic instruction – the following: in a fish
kettle – with lid that can be securely fixed, you may carry
primus-type stove, methylated spirit container, matches, 2
knives, 2 forks 2 spoons, one frying-pan, one billy-can, 2 plates
and 2 mugs. The fish kettle should be lashed to one of the bilge
stringers. This is from practical experience in a wooden dinghy.
Should the boat be of glass-reinforced plastic the question of
stowage may also beg the question of a glassfibre container
instead of the old-fashioned fish kettle. Nowadays there is a wide
choice of canteen sets ranging from the one-man type consisting
of two frying-pans with long detachable handles, 5-inch
diameter saucepan with lid and detachable handle and half-

pint mug. Weight about 12 oz and price about 13*s* 6*d* to much more ambitious sets costing anything from 30*s* to £3 13*s* 6d. In stoves too there is plenty of variety, ranging from the 'optimus' petrol stove to portable Calor gas stoves and, of course, the ubiquitous primus paraffin stoves which come in several sizes. However, it would be as ridiculous to lay down hard-and-fast rules as to turn this into a brochure from a store selling camping equipment. The point is that you should be able to stow all cooking and eating gear into one container, itself easily stowed. You will further need a container for spare light nylon line, screws, nylon for sail repairs and a palm, needle and sail-twine, a torch, etc. It is a good idea to carry (if you can) a hurricane lamp (a half-pint lamp will burn paraffin for twenty-four hours). It will be of service not only as an anchor light but for cabin illumination. They cost about 11*s*. Most of this gear in containers should be stowed aft; keep the bows clear for the anchor, about 8 fathoms of anchor warp (nylon) and some spare line (have all running rigging the same diameter). A fresh-water carrier should be lashed amidships one side of the centreboard casing.

Such a list has no pretensions to being exhaustive, but it will serve as a guide to compiling your own list and engaging in the fascinating jig-saw puzzle of stowage, bearing in mind the two very important factors of moving about under way and of correct trim under sail.

For navigational equipment I suggest the following. You will need at least one chart, depending on how far you are intending to cruise. I have always found Standford's coloured charts excellent. They fold up, a good point where space is at such a premium but above all they are fairly large scale and have larger scale inset diagrams giving details of harbours and harbour approaches. They also have chartlets inset showing tidal streams and, for the very lazy, many courses in different directions already marked in red!

You will need a reliable compass (a card compass, not just a needle) and best of all a gimballed liquid compass. Although nine times out of ten a hand compass is perfectly adequate, in rough weather the former provides the only really accurate way of steering the right course. Reed's *Nautical Almanack* provides all the tidal information you need as well as information on practically everything to do with boats and the sea. You will need a 2-inch radius protractor and a 7-inch rule and several (sharp) pencils.

Now a word or two about the type of dinghy which is suitable for cruising. For single-handed cruising a 12-foot dinghy is about right. Ten is a little small and fourteen too large. This is only a rough guide, because a lot depends on the physical attributes (or not as the case may be) of the cruiser. A light man should not have too large a boat because a dinghy depends on the weight of the man (or men) sailing her to keep her upright when sailing. So it is the height of foolishness if you are a lightweight to choose too large a boat just to get a bit more room to move about in at anchor. Another thing too is that our light friend could easily find himself in difficulties handling a heavy 15-footer up a beach, even though nowadays GRP boats are infinitely lighter than some of the old wooden ones.

On the other hand for two people 14 or 15 foot is ideal for cruising. There is a wide choice available today. I would advise not too racy a type. For example, for cruising purposes I would choose a *National Enterprise* rather than an *International 14*. For single-handers the *National Solo* class dinghy is quite a good bet. Let us take a quick look then at the *National Solo* and the *National Enterprise*. The *Solo* was in fact designed for single-handed racing, but it has a large cockpit and is quite suitable for cruising. Designed by Jack Holt, the *Solo* is built in double-chine construction of plywood. Dimensions are: LOA 12 ft 5 ins (3·78 m); beam 4 ft 11 ins (1·49 m); draft 6 ins (0·152 m); and with centreboard down 3 ft 7 ins (1·092 m) the sail area is 84 sq ft (7·80 sq m).

The *Enterprise* is also double-chine plywood. A very popular class, the measurements are as follows: LOA 13 ft 3 ins (4·038 m); beam 5 ft 4 ins (1·625 m); draft 6½ ins (0·165 m); and with centreboard down 3 ft 3 ins (0·990 m); the sail area is 126 sq ft (11·70 sq m). This dinghy is excellent for cruising.

In conclusion, I would like to emphasise that there is nothing inherently dangerous in dinghy cruising. To handle a small boat of this sort calls for skill in handling, judgement, seamanship, endurance and sometimes guts. For a newcomer to attempt a long and difficult cruise single-handed would on the other hand be the height of folly. Learn slowly, gradually making more ambitious cruises until you have the confidence in yourself and your boat to cope with whatever the weather may send you.

CHAPTER EIGHT

Learn to be a Seaman

(1) Knots and Splices

It is more than probable that many of my readers can tie at least the more generally used seaman's knots: the clove hitch, the reef knot, the rolling hitch and the bowline. I have allotted each knot a paragraph to itself with a heading so you can skip the ones you know; and if you know the lot, including how to make an eye-splice in 16 plaited nylon, skip the chapter!

But let us first learn how to stop the ends of our rope from unravelling. Nowadays synthetic-fibre rope is in general use and very good it is. It can be prevented from unravelling by lighting the end with a match, which fuses the end. This, while working all right with some rope, does not in my experience, always work. Again, not all rope used will necessarily be synthetic and then you might have to be working on deck in a strong wind that no matches will light it. What I am really trying to say is that it is important that you should know how to whip ropes' ends! There are two easily learnt methods; the common whipping and the sailmaker's whipping; to understand how to whip, splice or tie knots, it helps to look at drawings, so I have done some.

Common Whipping

Look first at figure 60. Get a short length or whipping twine. Lay it parallel with the rope to be whipped. Work away from the end passing the twine seven or eight times round both twine and rope as shown. Loop the remainder of the rope, hold the free end down and continue whipping with the looped part. Before you run out of twine pull the free end until the loop is pulled through, cut off any of this end that projects and you should have a neatly whipped rope's end.

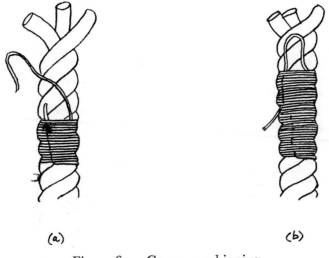

(a)   (b)

Figure 60.   Common whipping

Sailmakers' Whipping

Unlay (separate) the three strands of the rope as shown in figure 61, passing a loop of twine over one of them. Notice that one end of the loop must be longer than the other. Pass the ends between the other two strands. Lay up the rope again and whip the laid-up rope with the longer of the two ends of twine. You simply wind round the rope working towards its end. As you reach this pass the loop which I have drawn in black over the strand as shown in figure 62. Pull taut by the short end of the twine, and pass the latter between the strands and tie it to the long end with a reef knot. For a neat job get the reef knot between the strands. Trim loose ends, and there is your sailmakers' whipping.

In days when sails were reefed by tying the rolled-up bunt with lines called reef points, every seaman had to know the correct knot for this most important part of sail handling. The knot had to be simple to tie; certain of not slipping once tied and easy to untie when the time came to shake out the reefs. So the reef knot was evolved; the classic knot that every scout, guide, cub, brownie, and of course naval cadet, knows. This is a legacy of tradition. In point of fact, the reef knot has rather limited uses. It joins rope yes, but only of equal thickness. If you use it to join one thick and one thin rope's end, the knot will slip and you must use a sheet bend. Nowadays many yachts have roller reefing, and others use lacing through eyelets in the sail. For the reefing function of our knot has diminished. Nevertheless, you do quite often have to join ropes of equal (or very nearly equal) size so for that reason, and for tradition, let us learn to tie it.

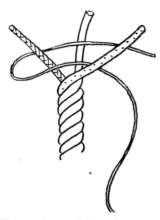

Figure 61. Sailmaker's whipping (i)

Figure 62. Sailmaker's whipping (ii)

The Reef Knot

Figure 63 shows how. Hold the two ends. Pass them over, the left *over* the right, followed by the right *over* the left. The end in your left hand goes over the end in your right hand and then back from the right over the left and so under the loop you have made. Perhaps another good reason for this knot's priority in all books on knot tying is its classic simplicity. Let's now see what we do when the two ropes' ends to be joined are of distinctly unequal thickness.

Figure 63.   Reef Knot

The Sheet Bend

This name too comes from the sails. In early days of sails, the sheets were 'bent' to the clews of the sails with this knot. Today we use hooks, but the knot has many other uses. To tie it, take the larger of the two ropes and make a loop. Pass the end of the smaller rope *up* through it. Then *over* the heavy rope, *under* its two ends, back *over* the other side of the heavy rope and so *under* itself and back *over* the loop of the heavy rope. If that is too much for you, look at figure 64. Let us now look at knots (which attach ropes to posts, spars, bollards, etc) called 'hitches'.

Figure 64.   Sheet Bend

The Half-hitch

This is the simplest form of hitch. Figure 65 illustrates it and I think needs no further comment. To make this a more secure and more useful knot, two half-hitches are necessary; and better still is to take one turn round the post (or whatever) before making your hitches. If you look at figure 66 you will see at once that it is a safer knot. This knot can be used for securing to posts, bollards and rings on quays or the ring of an anchor (although a fisherman's bend is preferred by some as it jams the first hitch); but the classic hitch for securing to posts, spars, etc is the clove hitch, a very useful knot indeed.

195

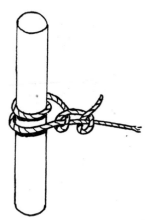

Figure 65.   Half-hitch   Figure 66.   Round turn
                                            and two half-hitches

The Clove Hitch

Figure 67 illustrates. Pass the rope round the spar, cross it over
itself and back through itself. As a piece of quite impressive
knotmanship, if you want to make fast to a bollard or king post,
you can, while approaching the king post with an air of non-
chalance, make a loop, make a second the same size *below* the
first; pass this second loop *over* the first, slip both over the king

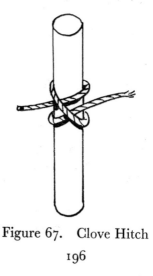

Figure 67.   Clove Hitch

post, haul taut and walk away looking superior. However, if you made a clove hitch on, say, a spar and the pull of the strain was not at right-angles (or nearly so) to the spar, but say down it; you will see, when the strain comes, on, your hitch sliding slowly down the spar and you won't feel superior at all. That is unless you have tied a . . .

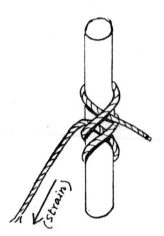

Figure 68.   Rolling Hitch

Rolling Hitch

As you will see from figure 68, this is tied by taking *two* turns round the spar *over* the *long* end of the rope (the end which the strain will come on). Make a third turn with the short end, and pass it through the *second* turn in the opposite direction to the longer end. This knot can be relied on not to slip provided that the strain comes on the end which passes under turns one and two as shown in the drawing. It can also be used to make a line fast to a rope like a halyard or even to a part of the standing rigging, say a shroud. You will soon come to realise its uses and of course its limitations.

You should be able to make a good loop in a rope, and for this there is no better knot than . . .

The Bowline

This is an easy knot once you have got the knack. Look at figure 69. For the purpose of describing this knot I will use the time-honoured words 'fall' and 'standing part'. The former is the shorter end you are tying with. The latter is the longer or more static end. Hold the fall in your right hand; place it over the standing part which you are holding in your left hand. Now, without letting go the standing part, move your left hand higher up on it and form a loop. You will now have a loop in your left hand and the fall in your right hand and the fall goes up through the loop, the standing part being under the loop. Pass the fall under and around the standing part, and down through the loop, haul taut; and there you have it. If you want to make a permanent loop, you can do this by means of an . . .

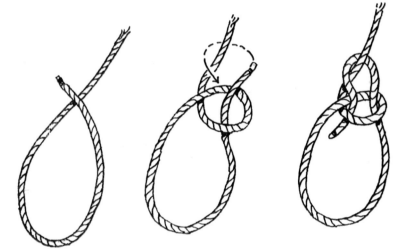

Figure 69.   Bowline

Eye-splice

Figure 70 shows the eye-splice in four stages. The method is as follows; whip the free end leaving about 4 inches, which you then unlay (separate the three strands). Whip these strands. Make the loop of the size you want, holding the standing part at the place you are going to insert the free end. Open the standing part by twisting the rope against the lay. Take a fid, or marlin spike (or screwdriver) and insert it under one of the opened strands and under it insert one of the free strands (the middle one, in the drawing coloured black). Now insert the spike under the strand above and tuck in the next strand (the white one, see the drawing). Now turn the splice over so that you can insert the remaining (hatched) strand. Pull each strand taut and repeat the process. Before the third time around, it is a good idea to shave the strands or take out some of the fibres. This thinning of the strands makes a more streamlined and neater splice. Three tucks as these three stages are called is usually enough, but for a really expert and secure as well as a good-looking splice, shave still more and put in a fourth tuck. It is a good idea to whip the splice with marline or twine with one of the whippings we have already learnt.

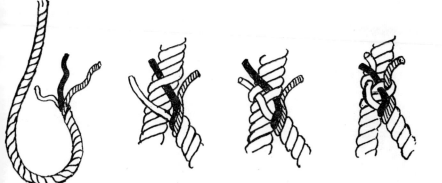

Figure 70. Eye Splice

Plaited Rope

So far the knots that I have described can be tied in hemp, or manila or coir or any rope of man-made fibre – it doesn't matter. However there is a lot of plaited line about in man-made fibre ropes (and very useful it is for sheets for example). You won't get anywhere trying to splice an eye into 8 or 16 plait nylon rope in the manner we have just been looking at. For this, the technique is as in figure 71. Unpick the rope for say, eight times its circumference and make your loop. Plaited ropes consist of a layer plaited over a core. To unpick the rope use a fid or spike or something slightly blunt at the point so that you part the yarns without splitting them. The method of crossing over the two lots of parted yarns is easy to follow from the drawings. At each cross haul the ends good and taut (you can tie them at intervals with thread to hold them). Shave the last inch or so, and as in the final drawing, whip the splice. This method makes a strong and neat eye-splice.

The study of seaman's knots is a fascinating one and there are several good books on the market for those who want to pursue this subject. A good definitive work is *The Ashley Book of Knots* by C. Ashley (Faber and Faber), but you can make your own choice. From the point of view of the beginner in cruising, the knots I have given you here will do all you are likely to need. They can serve as a foundation on which to build, but if you can tie them all quickly and safely you won't come to much harm!

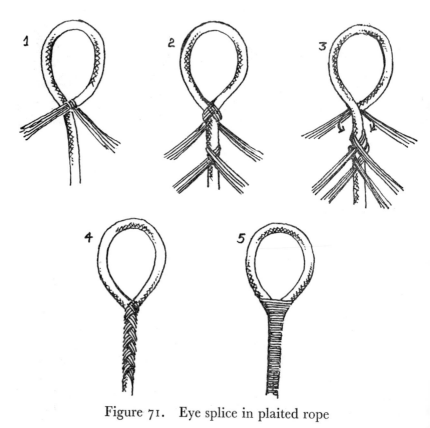

Figure 71. Eye splice in plaited rope

(2) General Maintenance – painting and varnishing

The modern trend of do it yourself has long been the fashion with boat owners. It is not only money saving, it is fun. The real question is – how much time have you? A lot depends, of course, on the size of your boat. Where you keep her for the winter is also relevant. If you house your vessel in a well-lit shed in your garden; then painting, varnishing and fitting out in general can be done by you and your friends in comfort during the early spring. Most of us are less fortunate. There are four ways of laying up a small cruising yacht. The most costly is to haul out and let the boat spend the winter under cover in a shed belonging to the local yacht yard. Next in price is to haul out and keep the boat under covers in the open. Thirdly, you can leave her in a mud-berth, where she will be afloat part of the time as the tide ebbs and floods. The fourth method is to leave her afloat on moorings; all right in some climates – the Mediterranean for example; not so good in more northern latitudes because of increased exposure to the elements and the risks of damage by ice.

If your boat is of a size that can be trailed and you have somewhere at home to put her for the winter then you have no problem other than that of hauling, or craning her out of the water and this is usually quite simple to arrange. If you are housing her with a yard for the winter, they will haul out at the appropriate moment. This is decided by the place she will occupy in the shed. Storage of twenty or thirty yachts in a large shed needs a lot of planning and for this reason alone, the yard will be very grateful to you if you tell them when you wish to lay up; and having done that see that the boat is ready at that date! It is even more important to let the yard know when you want your boat to be launched in the spring, because the order of spring launchings will determine, to a large extent, the positioning of the various yachts in the shed.

Now as I have said, the amount of work you do yourself will depend on the time you have available. It will, of course, also depend on inclination! But there is another factor. It is accepted that, if you lay up with a yard, they will get the fitting out work or at least some of it. No yard wants to fill their sheds with yachts which are going to be entirely fitted out by their owners. Some yards certainly are quite prepared for owners to work on their boats, but many are not. So the amount of work you do may well be limited by this.

There are indeed many jobs which for one reason or another are best done by the yard, for example stepping the mast (unless it is in a 'tabernacle' housed on deck. Putting on thick, tacky anti-fouling paint is a laborious business; and so is re-canvassing a deck! Painting and varnishing can take a surprisingly long time if done thoroughly, but they are pleasurable jobs. So let us start off by considering these two items on the fitting out list.

First clean the hull and let it dry. The final effect will depend largely on the thoroughness of your preparation. If the existing paint is in poor condition, if you wish to change colour, and especially if there are many layers of old paint underneath, it is advisable to get down to bare wood. If your boat is made of GRP and is brand new, you may not have to paint her hull the next season, but the third one you will (and quite possibly the second). GRP hulls get scratched and marked by dinghies, other yachts, quay sides, posts, etc just as wooden hulls do. The only thing that is different is the method of stripping off the paint. In the case of GRP, the answer is to use a paint stripper (like the International Paint Company's 'Pintoff'). If your boat is built of aluminium you can use a stripper but if she is of steel, then you will have to chip the paint off (and personally I should get the yard to do that).

With a wooden hull you can either use a stripper or burn off the paint with a blowlamp and scraper. Largely a matter of personal taste. Some say a stripper is easy to handle. Others maintain as hotly that only a 'burn-off' will get all the pigment out of the wood. The only thing you must not do is use them together because strippers are inflammable; and no double-entendre is intended by that. If the hull paintwork is in good condition then after a good wash down and dry off, roughen the surface well and sandpaper so that the undercoat will adhere properly.

Examine the hull. Stop up any hollows, for example dents or the round dowel houses on the top of counter-sunk screws which have lost their dowels; the dowel being the round piece of wood shaped to fit neatly above the counter-sunk screw so as to give the hull a smooth surface. Spot paint any bare patches. Now rub down, using sandpaper (water sandpaper is best) and dry thoroughly. The number of undercoats you give will depend on the condition of the paint. If it is bad give two. If you have stripped to bare wood, then you will certainly need two. Rub down each undercoat slightly to give an adhesive surface for the next coat.

There is much talk nowadays of polyurethane paints and varnishes. The principle difference between conventional paints and one-can polyurethane paints is that with the former, once you have primed and made good the surface, you build up with undercoats finally putting on the top coat of enamel for a glossy, waterproof finish. With polyurethane paints there is no basic difference between the undercoat and the enamel, except that the latter is glossier. You can build up in fact using enamel only, provided you matt each coat well before applying the next. (This is not so necessary if you use undercoating.) When using one-can polyurethane paints fill all holes and irregularities with white stopper. When the surface has been built up, sand down smooth for the painting. When using conventional paints you should prime the wood well before applying your stoppers. If you are changing from conventional paint to polyurethane it is advisable to strip right down to the bare wood. Polyurethane paints and vanishes are tough and look well, and many people now use them.

So far we have talked of painting the hull, but at this point we should consider the deck, because before you start painting the hull it is best to paint the deck. Decks, as we have seen, can be of wood, canvassed wood, plastics or metal. If the deck is in good condition you need only wash down, dry off, paint with waterproof undercoat and finish with a coat of deck paint. If the deck is in poor condition you have got a bit of a problem on your hands! If of wood or plastic a paint stripper will do the job. If of steel it means chipping before repainting with special primer, undercoat and top coat. If canvassed over wood and it is in bad condition you will have to strip off and re-canvas – and that job too, I would be tempted to give to the yard!

To advise on this question of what to do yourself and what to give the yard is very difficult, but it will be obvious that so much depends on the three factors of how much time you have, how much knowledge you have and how much your particular yard are prepared to let you do. As a rough guide I would advise letting the yard go over the hull for you after the winter season and examine it carefully with all their accumulated knowledge and experience. Stepping the mast is much better done by the yard and I should (personally) let them set up the standing rigging – the two jobs go together. (You can reeve running rigging if you want to, but remember to reeve halyards before the mast is stepped; and don't forget the burgee halyard!) Again, as I have said before it is usually best to let the yard put on the anti-fouling. Not only is it a tedious job but it has to be worked in with the launching which the yard will be doing since a lot of anti-foulings must be immersed within twenty-four hours of painting. When you bought your boat if she was second-hand, your surveyor will have had several if not all, keel bolts drawn and tested, but if you are in any doubt when the yard examines the hull they can knock out the bolts a little way to see what their condition is.

Let us now turn to varnishing. The old copal varnishes have today been virtually superseded by synthetic varnishes, which are tougher and indeed glossier. Many people prefer polyurethane varnishes. These present no problem except that if you are changing to polyurethane it is wise to strip down to bare wood. If polyurethanes are applied over conventional coating they don't always adhere properly, lose their water resistance and break down.

One of the greatest benefits of modern varnishes is the shorter drying time. They take only three to four hours to dry, and the polyurethane varnishes are quicker still.

If your varnish is in good condition all you need to do is rub down well and re-varnish. If it is in bad condition then use a stripper, working a small area at a time and get down to bare wood. In this connection an electric power sander is a wonderful tool – but use it with caution! If the weather has got in and stained some of the wood you can remedy this by applying bleach (with a clean brush) to the dark spots. Bleaching takes a little time, so don't be impatient. You can make a good bleaching solution from oxalic acid crystals. When you have finished bleaching to your satisfaction brush off the small crystals that remain on the wood and *don't* breathe them! Having got the surface clean and free of dark spots any large indentations in the wood should be filled by grain filler. This can be obtained in various shades. To thin it you use either white spirit or varnish. The object of grain filler is to provide a perfectly smooth surface on which to varnish. Now we can begin varnishing. Use a clean brush (and certainly not one that has been used for painting) and brush the first coat well into the fibres. Use a small tin if you can and don't stir the varnish. The final coat application is an art. I was once told by an old and expert painter to 'flow' the varnish on for the last coat, rather than brush it. Also don't apply it too thickly. If building from bare wood, I should put on six coats, roughening the surface with sandpaper a little to get good adhesion. Six coats may sound a lot but if you varnish carefully your wood will retain its natural light colour and you will only need a wash and a light coat or two for several subsequent seasons.

Another job you can do is examine the sails. Check batten pockets, tablings and slide fastenings. This is a pleasant job on a sunny spring day. If your cruiser is a power vessel, the extent of your examination of the engine (or engines) will of course depend on your knowledge and experience; and the same applies to owners of sailing craft with auxiliaries. If the engine has been properly laid up for the winter there should be no problems.

Don't forget to take a look at your ground tackle (anchors, cables, warps, etc) and it is a good idea to mark the cable with paint at, say, one fathom intervals. You can use different colours if you like, after the manner of a lead-line. Another pleasant job the owner can do is to examine all cordage; whipping loose ends, tucking in any eye-splices where needed, etc. In the interior of the boat there is much you can do. The galley, for example, and light fittings. However, there are two jobs below decks which periodically requires attention that are (to me at all events) somewhat irksome. They are cleaning and re-painting the bilges and the re-painting of painted wood work. The latter like re-varnishing below is all right provided you have plenty of time at your disposal. There are always lots of little nooks and corners that make this job quite a long one. At least, this is my experience.

So once again we get back to the question of time and inclination. One owner's delight is another's purgatory. One last point. Having worked out with the yard what you personally are going to do, make a list of the jobs in the order you intend to do them, when you see them in writing you can tell if you are attacking the problem in a methodical way. Also on that list put down the materials and tools you are going to need. Doing this has a further advantage in that the mere making of such a list in winter makes the spring launching seem less far away!

CHAPTER NINE

Bad Weather

(1) Under Sail

At first sight a gloomy expression, the words 'bad weather' need by no means evoke feelings of despair provided you know what to do. To carry this argument further, once you have experienced foul weather at sea it loses much of its power to worry. Once you have seen for yourself how well a properly designed and equipped yacht can ride out a storm you will face subsequent bad weather with confidence. However that properly designed vessel must be properly handled; so, although there is absolutely no substitute for experience, the following will I hope be helpful by reducing the problem to various positive actions to take should you meet up with a gale or two at sea. Of course, with cruises of moderate length, provided you have prepared the passage (see chapter five) carefully enough from the point of view of having to shelter and have studied the barometer and listened to the weather-forecasts, you are unlikely, under normal conditions to meet up with winds of gale force. Nevertheless, if you intend to cruise well offshore, there will come a time sooner or later when you and your ship will be tested, and having been tested and not found wanting, that gin in the cockpit, when it is all over, tastes like – well, choose your own brand of nectar!

In our cruise in chapter five we learned when and how to reef the mainsail, and to change headsails, but fortunately that time no very severe gale arrived to test us. We had admittedly to choose between running before the wind or taking temporary shelter in a protected bay. Let us assume now that no shelter is handy, the wind force is increasing and the falling barometer confirms that it is likely to continue to increase. Under the circumstance we can (i) heave-to and ride out the gale, (ii) ride out the gale to a sea anchor or (iii) run before the gale using a sea anchor to give control.

The decision to heave-to comes when the seas get too big for our boat and too much water is coming aboard. To heave-to, trim the (I presume already reefed) mainsail and helm as if you were going to sail to windward, while the jib is hauled to weather. An important thing to remember when heaving-to, if you are running, is that a vessel before the wind has the speed of the latter reduced by her own speed. It is difficult to judge the real force of the wind when you are running; and so it is a good plan to bring the wind on the beam from time to time to see how much it is increasing. When the moment comes to heave-to, choose a relatively calm patch, that is to say, of smaller waves to round up with the helm hard-down.

Yachts vary quite a bit in their behaviour when hove-to. Experience will tell you whether it is safer (and more comfortable) to put your own boat before the gale rather than heave-to. Some boats heave-to very well; others range about. As the yacht comes right up into the wind; the mainsail will flog about until the headsail (sheeted to weather) pushes the bows to leeward and the mainsail fills again. It may help to use the second of our three tactics and lie to a sea-anchor. There are some people who have no use for a sea-anchor. It is, I suppose, a matter of personal opinion, but I have at least one friend who has sailed round the world and pays great tribute to his sea-anchor's assistance in riding out bad storms. A sea-anchor consists of a canvas bag open at both ends; one opening being much bigger than the other so that the bag forms a cone or drogue. The large end is held open by an iron ring or in the case of the *Voss* anchor (invented by Captain J. C. Voss) by diagonal cross-bars.

A short length of chain, made securely fast inboard, is led over the bows, through a fairlead. To it is made fast a stout warp which terminates in the anchor. To the small end of the sea-anchor is bent a 'tripping' line. This has two uses. It enables the anchor to be hauled in small end first when it is no longer needed and secondly you can use it when running before heavy seas. Which brings us to tactic number three. To control the

Plate 19   *Lundy*

Plate 20   *Jaunty 22*

Plate 21   *Jaunty 20*

Plate 22   *Senior 32*

Plate 23   *Cheverton Champ* (*a*) and (*b*)

Plate 25 *Oceanic*

Plate 26 *Ranger 27*

Plate 27   *Nozomi*

ship's speed you can use the tripping line by bringing it into play so as to allow a big wave to pass harmlessly without breaking. You should tow the drogue at about 5 fathoms (30 ft) (9·14 m), the tripping line taking the strain. On the approach of a big sea, slacken the tripping line, let the sea-anchor warp take the strain. It will at once operate and check the boat's way until the big-fellow has passed. This is really a method of keeping the yacht moving as fast as is consistent with safety. Running unchecked before big seas has its dangers. Many famous long-distance cruising men, from Captain Joshua Slocum onwards have advocated the wisdom of not running too fast. Even towing warps or cable to part the seas and make them break astern of you can be very useful at times to avoid being pooped. The latter can of course be dangerous, but it is always (and I speak from chilly experience) unpleasant!

(2) **Under Power**

We have been considering some aspects of bad weather at sea mostly from the point of view of sailing yachts or motor-sailers. Let us look at it from the motor-cruiser's angle. When punching into almost head-on seas the most natural reaction – to throttle down – is the correct manoeuvre. It is really when the wind is on the beam or the quarter that, in the case of power vessels, an unpleasant danger manifests itself. This is the danger of excessive rolling. If the boat happens to be rolling away from a sea as it comes to her, and if her natural period of roll continues to coincide with the seas, each wave will increase her roll and she will be in serious danger of capsizing. The right way to deal with this is to alter course, or if that is for any reason undesirable, to increase or decrease speed so that the continuity is broken. If your yacht carries steadying sail, this is a great help particularly when there is a strong beam wind, but even in a heavy swell without wind. With single-screw motor yachts some sort of sail is very desirable in case of engine failure. Motor-sailers have no such problem of course and motor-cruisers with twin engines have the added security of the second engine; but with a single-screw – I personally recommend being able to set even a very modest amount of sail. With a small motor-cruiser, plan your passages carefully so that should bad weather overtake you, you can get to shelter in time possibly to anchor and see the gale out. Motor-sailers like the *Spey* or the *Nicholson 38* will take such weather in their stride, but if yours is a small vessel, perhaps single-screw, with a large open cockpit, use your head and don't ask her to do more than is fair and sensible.

(3) Simple Weather-forecasting

To end this chapter, a word on do it yourself weather-forecasting. This is a fascinating subject. It is also quite a large one and there are several excellent books that deal with it. However, a book of this nature can only deal with the matter briefly. Nevertheless, it can, I hope, teach you the rudiments and put you on the right track for further study once your enthusiasm is aroused – which incidentally, in its variety of subject-matter, is exactly what this book is intended to do!

To forecast the weather you need a barometer and an observant pair of eyes. Let's consider the barometer first.

The type most usually found in small boats is known as an aneroid barometer. This registers atmospheric pressure. It consists of a chamber almost empty of air, so that the pressure outside it is always greater than the pressure inside. One wall of the chamber consequently is always tending to move inwards towards the other. It is prevented from doing this by a spring. It will be clear that the amount that the spring is able to hold it back varies with the pressure of the atmosphere. The spring is connected to a pointer which moves round a graduated dial. A barometer of this nature is a sensitive instrument and reflects every small movement of the spring. By noting a sequence of pressure readings on the dial you can tell whether the atmospheric pressure is falling, steady or increasing. This is a wonderful help in weather-forecasting, since a law of nature decrees that wind blows from an area of high pressure to a low one. A single reading of the 'glass' as it is often called is virtually useless. Only when you have three or four successive readings over a period can you begin to predict a change in the weather.

Of course everyone knows those attractive old wall glasses which bear the legends 'Fair', 'Change', 'Rain', 'Stormy', etc, and there is some truth in these since a high glass usually means fine weather and a low glass, bad weather, but it is nevertheless in the *movement* of the glass, up or down, allied to a study of the sky's appearance, the direction of the wind (or winds) and cloud formations and movements at various altitudes that we will find the data on which to base our forecast.

So let us take a look at some of these cloud formations. Let us consider them in groups according to height, starting with the highest – that is above 20,000 feet.

Cirrus. These are the 'mare's tail' clouds of childhood, so called because of their feathery formation something like a flowing tail. They are usually white and are found at heights of from 4 to 5 miles. They indicate the coming of wind.

Cirrocumulous. These small globular masses of cloud are found also between 4 or 5 miles up. They are white with no shadows. Sometimes they take up a rippling formation like the scales of a fish, which has given rise to the term – a 'mackerel' sky. Like cirrus, they indicate wind.

Cirrostratus. Once again these are high clouds (4 or 5 miles), they have a white hazy look as they spread over the sky and they foretell bad weather, and the approach of a depression.

Next comes the middle group of cloud formations, found between 20,000 feet and 6,500 feet up.

Altocumulus. Everybody knows these with cotton-wool appearance, in fairly large, flattened masses, but they can also take up a 'mackerel' appearance, in which case, they mean wind. They are found between $1\frac{1}{2}$ to 4 miles up.

Altostratus. Also found between $1\frac{1}{2}$ and 4 miles, this formation looks like a veil of grey.

In the low group, that is from close to the ground to 6,500 feet, we have the following:

Stratocumulus. Rounded masses of cloud which cover a great deal of the sky, with pronounced shadows in the lower parts.

Stratus. Found very low down, covering much, if not all of the sky, fog-like.

Nimbo stratus. Like stratus, but dark, waterlogged, full of rain!

To cheer up a bit we can consider now the formation called simply:

Cumulus. These large, thick clouds, with a marked vertical (rising) development mean fine and settled weather. However, should they become waterlogged, they are known as . . .

Cumulonimbus. They may go away or they may not, depending on conditions but if they develop an 'anvil' shape at the top (*Hybrid cirrus*) it is a fair bet that thunderstorms will occur.

Now these brief descriptions and definitions fall a good way short of a serious study of weather conditions and forecasting, but like the old saws (red sky at night, sailors delight, red sky at morning sailors warning, etc), they are based on sound observation and should prove a useful guide.

Let us now consider the development and course of that most familiar phenomenon, the depression. Depressions are very common. They are part of the circulation of the earth's atmosphere in the temperate latitudes that lie between the polar and the equatorial regions, and as cruising yachtsmen, we become pretty familiar with them though not necessarily friendly!

What happens is this. When a stream of warmer air from the equatorial region trespasses into the cold air of the polar region a depression begins. The warm air, turning into the cold air-stream rises over it (warm air rises) it cools, and we get rain. This is known as a warm front. Here we see cirrus clouds high up as a first warning. As this front approaches, altostratus clouds form until eventually nimbo stratus covers the sky and heavy rain results. As the front passes, the temperature at sea level rises and the rain stops. Now we see stratus clouds, low down, and we probably have drizzling rain. This is the warm sector of the depression.

Following behind it comes the cold front, which in its turn forces up the warm air, this air rises quickly and we get more rain, but of shorter duration, this passing of the depression is confirmed by a falling temperature, squally winds and rain. Finally the wind veers, the cumulo nimbus clouds disappear and with the improvement of the weather, fine cumulus clouds arrive to improve our spirits. But quite possibly not for long!

The weather behind a depression is frequently unsettled and line squalls and thunder are not uncommon. Depressions are said to move at from 20 to 30 miles an hour but that is a generalisation. Some move faster while others remain relatively

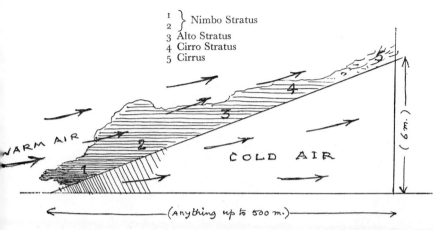

Figure 72. Depression; diagram of warm front

stationary. Look now at figures 72 and 73, which illustrate the sequence of events I have described. You will notice the various cloud formations and their heights. With this observation, and with the fall in pressure that your aneroid barometer will have indicated, you will be able to forecast the ensuing weather surprisingly accurately. A depression is really a fall in baro-

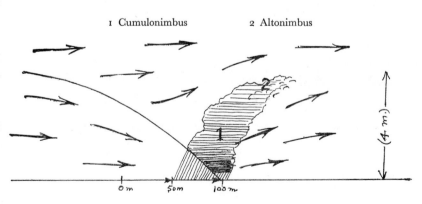

Figure 73. Depression; diagram of cold front

213

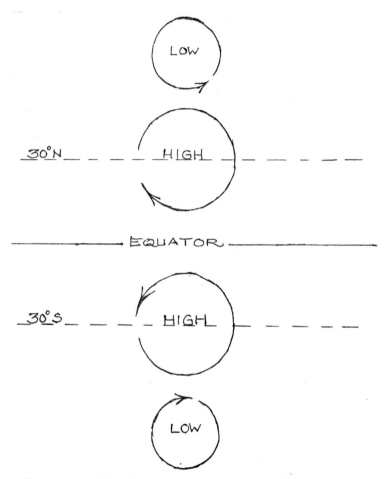

Figure 74. The five pressure areas on the earth's surface

metric pressure, as a warm air-stream, meeting a cold air-
stream rises. We in the British Isles are certainly familiar with
depressions. Ours begin in the North Atlantic Ocean, many
miles away; but as I said depressions can occur anywhere in the
temperate latitudes. They are part of the natural order of things.

A word now about wind. Look at figure 74. This indicates the
five areas of pressure on the earth's surface. Near the Equator
is an area of low pressure caused by the hot air rising. On each
side are two areas of high pressure (between latitude 20° and
latitude 40° north and/or south), and on either side of these the
two polar areas, north and south.

The earth, spinning about on its axis gives a twist to the air-
streams flowing from high pressure areas to low, and so we get
the regular pattern of winds we all know, the Westerlies north
and south and the Trade Winds. Figure 75 will show what I
mean. These are the winds which seamen have used from time
immemorial and they are just as useful to the yachtsmen today.

Often, during the weather-forecast programmes for shipping,
the expression force 4, force 7 is used. This refers to the Beaufort
Scale, so called after Admiral Sir Francis Beaufort who
introduced it in 1805. It runs from force 0 to force 12. Expres-
sions like moderate breeze, fresh breeze, fresh gale and strong
gale are used. They always seem to me to be ambiguous. It is
better to relate the scale to miles per hour of the wind. Here it is:

Beaufort Wind Scale	Wind speed in Knots
0	0 (Calm)
1	2
2	5
3	9
4	14
5	18
6	24
7	30 (Moderate gale)
8	37
9	44
10	52 (Whole gale)
11	60
12	68 (Hurricane)

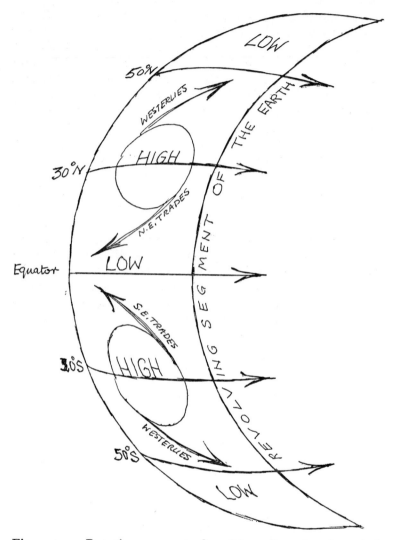

Figure 75. Rotating segment of earth's surface, showing wind pattern

One final word. Remember that if you are sailing at 5 knots into a 20-knot wind, you increase that wind's force to 25; and if running before it, you reduce it to 15. A truism perhaps, but it is surprising how often people forget it!

CHAPTER TEN

A Word about Design

We have already seen that for a displacement yacht (as opposed to a racing dinghy, speedboat, high-speed cruiser or any vessel which planes along the surface of the water rather than cuts through it) there is a formula which gives an approximate maximum theoretical speed, the formula being:

$$1 \cdot 4 \sqrt{\text{load water-line (in feet)}} = \text{maximum speed in knots.}$$

Although as I said this gives an approximate theoretical speed, it provides a useful yardstick. Now what in fact does this tell us? It must be obvious that water-line length is the key to speed in a displacement hull. But the more of the hull there is immersed in the water the greater the 'skin' friction. Therefore, for a boat to be fast water-line length and light displacement are essentials. To get stability we need a fairly deep draught and moderate beam. We have just described the average class racing yacht. For boats designed to sail offshore certain modifications must be made. If the bows are too fine much water comes aboard and at times buoyancy will be lacking where it is needed. A very deep draught often results in a tiring motion in a seaway. Again, very light displacement means cramped living accommodation – an important point, for the cruising man lives aboard.

And so we see that the average cruising yacht represents an attempt to strike a happy mean between seaworthiness and comfort, and speed. I have stated elsewhere in this book, while discussing the international aspects of sailing, how designers in different countries are tending to profit from each other's experiences; and former differences are tending to disappear. Let us take as an example of this in the basic yacht types of Great Britain and the United States. If we go back in time to the period when yachts and work-boats were of similar design, we find that in America the tendency was towards a shallow-draught hull, often with a centreboard, and broad beam. The British yacht on the other hand was narrow and deep. This tendency was also encouraged by the rating (racing) rules of the period. In the 1800s these differences are most marked. Now that the two trends have (and are still) converging we find that in Britain yachts have more beam while in the USA the centreboard has lost some of its importance. Even so, the average American yacht still has more beam than her British sister; while we have fewer centreboarders. What then are the features that our dream boat should embody? Moderate displacement is one, with a hull that has a good depth of keel and fairly high freeboard, and as much beam as is consistent with a good sailing performance. Broad beam apart from providing more space below decks and wider decks to work on above, has the great advantage of producing a moderate angle of heel – a real boon on long passages. So we want our beam to be as broad as possible within the limits of the design. These limits are changing. The late Charles E. Nicholson, well-known British designer, once remarked that 'nothing stopped a boat like beam'. Today, his nephew Charles A. Nicholson thinks differently and his boats are not only relatively 'beamy', they are fast! Beam then, produces desirable 'stiffness' (absence of extreme heel).

Consideration of the design of a cruising yacht falls conveniently into three categories; speed, comfort and seaworthiness. With modern rigging and sails, it is no problem, given sufficient wind, for a contemporary cruising yacht to reach her theoretical maximum speed. It is doubtful whether designers in the future will be able to achieve much more in the way of high average speeds unless they hit upon something fairly revolutionary.

Multihull yachts, catamarans and trimarans are not revolutionary since they embody principles discovered years ago, but they are able to achieve very high average speeds, especially if the passage does not involve much tacking. Multihulls are apt to be slow going about. Because of their design and their light displacement (the very factors that produce their speed) there are many cruising men who prefer a single-hull displacement vessel for serious offshore work. 'Cat' designers (and quite a few owners) disagree; although one acquaintance of the writer, after experiencing running for many miles before a force 7 wind on crossing the Altantic Ocean eastwards was vocal in his preference for a 'mono' hull. As I wrote in chapter one, this is as yet a problem unresolved. The great American designer Nathaniel Herreshoff, who was experimenting with twin-hulled craft as far back as 1870, is on record as saying: ' . . . It is my belief that a single-hulled sailing machine can not be developed that will have a higher average speed than the multi-hulled craft . . .'

As far as comfort goes the multihull offers good accommodation below decks and a roomy deck to work on, but there exists the problem of capsize. A single hull with an adequate ballast keel is safer. With the advent of more beam the single-huller need not be uncomfortable below. The absence of a marked angle of heel in the multihull is however an advantage where comfort is concerned.

Let us turn for a moment to the design of power craft. The question here resolves itself into whether you want a fast boat that planes the surface or a slower displacement-type hull that will be more seaworthy. If your aim is to cruise, then the former are really no use to you and some sort of compromise will have to be made. Nevertheless, there are yachts, like the *Bertram 25* in which short cruises can be made in safety; this particular vessel achieving speeds of over 40 knots! The same firm make the *Bertram 37* which attains speeds of 30 knots and for a 37-foot boat with every comfort below this is very good. But you pay for it! This vessel costs £22,900! With the *Jaunty* class, say the 24-footer, we have a thoroughly seaworthy little vessel that chugs along nicely at speeds of 7–8 knots. This sort of boat is based on a traditional displacement work-boat hull with a powerful beam. With the *Bertram*-type boats the high speeds come from the powerful engines lifting the 'V' bow section out of the water so that the flat sections of the after part can plane in the groove cut by the fore sections. Part of the secret (of the 25-foot *Bertram* for example) lies in the very substantial beam (9 ft 11 ins (3·022 m) on the 25). Between these types lie a variety of compromise.

CHAPTER ELEVEN

The Domestic Angle

(1) Cooking and the Galley

Fifteen to twenty years ago, it was not at all uncommon to find a yacht in which the galley was situated right up for'ard. This was of course a legacy from the affluent days of the paid hand, who lived and had his being in the fo'c'sle and cooked up there too. There is a theory, which I have often proved, however much of an old wives yarn it may sound, that air in a yacht travels through from aft forward, no matter how she is lying relative to the wind, under normal conditions. This has been suggested as the reason why the galley always used to be stuffed right up in the fore peak. But I doubt it. I think it was up there so that the paid hand or skipper could cook on it without having to disturb the owner and his guests; and it is of course a naval tradition of long standing that the officers lived aft, and the crew for'ard!

Today all that has gone, except in very large yachts owned by those lucky people who manage not only to make a lot of money but, far cleverer, to hang on to it. Nowadays the galley is to be found amidships or slightly aft of that – where the beam is greatest and the motion least, and the cook is given pride of place for his arts and crafts. Ocean racing devotees lay great emphasis on this honourable position for the galley, because a crew lives on its stomach just as much as an army is said to march on it. A crew 'steers, hands and reefs' better if it is a well-fed crew. No one would disagree with this; and of course in ocean racing, stamina and morale, so closely related to feeding well and regularly, win at least half if not 75 per cent of ocean races.

In cruising, which tends to be more leisurely, it is still most important to eat proper hot meals, and a little thought given to the planning of the galley will pay good dividends.

The cook should be able to work properly under way. The stove must be slung in gimbels and the galley so arranged that the cook can 'chock' himself off in there with everything he (or she) needs to hand without having to shift position. There are many makes of stove on the market nowadays; both paraffin burning and bottled gas. The latter now smells so that leaks can be traced. Even so, turn it off *at the cylinder* after each use because pipes and joints can leak and gas in the bilges has blown up more than one yacht! Plan the galley so that things don't rattle about when stowed and the ship's motion is lively. It is, of course, really a matter of commonsense. Adjustable slats to take a variety of sizes of plates or mugs or cups and keep them firmly wedged are important; and any drawers must be not only easily opened with one hand (or even one finger) but at the same time self-securing when shut so that they will not open as she heels and cover you and the cabin with their contents.

(2) Sleeping and Keeping Dry and Warm

The amount of our lives we spend asleep is sufficiently large to provide the subject for a paragraph in 'believe it or not?' Frequently quoted by makers and sellers of beds and mattresses. Although it may seem on the average cruise that one spends all too little time in one's bunk, being frequently disturbed by such cries as 'all hands on deck for reefing the mainsail!' Yet one does spend a sufficient period sleeping to warrant a lot of thought on the subject of berths. Indeed the safety of the ship (and those aboard her) depend (in bad weather especially) on the simple factor of the crew getting enough rest for each to do his job properly when called upon.

Now this may all read like a preliminary to a plea for silk sheets and feather beds of vast dimensions. Far from it. The worst mistake you can make is to have your berths (*a*) too big and (*b*) too soft; for if you do, you will bounce about and roll out of them on to the deck as soon as the motion gets a bit lively. Two feet of breadth is quite adequate and there should be a leeboard on the inboard edge to stop you falling out when she rolls. If your berth is not too wide and not too springy you will *feel* secure and you will sleep better! Sir Francis Chichester's quarter berth in *Gypsy Moth IV* was very narrow. It was, however, wet; which brings me to my next point – dryness below decks.

Imagine your feelings if, having gone to a warm bed at home on a stormy night you are suddenly awakened by a douche of cold water in the middle of the bed; or again by an incessant drip, drip, from the deck head landing on your head! Yet this state of affairs is regarded by some yachtsmen as an inevitable evil. 'All boats "work" a bit in a seaway!' How often have I heard that! And yet it is not inevitable at all. In a modern yacht with decks and hull moulded in GRP, provided she is properly built, there should be none of these leaks. The same applies if the deck is of plywood. If of tongued and grooved planking canvas covered and painted, leaks *may* appear but you can stop them. It is, I admit sometimes quite difficult; since water can be getting in for example right up forward and then running under the canvas to reappear as a leak further aft. (Almost inevitably over a berth!) If this happens you must examine your decks very carefully especially along the covering board and the margin. That is to say the two 'outer' planks, the former being the board covering the outside deck planks and the latter the planking nearest cockpit or coachroof coamings, or hatches. The canvas of a canvas covered deck will usually be tucked under the covering boards and margins and as water tends to collect there is a weak spot. The canvas around here will rot more quickly. If a thorough examination of the deck reveals no obvious weak points you may be faced with re-canvassing the whole; a tiresome prospect but worth effort (and/or money). Another source of leaks is round the mast. If it is stepped on the keel make sure that, where it passes through, the deck is protected by means of a mast-coat; in other words a collar, lashed tightly round the mast about six inches above the deck and tacked (or secured depending on the material of which the deck is constructed) to form a leak-proof skirt where the mast enters the deck.

But probably the worst offenders are hatches, especially round their forward ends. In thoroughly up-to-date yachts the design of hatches has been so improved as to minimise leak risks. In older yachts a strip of rubber along the forward end of the hatch will often work wonders.

If your decks are of laid teak or pine planking the best antidote to leaks is to see that all seams (and that means *all*) are thoroughly caulked.

We have so far been talking about keeping dry below decks, but it is worth giving a little thought to keeping dry above decks too. This consists mainly in the appreciation (and acting up) a simple maxim: it is much easier to 'keep' dry than to 'get' dry. The active interpretation of this maxim being to don your oilskins when the bad weather begins and not half an hour or so later! It may sound surprising to the newcomer but many people defer putting on their 'oilies' until they themselves are thoroughly wet. There used to be a reason for this in that the old-fashioned 'oilskins' were heavy, intractable cumbersome things. Nowadays oilies are of plastic and are pliable and moreover far more skilfully designed. Coats can be long or short and there are excellent waterproof trousers to match. If you can wear woollen garments underneath your oilies they are far warmer than cotton, etc. Wool does not become cold when you sweat; and everybody sweats a bit under oilies. Clothes designed to keep moisture out will also tend to keep it in, so it is absorbed by whatever garments you are wearing below. If those garments have also become thoroughly rain and spray-soaked the situation is aggravated. So you can see that the afore-mentioned maxim is a sound one.

The 'oily' trousers should be long enough to come over your sea boots (I use light, half-length boots that can be kicked off easily). It is worth remembering to put the trousers on before the boots, so you don't risk tearing them. Also watch that you don't have the sleeve ends of a sweater projecting beyond the oilskin coat cuffs because water will soon soak right up to your elbows. The same applies to your neck – button up tightly round the neck. If necessary, a soft light towel scarf round the neck, outside the oilskin neck band helps to stop your own neck getting sore. Make sure your oilskin suit has pockets. Once donned you don't want to find yourself scrabbling inside your oilies for a knife or marline spike. Personally, I have my knife and spike on a lanyard round the waist with the former tucked into a handy pocket. The same lanyard has a pair of sister hooks attached to part of it so that one can attach oneself to the ship (stanchion, guard-rail, pulpit, etc) when working on the foc's'le in bad weather. Falling overboard is not only foolish and very dampening; it can be fatal!

CHAPTER TWELVE

Sea-sickness and other Maladies requiring First Aid at Sea

Any ship which cruises should have a first-aid box or medicine chest. In addition she should carry some book on practical first aid, an excellent one being the St John's Ambulance Association handbook.

What the medicine chest contains is a matter of individual opinion and experience. The following list should, however, provide a good basis:

Iodine
Disinfectant (Lysol, etc)
Zinc ointment
Boracic crystals
Soloids of sublimate of
  mercury
Eno's fruit salts
Calomel
Epsom salts or Andrew's liver
  salts
Castor oil
Olive oil·
Calamine lotion
Bicarbonate of soda
Brandy
A small tin of Antiphlogistine

Disprin tablets

Alka Seltzer tablets
Codeine tablets
Beecham's powders
Quinine tablets
Dramamine or Avomine
Chloretone (in 10-grain cap-
  sules)
Kwells tablets

Boric lint
Cotton-wool
Gauze dressings
Dressings for burns
Two or three triangular band-
  ages
Sticking plaster
Elastoplast or similar dressings
Oil silk

Roller bandages	Hot-water bottle
	Surgical needle and sewing
Splinter tweezers	silk
Scalpel	Medicine glass
Surgical scissors	Finger stalls
Thread and needles	Two clinic thermometers
Safety-pins	

In practice few yachtsmen of my acquaintance carry half as many things and, of course, a lot depends upon how far afield you intend to go. But, even so, if you are going offshore at all, the wise skipper takes precautions against the day when somebody in his crew is going to need first aid and need it at once and not in five or six hours' time.

Sea-sickness

This, being perhaps the most common ailment at sea, has pride of place.

Prevention: this is far better than cure and consists of avoiding greasy food, acids and over-indulgence of any kind for several days before going to sea. It is amazing the difference this makes.

At sea: take Eno's fruit salts and keep the bowels open.

The best anti-sea-sickness preparations that I know are Dramamine and Avomine. Other cures are: Kwells and Mothersill. Both of these work on some people. Two 10-grain tablets of Chloretone taken before sailing also act well on some and may be supplemented after some hours by a further 10-grain capsule in perfect safety.

Cure: some drugs, like Dramamine, work on some people when they are actually feeling sick, but it is best always to take them before you feel sickness coming on.

In a mild attack: eat dry foods – biscuits, cold chicken, also glucose barley sugar. Keep in the open, if possible, and try and concentrate on work of some sort.

In a bad attack: lie down with head low, keep warm and eat dry foods as above, even if it is a great effort to do so.

It is agreed by most doctors that sea-sickness is very largely a disorder of the nervous system. The amount of tolerance that training and familiarity with the sea will produce varies considerably (see figure 76). It has been said of sea-sickness that it can be divided into two phases – in the first you think you are going to die, in the second you are afraid you aren't!

Here are some other common ailments and their appropriate treatment.

Figure 76.   Sea-sickness – 'The amount of tolerance varies greatly'

(1) Boils

A bad boil is generally treated by hot fomentations. Soak a piece of boric lint in boiling water, wring it out and apply to the boil hot. Cover the lint with a square of oil silk and bandage. A little cotton-wool will further help to keep the heat in and of course, where suitable, plaster strips may be used in place of a roller bandage.

(2) Burns and Scalds

Remove any clothing near the affected part – but do not remove clothing stuck to the skin. (It may be necessary, to comply with this, to cut seam stitches with a knife.) Cover the burn with a sterile dressing or, of not available, a clean laundered towel. Do not prick blisters or apply any ointments or lotions to the wound. In the case of scalds remove the hot, soaked clothes at once, then treat as a flame burn. If the patient can quickly be got to hospital give nothing by mouth, if not, frequent cold drinks may be given.

If a person's clothing catches fire he should at once throw himself on deck and roll over and over and check the flames until help arrives. A better way still, if practicable, is to wrap a rug or blanket round the burning part and exclude the air. Always remember with burns that the thing to be done as soon as possible is to exclude the air.

(3) Constipation

Owing partly to lack of exercise this is a frequent malady aboard ship. Two grains of calomel relieve it.

(4) Minor Cuts

Wash any cut (in antiseptic) and then to a very small cut apply iodine. If a large cut this might sting badly and cause an iodine burn. Afterwards apply a lint dressing and bandage it or fix it with plaster.

(5) Deep Cuts

A bad cut must be treated with great care and promptness. Dissolve a solid of sublimate of mercury in a pint of warm water, and wash the wound very thoroughly, first plain warm water, and then with the solution. The person dressing the wound must scrub his hands in disinfected hot water. He should then sew up the wound with an interrupted stitch using surgical sewing silk. Remember that the surgical needle must be boiled for a good twenty minutes to sterilise it. When the wound has been stitched, it should be swabbed with a solution of sublimate of mercury, as before, and covered with a gauze pad, and then bandaged. If the wound persists in bleeding the limb should be kept raised.

(6) Drowning

(*a*) Where the patient does not appear to have suffered at all from being immersed: remove clothing at once; dry well; put on dry clothes; give a hot drink and rest a while.

(*b*) Where the patient is suffering from temporary exhaustion: remove clothes, dry, put to bed between warmed blankets (if necessary circulation promoted by massage), give a hot drink beef tea, etc) and rest; and if possible, go to sleep.

(*c*) Where the patient is suffering badly, but is still breathing: remove all tight-fitting clothing, lay down on deck and turn on his or her side. The application of smelling-salts will assist normal breathing.

(*d*) Where breathing has stopped: this is, of course, the most serious case. Again lay on deck, loosening tight clothing, but this time the patient should be face downwards, with the head inclined slightly to the right. Handle the patient very carefully and do not force him or her to adopt a position, but do not allow him or her to lie face upwards. Clear the mouth of any slime and begin artificial respiration. Do this as follows: kneel astride the patient facing towards the head. Put your hands on the small of the back, the fingers spread out over the lower ribs and the thumbs almost touching. Now lean steadily forward putting your weight on your hands, and exerting a downward pressure on the patient, and so driving air (and water, if any) from his lungs. Next swing back, rapidly releasing the pressure. This should cause him or her to inhale. Keep your hands in position on the small of the back; repeat this every four of five seconds in a regular rhythm. You are in point of fact producing a breathing motion in the lungs similar to that caused by natural breathing and you must carry on, for a long time if need be, until natural breathing is restored. Once this is so – and make quite sure before you stop the artificial respiration – turn the patient face upwards and by massage endeavour to promote circulation. The blood-stream should be massaged upwards towards the heart along the inside of the legs and arms and on the back, rubbing in every case towards the heart.

The patient should be warmed by applying hot-water bottles or heated flannels to the arm-pits, the soles of the feet and the pit of the stomach. A hot linseed poultice applied to the chest will relieve pain in breathing.

As soon as the patient has recovered somewhat and appears to be fully restored to life, remove the clothes and dry thoroughly, rubbing towards the heart. Then wrap the patient in warm blankets and put to bed in a well-ventilated room or cabin. Give a teaspoonful of warm water to see if the swallowing powers have returned, and if so, give some weak, warm brandy or beef tea. Encourage the patient to go to sleep and keep continuous watch in case breathing should again fail. If it does, resume artificial respiration as before and without any delay. Remember never to start off by giving the patient stimulants, and do not put the patient into a hot bath as this could well be very dangerous.

An important method that you should know, of reviving an apparently drowned person is by artificial ventilation sometimes called the 'kiss of life'. Again immediate treatment here is vital and seconds count. Lay the patient on his back, use your finger to clear the mouth and remove false teeth, extend the head by supporting the nape of the neck and pressing the forehead backwards; press the angle of the lower jaw forwards from behind or pull the jaw forward with the thumb in the mouth, then place the heel of one hand on the forehead to keep the head extended and pinch the nostrils closed with the finger and thumb. Now take a deep breath; open your mouth wide sealing your lips around the patient's mouth. Blow into his lungs until they are full; now remove your mouth and watch the patient's chest fall. Repeat the procedure giving four or five inflations to saturate the blood with oxygen. If the patient's mouth is damaged, injured, close it and blow through his nose. In the case of small children it may be necessary to seal your lips round both mouth and nose. If after four or five inflations the patient's colour remains blue-grey it is likely that the heart has stopped beating in which case the method of artificial respiration already described must be started.

(7) Food-poisoning

Make the patient sick. One way of doing this is to make him or her drink a large amount of salt-water or mustard and water. Afterwards give a good dose of Andrew's liver salts or Epsom salts.

(8) Sore Throat

Gargling with a solution composed of a teaspoonful of carbolic acid in half a pint of warm water will do much to alleviate the discomfort of a sore throat.

(9) Splinters

Clean the surrounding skin with iodine. If you can get at the splinter with tweezers it should be simple to extract it. If not, you may have to snick at the skin until you can get a hold of the splinter with the tweezers. Do not use a knife or needle for this, unless they have been boiled for at least twenty minutes. The hands, of course, should be washed well in disinfectant water. Having extracted the splinter, dress the wound so as to keep dirt out of it. A deep and particularly stubborn splinter may be worked to the surface by hot fomentations.

(10) Stings

Wasps and other uncharitable insects do find their way aboard. A fresh raw onion cut across the root will produce a milk-like fluid. This should be applied direct to the stung part and then a clean piece of ordinary soda should be rubbed gently over the same place.

(11) Sun-burn

Calamine lotion applied night and morning will normally give relief. In bad cases you should apply Nikalgin jelly over the burnt part.

This concludes the brief list of the more common accidents. Remember in all cases which are serious to send for a doctor as soon as possible. First aid is just what its name implies; a number of immediate measures, pending the arrival of professional treatment.

CHAPTER THIRTEEN

The Seaman's Language
A Glossary of Nautical Terms

ABACK. When a vessel is on the starboard tack, the sails are said to be aback when the wind blows on their port-hand side and vice versa.

ABAFT. Behind, eg 'aft of'.

ABAFT THE BEAM. Bearing more than 90° from dead ahead.

ABEAM. At right-angles to the centre of the fore-and-aft line.

ABOARD. On or in any vessel. On board.

ABOUT. *See* 'Tacking'.

ADRIFT. Broken away.

AFLOAT. Waterborne.

AFT. Behind. To go – to go to the after part of a vessel.

AFTER PART. The hinder part of a vessel.

AGROUND. Not waterborne.

AHEAD. Directly in front of.

A'LEE. 'Helm a'lee' indicates that the tiller has been put down to leeward.

ALOFT. Above the level of the deck. To go – to go up the mast by one means or another.

AMIDSHIPS. The point of intersection of an athwartships line across the vessel midway between the stem and stern. Also, when the tiller and/or rudder are pointing along the ship's fore-and-aft line.

APRON. A piece of timber abaft the stempost.

ASTERN. Behind the vessel.

ATHWART. Across.

ATRIP. The anchor just broken out of the ground.

AVAST. Stop, eg avast heaving.

AWASH. With water washing over.

A'WEATHER. Towards the wind; eg staysail a'weather – when the staysail is sheeted to windward.

AWEIGH. When the anchor is clear of the ground.

BACK. *See* 'Aback'.

BACK, TO. To increase resistance to a strain by some means.

BACKING (*of the wind*). When the wind's direction shifts against the sun (anti-clockwise).

BACKSTAY. Standing rigging from a masthead to the stern of a vessel to take the forward strain of the mast.

BAGGYWRINKLE. An anti-chafe made from rope and served round wire and spars where required.

BAIL. To remove the water from a boat with a bailer, bucket or other contrivance.

BALLAST. Weights placed in a ship to counterbalance the overturning effect of the wind upon the sails.

BALLOON CANVAS. Full-cut sails used in light airs.

BAR. A shoal formed across the mouth of a harbour or river, etc, by tidal action.

BARE POLES. With no sails set.

BARK (BARQUE). A three-masted vessel, square-rigged on the fore- and mainmasts, and fore-and-aft rigged on the mizzenmast.

BARQUENTINE. A three-masted vessel, square-rigged on the foremast and fore-and-aft rigged on the main and mizzen.

BATTEN DOWN. To secure all hatches, skylights, etc.

BATTENS. Light pieces of wood fastened across the sails to keep them to a designed shape.

BEACON. A guiding mark to assist navigation.

BEAM. A transverse timber which supports the deck.

BEAM. The width of a ship at her widest part.

BEAM. A bearing at right-angles to the centre of the fore-and-aft line of the ship.

BEAM ENDS, ON HER. A ship flung on her side.

BEAR AWAY. To move away from.

BEAR DOWN ON, TO. To move directly towards.

BEARING. Direction referred to the fore-and-aft line of a ship (eg on the bow beam or quarter) or to the compass meridian.

BEAR OFF. To shove away from (with a boat-hook, etc).

BEAR UP. To keep and move away from the wind, by putting the tiller up to windward.

BEATING. To sail a course directly to windward (*see* 'Tacking').

BEAUFORT SCALE. A numerical notation of wind force.

BECKET. A loop.

BEE-BLOCKS. Sheaves fitted to either side of a boom end as leads for reef earings.

BEFORE. In front of.

BELAY. To secure a rope with figure-of-eight turns round a belaying pin, cleat or bollard.

BELAYING PIN. A movable pin of metal or wood through a rail or bar, etc, for the purpose of 'belaying' a rope.

BELL BUOY. A buoy containing a bell that is rung by the sea's motion.

BELLS. Time on board ship is announced by the strokes of a bell.

BELLY. The curve of a sail.

BEND TO. To secure one thing to another.

BERMUDA RIG. A rig in which the mainsail is three-cornered, or jib-headed. (Slang: 'Leg of mutton'.)

BIGHT. An unknotted loop in a rope; also used of any part of a rope between the ends.

BILGE. That curve of the under-body on which a boat rests when taking the ground.

BILL. The point (of a hook or an anchor).

BINNACLE. The housing of the mariner's compass.

BITTS. Strong vertical posts through the upper deck of a vessel with a crosspiece connecting them. Used for securing cables, etc.

BLUFF. Steep-to; bluff-bowed (of a vessel – wide-bowed.)

BOBSTAY. A stay from the stem near the water-line to the bowsprit end, which stays the bowsprit, and prevents it from lifting.

BOLLARD. A short heavy post on a ship or jetty to which ropes may be secured.

BOLTROPES. Roping sewn round the edges of sails.

BONNET. An extra piece of canvas which is laced to the foot of a square sail to increase its area.

BOOM. A spar used to extend the lower part of a sail. It takes its name from the sail it extends (namely main boom, mizzen boom).

BOOMKIN (BUMKIN). A small spar, projecting from the ship's side to give a fair lead for sheets.

BOOT-TOPPING. The scrapping and repainting of a vessel's water-line.

BOTTLE SCREW. A screw-threaded frame which turns on two threaded pins, each fitted with an eye; for setting up rigging.

BOTTOM. The underwater body of a ship.

BOWER. The principal anchor, carried at the bow.

BOWLINE. A knot forming a loop.

BOW LINES. The curve of the forepart of the body of a vessel considered in sections parallel to the fore-and-aft section.

BOWS. The sides of the forward part of a ship.

BOWSPRIT. A spar projecting forward from the stem-head.

BRACES. Ropes secured to the yard-arms of a squaresail yard, and which control its fore-and-aft movement.

BRAIL. A rope encircling a fore-and-aft boomless sail to gather it in to its mast or spar. Used principally with spritsails.

BREAK. To break out; to wrench an anchor from its holding in the bottom.

BREAKER OR BARRICOE. A small barrel for carrying fresh water.

BREAST-HOOK. A piece of timber placed across the bows of the ship to keep them together, and strengthen them.

BRIDLE. A rope, chain or wire used for connecting two objects.

BRIG. A two-masted square-rigged vessel, but with a fore-and-aft mainsail, driver or spanker on the aftermast.

BRIGANTINE. A two-masted vessel, fore-and-aft rigged on the main and square-rigged on the fore.

BRING TO. To stop the ship; or to take turns with cables round a capstan.

BRING UP. To come to anchor.

BROACH TO. To swing suddenly into the trough of a sea broadside on.

BROAD REACH. When the wind is abaft the beam (between reaching and running).

BULKHEADS. Upright partitions dividing the ship into several compartments.

BULL'S-EYE. A hardwood round thimble.

BULWARKS. The sides of a ship that extend above the deck level.

BUNK. A bed, on board ship.

BUOY. An anchored float distinctively shaped and coloured, that indicates the position of something beneath the surface.

BUOY, MOORING. A buoy to the ground tackle of which a ship may be moored.

BURGEE. A swallow-tailed signal flag; a triangular distinguishing flag denoting membership of a given yacht club.

BUTTOCK LINES. The curve of after-part of the body of a vessel considered in sections parallel to the fore-and-aft section.

BY THE HEAD. A vessel trimmed to be deeper forward than aft.

BY THE LEE. Sailing, when running, with the wind blowing over the same quarter as the mainsail.

BY THE STERN. Opposite of 'by the head'.

CABLE. As a measure of distance, 200 yards (100 fathoms), ie about one-tenth of a nautical mile.

CABLE. The rope or chain of an anchor; a stout, thick rope.

CANT, TO. To turn or list.

CAPSTAN. A machine for heaving or veering a cable.

CAREEN. To heel a vessel over in order to get at her bottom.

CARRY AWAY, TO. To break or part.

CARRY WAY, TO. To continue to move through the water.

CARVEL. Method of building a boat with a smooth surface, the planking being edge to edge.

CAST. To pay a ship's head off by sails to bring the wind on the side required.

CAT. Concerned with weighing and lifting of an anchor, eg cat head, cat davit, cat pennant, cat purchase.

CATAMARAN. Vessel with two hulls joined together by beams. A large floating platform or stays.

CAT'S PAW. In a period of calm, a local temporary roughening of the surface; also a twisting of a rope in two loops through which a block may be hooked.

CAULK. To make watertight by driving oakum into the seams between planks.

CENTREBOARD, CENTREPLATE, DROP-KEEL, DAGGER-PLATE. A fin of wood or metal which can be lowered through the bottom of the boat to diminish leeway.

CENTRE OF BUOYANCY. The centre of the immersed volume of a vessel.

CENTRE OF EFFORT. The balancing point of a sail plan.

CENTRE OF GRAVITY. The point of resolution of all weights contained in a vessel.

CENTRE OF LATERAL RESISTANCE. The balancing point of the underwater profile.

CHAFE. To rub.

CHAIN-PLATES (CHANNEL-PLATES). Ship side fittings taking the lower end of the shrouds.

CHART. A map used solely for purpose of navigation or pilotage.

CHECK. Of a cable, to stop progress. Of a sheet or halyard, to ease out a little very slowly.

CHOCK-A-BLOCK (BLOCK AND BLOCK, OR TWO BLOCKS). When the two blocks of a tackle come together. (Slang: 'two-blocks' or 'chokker' – 'fed up').

CLAW OFF, TO. To work to windward off a lee-shore.

CLAW RING. A device for attaching the sheet block to a roller reefing boom.

CLAW TO WINDWARD, TO. To work slowly to windward.

CLEAT. A shaped piece of wood or metal to which ropes may be secured.

CLENCH. To turn over the point of a nail.

CLEW. The junction of leech and foot of a sail.

CLINKER (CLINCHER, CLENCHER). Method of building in which each side plank overlaps the one below.

CLOSE-HAULED. Sailing as close to the wind as possible with all sails drawing.

CLOSE-REEFED. With all reefs pulled down.

COACHROOF. The raised part of a cabin or cabin top 'inboard' of the sides, constructed for 'headroom' in small boats.

COAMING. A vertical protective erection around hatches, etc, which prevents water or anything entering, or anything falling in from the deck and to which coverings are secured to batten down. It is also a raised wood rail round a 'well' or 'cockpit' in small boats.

COASTER. A very light 'full-cut' headsail.

COCKPIT. The lower part of yacht's well.

COMPANION. A ladder or stairway.

COMPASS. A navigational instrument which indicates a north point.

COMPOSITE (CONSTRUCTION). (A ship) built with an iron frame and wooden skin.

CON, TO. To direct the helmsman.

COUNTER. The projection of a ship's hull abaft her sternpost.

COURSE. The angle made by a ship's track and a meridian; the lowest sail on each mast of a square-rigged ship except the mizzen.

COVERING BOARD. The outer plank of the deck which covers the heads of the frames.

CRADLE. A frame which holds a vessel upright out of the water.

CRANSE-IRON. The iron ring at the end of the bowsprit.

CRINGLES. Eyelets worked into the roping of a sail.

CROWN. The point at which the arms of an anchor join the shank.

CRUTCH. A trestle for supporting the gaff and boom (*see* 'Gallows'). A metal contrivance on a boat's gunwhale which serves as a fulcrum for an oar.

CUTTER. A single-masted fore-and-aft rigged vessel carrying more than one headsail.

DAVITS. Cranes for lowering and lifting boats.

DEAD-RECKONING. The calculation of the position of a ship, based upon her course and taking into consideration the continued influence of winds, currents and leeway.

DEADEYES. Circular pieces of hardwood with sheaveless holes, used for setting up the lower ends of standing rigging (by means of lanyards).

DEADLIGHTS. Metal shutters to protect the glass of scuttles or portholes.

DEADWOOD. Wood filling pieces between the stem and sternpost and the keel.

DECK. A horizontal partition of a boat.

DEEP. An unmarked graduation of the hand lead-line; an area of deep water between stretches of shoal.

DEVIATION. The amount of compass needle deviates in an easterly or westerly direction from the magnetic meridian due to the influence of metal in the ship.

DIAGONAL BUILD. A flush double-skinned boat with planks laid diagonally.

DINGHY. A small open boat, generally tender to a yacht. A small open sailing boat.

DIP, TO. To lower and rehoist a flag in salute.

DIPPING LUG. A lugsail, the tack of which must be passed or dipped round the mast when going about.

DISPLACEMENT. The amount of water in tons displaced by the underwater volume of the vessel.

DOGHOUSE. A raised protection carrying abaft the cabin.

DOG VANE. A wisp of bunting in the weather rigging.

DOGS OF THE CAPSTAN. Small projecting lugs to prevent the cable from rendering.

DOLPHIN. A mooring staging not connected with the shore.

DOUBLE-CHINE. Two chines along each side. Chine is the intersection of the straight sides with the flat bottom planks of a boat.

DOWNHAUL. A rope used for the purpose of hauling anything down.

DOWN HELM, TO. To put the tiller to leeward, ie down wind.

DOWSE, TO. To take in sail, strike spars quickly, or put out a light.

DRABLER (DRABBLER). A shallow squaresail laced at the foot of a bonnet.

DRAUGHT. The maximum underwater depth of a ship.

DRAW, TO. (*of sails*). To fill.

DREDGE. Process of dragging an anchor at short stay along the bottom to give steerage way in a tideway.

DRESS SHIP, TO. To display flags.

DRIFT. The rate of a current in knots; the unassisted movement of a ship.

DRUM HEAD. The head of a capstan.

DUCK. A cotton cloth used for light sails or boat sails.

DUTCHMAN's LOG. A primitive means of measuring the speed of the ship through the water.

EARINGS. Ropes for securing the clew of the sail to the spar.

EASE, TO. Of a rope (*see* 'Check'); of a ship, to luff for a dangerous sea.

EBB. The falling of the tide.

ECHO-SOUNDING. The method whereby electrical impulses from a vessel to the bottom are timed on their return.

EDDY. A local circular or spiral movement of water unrelated to the movement of the surrounding current.

ENSIGN. A flag carried by a ship to proclaim nationality.

EVEN KEEL. Neither 'by the head' nor 'by the stern'.

EYES. The extreme fore end of a vessel.

FAIRLEADS. Metal channels to prevent chafe and to guide the lead of a rope.

FAIRWAY. A navigable channel.

FAKE. A single circle of a coil of rope.

FALL. The hauling part of a rope.

FALLING OFF THE WIND. Paying off to leeward.

FALSE KEEL. A piece of wood bolted to the outside of the main keel.

FATHOM. A nautical measurement of six feet.

FAY. Thinning down surfaces before fastening them together.

FEND, TO. To push off.

FENDERS (FEND-OFFS). Pads to prevent a ship's side from chafe.

FETCH, TO. To make, or reach.

FID. A tapered piece of wood or iron used to limit the travel of a spar (bowsprit). A tapered piece of wood or iron used to enlarge holes in wood or iron.

FIDDLE. A bar of wood or metal fitted with small sheaves to provide leads for light running gear. Wooden partitions on a saloon table for use when feeding in rough weather.

FIDDLE-BLOCK. A pulley having two superimposed sheaves, the upper one being larger than the lower.

FIFE-RAIL. A piece of wood or metal containing a number of belaying pins.

FISH. To strengthen a spar with splints.

FLAKE, TO. To coil down in layers free for running.

FLARE. The concave upward curve of a vessel's bow; a flare-up light signal.

FLAT-ABACK. With the wind on the wrong side of the sails.

FLATTEN IN, TO. To haul in the sheets.

FLEET, TO. To haul the blocks of a purchase apart.

FLOOD. The rising of the tide.

FLOORS. Athwartship pieces of metal connecting the heels of a ship's frames (sometimes made of wood).

FLUKE. The extremity of an anchor arm; irregularities in the wind.

FLY. The horizontal measurement of a flag.

FLY TO. Come quickly up into the wind.

FLYING (*of a sail*). When its luff, when set, is not hanked to a stay.

FO'C'SLE. This is literally 'forecastle', formerly the cabin or 'castle' before the 'foremast' of a ship. Now generally used for that part of the 'foredeck' on its superstructure containing the 'anchors' and 'cables' or the 'crew' space below it, differentiated by 'on the fo'c'sle' for working 'cables', etc, and 'in the fo'c'sle' for crew space.

FOOT. The lower edge of a sail.

FORE. Forward.

FORE-FOOT. The junction of the stempost and the keel.

FORE-REACHING. Movement in a boat under sail dead into the eye of the wind when luffing or going about.

FORESAIL. The principal sail set on the foremast. (Note *not* on the forestay.)

FORETRIANGLE. The sail area forward of the mast usually measured along the foreside of the mast in 'cutters', 'yawls' and 'ketches' and of the foremast in schooners from the deck to the top of the highest 'sheave' used or headsails; and from the foreside of the mast (as already indicated) to where the line of the 'luff' of the foremost headsail (when extended) cuts the bowsprit, stem or hull.

FORWARD. On the foreside of.

FOUL ANCHOR. A turn of the cable round an anchor or an anchor caught up on anything.

FOUL BERTH. At anchor with insufficient swinging room.

FOUL BOTTOM. Uneven, rocky patches on the sea-bed (foul ground). An under-body coated with weeds or barnacles, etc.

FOUL HAWSE. Crossed or twisted cables.

FOUNDER, TO. To sink.

FOX, A. Twisted rope yarns (*see* 'Nettles').

FRAME. *See* 'Timber'.

FRAPPING. Binding.

FREE. Not close-hauled or with the wind aft.

FREEBOARD. The height of the deck from the water-line.

FRESHEN (*of wind*). To increase.

FULL (*of a sail*). Drawing well.

FULL AND BYE. Sailing as close to the wind as possible with every sail full.

FURL. To gather a sail up and secure it to its spar.

GAFF. A spar to which is bent the head of a fore-and-aft sail.

GALE. Forces 8 and 9 on the Beaufort Scale. A wind of from 47 to 55 knots.

GALLEY. A ship's kitchen.

GALLOWS, PERMANENT. A fixed frame for supporting the boom (*see* 'Crutch').

GAMMONING. The fastenings of a bowsprit at the stem.

GANG PLANK. A board used as a bridge from a ship to a jetty.

GANGWAY. A passage. The removable part of the bulwarks through which a ship may be boarded.

GARBOARD STRAKE. The planks or plates which lie next to the keel.

GATHER WAY, TO. To begin to move through the water.

GEAR. Used to describe all the tackle of a mast or sail and the steering apparatus.

'GENOA'. A large 'jib' for racing, overlapping the mast and 'sheeted' further 'aft' than a working headsail.

GIMBALS. A system of bearing rings to maintain an article in the horizontal position at sea.

GO ABOUT. *See* 'Tack'.

GOOD FULL. With the wind just freer than close-hauled.

GOOSE-NECK. A hinged metal fitting used to secure a spar to its mast.

GOOSED-WINGED. Running before the wind in a two-masted vessel when the sails of the aftermast are boomed out to the opposite side to those of the foremast.

GORGE. The swallow of a block.

GRAPNEL. The cable of a boat's anchor, not the anchor itself.

GRAPPLE OR GRAPPLING IRON. A small multiple-armed anchor.

GRATING. A cross-wood framework.

GRIPES. Canvas or webbing bands used to secure a boat in davits.

GROMMET. An endless ring of rope.

GRP. Glass-reinforced plastics.

GUDGEONS. Ring-shaped rudder fittings, through which the pintles pass.

GUNTER. A triangular-shaped mainsail the head of which is extended above the masthead by a yard which slides up and down the mast.

GUNWALE. The upper edge of a boat's side.

GUY. A controlling rope, usually on a spar.

GYBE, TO. When sailing, to bring the wind from one quarter to the other in such a way that the boom swings across.

HAKMATACK. A species of American larch used in shipbuilding.

HALYARD, HALLIARD. A rope used for hoisting anything.

HAMBRO LINE. A small line used mainly for seizing.

HAND, TO. To furl; of a patent log, to haul in.

HAND LEAD. *See* 'Lead'.

HANDSOMELY. Gently or slowly.

HANDY-BILLY. A small jigger; ie a purchase having a fixed double block fitted with a tail and a moving single block.

HANKS. Hooks or rings by means of which jibs and staysails are attached (by their luffs) to the stays from which they pivot.

HARD. A hard part, natural or artificial, on a soft shore.

HARD A-PORT, HARD A-STARBOARD. The order to use the maximum effective helm to make the ship's head go in the direction indicated by the order.

HARDEN (*of wind*). When a stiff breeze ceases to be gusty.

HARDEN IN. To flatten in sheets.

HATCH. An opening in the deck to go in and out by.

HATCHWAY. An opening with a movable cover (hatch) in the deck of a vessel.

HAUL, TO. To pull on a rope.

HAUL YOUR WIND, TO. To sail closer to the wind.

HAWSE. The distance between the stem of a vessel and the holding flukes of the anchor to which she is riding.

HAWSE, CLEAR. When riding to two anchors a ship is said to have a clear hawse when one cable has not fouled the other.

HAWSE, FOUL. A ship riding to two anchors with the cables crossed once or more.

HAWSE, OPEN. Moored to two anchors without a swivel.

HAWSE-PIPES. The holes in the bows of a ship through which the anchor cable runs.

HAWSER. A large rope or cable of rope or steel.

HAWSER-LAID. With the strands laid up as in a hawser.

HEAD. The fore end of the ship.

HEAD OF A SAIL. The upper edge.

HEADS. Lavatories about ship.

HEADSAILS. The sails forward of the foremast.

HEAD SHEETS. The floor-boards in the bows of a boat.

HEART. A central strand in a rope of even numbered strands to fill up the cavity in the centre.

HEAVE, TO. To haul; to throw.

HEAVE IN SIGHT, TO. To come in view.

HEAVE SHORT, TO. To shorten in the cable to 'short stay'.

HEAVE TO, TO. To stop; to take way off; to keep as near as possible head on to a heavy sea at minimum speed to secure steerage way.

HEEL. The after end of the keel; the butt of a mast; the inclination of a ship.

HELM. The tiller or wheel.

HELM DOWN. The opposite to 'helm up' (helm a'lee).

HELM DOWN, TO. To move the tiller towards the wind so that the ship's head goes to leeward (helm a'weather).

HITCH, TO. To make a rope fast to an object, not to another rope.

HOG, TO. To scrub thoroughly.

HOGGING. The convex longitudinal strain on a vessel.

HOIST, TO. To haul aloft.

HOLY STONE. A soft porous stone used for scouring woodwork.

HOOPS. Rings holding the luff of a sail to a mast.

HORSE. A bar, rail or wire running athwartship across a vessel's deck on which a sheet travels.

HOUNDS. Projections which support the trestle trees of a mast; that part of the mast from which the upper end of the lower standing rigging is set up.

HOUSE FLAG. A personal flag.

HOUSING. The part of a mast or bowsprit inboard; of a topmast lowered but not struck.

HOVE. *See* 'Heave'.

HUG, TO. To keep close to.

HULL. The body of a vessel, not including her masts and fittings.

HURRICANE. A wind of force 12 by the Beaufort Scale, ie of more than 64 knots.

INBOARD. Within the 'framework' of a ship, near or towards 'amidships'.

INHAUL. Opposite of outhaul.

IRONS, IN. A ship is in irons when she is head to wind and unwilling to pay off on either tack.

JACK-IN-THE-BASKET. A basket beacon.

JACK-STAY. A rigid length of iron, wood, wire or rope on which anything travels.

JACKYARD TOPSAIL. A topsail extended beyond the topmast by means of a small spar called a jackyard.

JACOB'S LADDER. A rope ladder having wooden rungs.

JAWS. The crutch at the mast end of a boom of gaff which bears against the mast (*see* 'Parrel').

JIB. The foremost headsail; appertaining to the jib, eg jib sheets.

JIB-BOOM. An extension of the bowsprit on which additional headsails are set.

JIGGER. A small mast stepped abaft the mizzenmast on which the spanker sail is set; the mizzensail on a yawl or ketch is sometimes called the jigger; a small purchase (*see* 'Handy-billy').

JOGGLE-SHACKLE. A long-jawed shackle used in cable work.
JURY. Makeshift.

KEDGE. A small anchor.
KEDGE, TO. To move a vessel by hauling on a kedge anchor.
KEEL. The lowest fore-and-aft member of a vessel.
KEELSON. A fore-and-aft timber connecting the floors to the keel.
KENTLEDGE. Shaped pieces of ballast.
KETCH. A two-masted vessel with the aftermast (mizzen) shorter than the mainmast, and stepped forward of the sternpost.
KILLICK. A stone used for anchoring on a foul bottom; (colloquially) an anchor.
KING POST. A vertical post on deck.
KNEES. Wood or metal crooks in the ship's framework; elbows.
KNIGHTHEADS. Vertical timbers on either side of the bowsprit.
KNOT. A nautical mile per hour (not a measure of distance).

LACING. A line securing a sail to its spar.
LAID UP. Unrigged and dismantled.
LANDS. The overlaps of clench-built planking.
LANYARD. Lashing.
LASH, TO. To secure with ropes.
LATITUDE. Measurement north or south of the Equator.
LAUNCH. To allow to slip into the water.
LAY. Of a rope, the direction left or right in which the strands of a rope or hawser are twisted; also 'go', ie lay aft, go aft; to put.
LAY OFF (*of a course*). To rule off.
LAZY. Extra, eg lazy guy, lazy painter.
LEACH OR LEECH. The after edge of a sail. In a squaresail, the vertical edges.
LEAD. A leaden weight on the end of a marked line (lead-line) used to find the depth of the sea.
LEAK. An accidental opening in a ship's hull which allows water to enter.
LEE. On the side away from the wind.
LEE BOARDS. Boards pivoted on the sides of shallow-draught vessels which, when lowered, increase the resistance to lee-way.
LEE-BOWING. 'Lee-bowing the tide' is a sailing advantage obtained by taking the tide on the 'lee-bow' in going to

'windward'. 'Lee-bowing' also means a racing tactic in which the 'give-away' boat goes 'about' on the 'lee-bow' of another so 'back-winding' her.

LEE-GOING TIDE. A tidal stream setting in the same direction as the wind.

LEE HELM. A vessel is said to carry lee helm when she tends to fall off the wind.

'LEE-OH!' A warning that the helm has been put down for going about.

LEEWARD (LOO'ARD). Down wind.

LEE-WAY. The angle between a ship's fore-and-aft line and her wake.

LEG. A tack.

LEG-OF-MUTTON SAIL. A triangular sail; the original slang name for the Bermudian sail.

LEGS. Stout baulks of timber, their upper ends bolted to the outside of a vessel through midship timbers near the sheer-strake and guyed fore-and-aft in a vertical position to support the boat in an upright position when laid ashore.

LET DRAW. To permit a sail to fill on the desired tack.

LET FLY. Let go sheets.

LET GO. Of an anchor, to let it fall into the water.

LIFE-LINE. A stout line rigged about the upper deck in heavy weather to provide handhold for the crew.

LIFT. A rope to take the weight of a spar (ie topping lift).

LIGHT AIRS. Forces 1 and 2 Beaufort Scale; wind of 2–6 knots.

LIGHT BREEZE. Force 3 Beaufort Scale; wind of 7–10 knots.

LIMBERS. Holes in the floors to permit the free passage for-and-aft of bilge water.

LINE. Small cordage.

LINES, HEAVING. Light lines weighted at one end (used for passing the end of heavy hawser).

LIST. The inclination of a vessel from the horizontal due to a transverse change in trim.

LIZARD. A short length of rope with a thimble or eye fitted in one end.

L.O.A. Length overall.

LOG. A contrivance by which the speed of a vessel is estimated.

LOG-BOOK. A day to day record of a ship's life.

LOG SHIP. A leg-of-mutton-shaped board dropped over the stern at the end of a marked line to ascertain the ship's speed.

LONGITUDE. Measurement east or west of the prime meridian of Greenwich.

LOOM. The handle of an oar; the reflection of a light.

LUBBER'S POINT OR LUBBER'S LINE. A fixed mark inside a compass bowl indicating the direction of the ship's head.

LUFF. Of a sail, its leading or weather edge.

LUFF, TO. To bring a vessel closer to the wind.

LUFF TACKLE. A working tackle with a double and a single block.

LUFF UPON LUFF. A luff tackle with a second luff tackle clapped on its hauling part, thereby trebling or quadrupling the power of the first.

LUG. A projection.

LUG, A BALANCE. A rig in which the tack of a boomed lugsail is made fast to the mast.

LUG, A DIPPING OR STEM. A lugsail rig in which the tack of a sail is made fast at the stem.

LUG, A STANDING. A boomless lugsail rig in which the tack is made fast to the mast.

LUGSAIL. A four-sided sail, its head bent to a yard (and its foot occasionally to a boom).

L.W.L. Load water-line.

MAINSAIL. The sail 'set' from the 'main mast'. The main mast is the principal and tallest mast of a ship, and the mainsail, the sail hoisted upon it, is the largest sail.

MAKE, TO. Reach (eg to make port); of tides, the increase of the tidal range and velocity from neaps to springs.

MAKE A STERNBOARD, TO. To make a vessel go astern under sail.

MAKE SAIL. To set the sails.

MAKE WATER, TO. To leak.

MAN, TO. To provide a crew for a ship, or for any given purpose, ie man the winch, man the falls.

MANILLA. A form of rope made from the fibres of Philippine Island hemp.

MAN-ROPES. Steadying ropes providing hand-hold when ascending gangways, companion ladders, etc.

MARL, TO. To take a number of turns of line round anything, each turn concluding with a half-knot.

MARLINE. Light, two-stranded line, suitable for marling.

MARLINE-SPIKE (MARLING SPIKE). A tapered wood or steel instrument for opening up the strands of a rope.

MARRY, TO (*of rope ends*). To join unlayed rope ends together strand for strand; (*of ropes and falls*) to hold two ropes together in order to haul on both equally.

MAST. A spar or system of pieces of wood or metal placed nearly perpendicular to the keel of a boat and used to spread sails or to support other spars on which sails are spread.

MASTHEAD. Top of the mast.

MAST STEP. A socket in the keelson into which the mast heel is stepped.

MEAN DEPTH. The depth below mean sea-level.

MESSENGER. A small rope bent on to a larger one and brought to the capstan in order to heave the larger one which by itself is too big to be brought-to.

MIDSHIPS. (*See* 'Amidships'.) Of the helm, the executive order to centre the rudder.

MILE. A nautical mile is equal to one minute of latitude at the Equator, and is universally accepted as being 6,080 feet.

MISS STAYS, TO. To hand up in the wind and fail to come about when tacking, instead of paying off on a new tack.

MITCHBOARD. A crutch-shaped piece of wood used to support the main boom on the rail when the mainsail is lowered in bad weather, and a trysail set in its place.

MIZZENMAST. The aftermast in yawls, ketches and in three-masted vessels (ie foremast, mainmast and mizzenmast).

MIZZENSAILS. Sails set from the mizzenmast.

MODERATE BREEZE. Forces 4 and 5 Beaufort Scale; wind 11–21 knots.

MOOR, TO. To lie to more than anchor; to pick up a mooring.

MOORED 'ALL FOURS'. Moored between anchors or cables from both bows and both quarters.

MOORINGS. Permanent anchors or heavy weights, etc, laid down in the bed of a harbour, to which a mooring chain is shackled. The mooring chain is hauled inboard and bitted by a vessel picking up moorings, it is pulled up on a length of rope (a buoy-rope), and its position is indicated by a mooring buoy. To 'slip a mooring' is to let it go, to cast it adrift.

MOUSE, TO (*of a hook*). To take several turns with yarn round the back and bill of a hook to prevent it jerking out of its hold.

NAIL-SICKNESS. Minor leaks in a ship's side caused by the galvanic action of sea-water on bare iron fastenings, nails, etc. The fastenings erode, leaving unplugged nail holes, through which the water percolates.

NAVEL PIPES. Metal lined openings in the deck through which the anchor cable runs from the chain locker.

NAVIGATION. The art of conducting a vessel in safety from one point to another.

NEAPED, OR BE-NEAPED. Left aground by a receding spring tide, so that the rise of the succeeding tide will be insufficient to refloat the vessel.

NEAPS. The smallest tides, having the lowest high-water and highest low-water of a tide cycle.

NETTLES. Two or three yarns laid up (twisted) between the finger and thumb left-handed. Sometimes called a 'fox'.

NIMBUS. Rain cloud.

NIP. The point at which a rope or cable bends sharply, ie round a cleat, block, or pin, or (of cable) over the lip of a hawse-pipe or fairlead.

NIP, TO (*of a hawser, etc*). To make it fast with a seizing.

OAKUM. The teased-out yarns of rope-strands, for caulking, etc.

OFF. Offshore (eg the wind taking off, blowing offshore); near to (eg anchored off Ryde); away from (eg off the wind).

OFF AND ON, TO STAND. To keep close to the land, but to keep on alternately closing and then withdrawing.

OFFING. The open sea at a safe distance from the shore; the open sea viewed from the security of a sheltered anchorage during a gale.

ON. Opposite of off; towards (eg a wind blowing onshore).

ON A WIND. Close-hauled.

OPEN (*of a boat*). Undecked; (*of an anchorage*) unsheltered.

OPEN HAWSE. Riding to two bower anchors without a swivel.

OUT. Away from the shore.

OUTBOARD. Beyond the ship's sides.

OUTHAUL. A rope used to haul anything out into position (eg a jib outhaul).

OVERBOARD. Over the side.

OVERCAST. When the sky is covered with clouds.

OVERFALL. Tide rip; shoal.

OVERHAUL, TO. To gain on: (of a rope) to slacken off; (of a tackle) to draw the blocks apart – opposite to 'fleeting'; (of gear) to examine and make ready.

PAINTER. A rope attached to the stem ring-bolt of a small boat, and used for securing the boat to anything.

PALM. A form of thimble which straps across the palm of the hand, and is used by sailmakers when roping or seaming canvas; (of an anchor) the flat face of an anchor fluke.

PARBUCKLE, TO. To roll a spar or cask, etc, up a slope or quay face, etc, using the bight of a rope.

PARCEL, TO. To wind overlapping strips of canvas tightly round a rope with its lay. To bind a mooring hawser with turns of rope or junk in order to prevent chafe at the point where it passes through a fairlead.

PARREL. A contrivance for keeping a spar close to its mast.

PARREL BALLS. Hardwood balls fitted to a parrel to give it a travelling and turning surface.

PARREL LINE. The piece of rope or wire on which the parrel balls are threaded, and which secures them to the parrel.

PART (*of a rope*). Standing part, running part, hauling part.

PART, TO. To break, to carry away.

PARTNERS. The supporting frame of a mast where it passes through the upper deck.

PASS, TO (*of a lashing rope*). To take securing turns with.

PAY, TO (*of a seam*). To fill with stopping. To coat a ship's bottom with anything except paint.

PAY OFF, TO. To allow a ship's head to swing away from the wind.

PAY OUT, TO (*of a rope*). To slacken hand over hand.

PEA. The point of an anchor or hook.

PEAK. The topmost corner of any sail but a squaresail. The outer end of a gaff.

PEAK. To set up on a gaff sail's peak halyard, until wrinkles begin to appear in the throat of the sail.

PENNANT (PENDANT). A triangular-shaped flag. A short piece of rope or wire, one end of which, the standing end, is made fast to a spar or sail, and in the other end of which is an eye to hold the hook or the upper block of a tackle.

PENNANT, REEF. A rope by which a reef-cringle is bowsed down to the boom end.

PIG. A cast piece of ballast.

PIN. The axle of the sheave of a block.

PINTLES. Metal elbows which take the gudgeons of a rudder's fittings.

PLAIN SAIL. Lower canvas.

PLUG. The stopper for the draining hole in the bottom of a boat.

POINT. One thirty-second part of the compass, ie $11\frac{1}{4}$ degrees.

POINT, TO. To weave the yarns at the end of a rope into a tapered point.

POINTING. A degree of closeness to the wind when sailing close-hauled.

POINTS, CARDINAL. North, South, East, West.

POINTS, REEF. Cords on either side of a reef band, used to tie up the unwanted foot of the sail when reefed.

POLE-MAST. A lower mast and topmast in one piece.

POOPED, TO BE. When running before a heavy sea, the seas overtake the vessel and fall on board the after part.

POPPETS. Pieces of wood which fill up the rowlocks of double-banked pulling boat.

PORT. On the left hand facing forward.

PORT TACK. With the wind blowing on the port side.

PRAM. Norwegian pattern dinghy.

PREVENTER. An additional stay set up to counteract the bending strain on a spar.

PURCHASE. A system of blocks for increasing haulage power.

QUANT. A long punting pole.

QUARTER. Half-way between the beam and right aft.

QUIET NUMBER. An easy, uneventful job.

RABBET. A notch cut in a timber to take the edge of a plank.

RACE. Locally disturbed water.

RACK, TO. To seize together with racking seizing round two ropes, one of which is subject to more strain than the other.

RADAR. An electronic device for obtaining bearings and distances.

RAFFEE. A triangular sail which is set above a squaresail in a fore-and-aft rigged ship.

RAKE. The inclination of a vessel's mast in the fore-and-aft line.

RANGE (*of cable*). To flake down on deck in large bights. Of tide, the difference between the rise and fall of any given tide.

RATTLING DOWN. To make ratlines.

REACH, TO. To sail with the wind free.

'READY ABOUT'. The warning that the helmsman's about to tack.

REEF, TO. To shorten sail.

REEF, SPANISH. To tie a knot in the canvas of a headsail.

REEF-BANDS. Strengthening bands of canvas across a sail through which reef points are passed.

REEVE, TO. To thread or pass through anything.

RELIEVING TACKLES. Temporary tackles set up to the steering gear to assist the helmsman in heavy weather.

RENDER, TO. To give; to operate freely.

RHUMB LINE. The shortest distance between two points, a straight line on a Mercator chart; a course cutting all meridians at the same angle.

RIDE, TO. To be at anchor or moorings.

RIG. The arrangement of a ship's mast, rigging and sail.

RIG, TO. To set up.

RIGGING (STANDING). The cordage which supports the mast and spars. (RUNNING). Which controls or is attached to the sails.

RINGTAIL. An extension fitted to the leech of a fore-and-aft mainsail.

ROACH. A curved edge to a sail.

ROCKERED. A rounded or curved keel.

ROGUE'S YARN. A coloured yarn found in the heart of the strands of all Government rope.

ROLL. Transverse motion on a vessel.

ROLLER REEFING. A method of reefing in which the sail is rolled up round a revolving boom.

ROUND TURN. One complete turn round anything.

ROUNDLY. Quickly and steadily (opposite to handsomely).

ROUNDS. The rungs of a Jacob's ladder.

ROWLOCKS. Square gaps for the oars, placed at intervals in the gunwale of a boat.

RUBBING STRAKE. An additional thick piece of wood, running the length of a boat and made fast on the outside of the planking a short distance below the gunwale, to protect the boat when lying alongside anything.

RUDDER. A flat plate hinged to the sternpost and used to direct the movement of a ship.

RUNNER. The purchase for tautening a backstay. Used often to mean a backstay itself.

RUNNING. To sail with the wind right aft.

RUNNING RIGGING. (*See* 'Rigging'.) Rigging which 'runs' through blocks, etc.

SALTINGS. Flat land, subject to part flooding with high tides.

SCANDALISE. To trice up the tack and settle the peak of a gaff sail.

SCANTLINGS. The dimensions of timbers used in a boat.

SCARPHING. Joining timbers together by tapering the ends and lashing or bolting them together so that the result is a constant thickness.

SCEND. The lift of the bows of a boat to the sea or swell.

SCHOONER. A vessel fore-and-aft rigged on the fore- and main-masts. (If the vessel has more masts, for-and-aft rigged on those as well.)

SCORE. The groove in a block which receives the strop.

SCULL, TO. To propel a boat with a single oar over the stern.

SCUPPERS. Apertures in the bulwarks to permit water to run off the deck.

SCUTTLE. To sink a vessel deliberately; a glazed aperture to admit light and air.

SEIZE. To fasten two things together with seizings.

SEIZINGS. Turns of line.

SEMAPHORE. A method of signalling.

SET A COURSE, To steer.

SET UP, TO. To rig; to tighten, of lanyards or shrouds; to flatten, of sails.

SETTLE, TO (of a sail). To lower a little and handsomely; (of a ship) to sink slowly.

SEVE. To bind line tightly round a rope against the lay.

SEXTANT. An instrument used in astronomical navigation.

SHACKLE. An iron fitting. D-shaped, U-shaped, saddle-shaped, etc, the open end of which may be closed by a pin, for connecting objects.

SHANK. The main body of an anchor.

SHEAVE. The wheel of a block.

SHEER. The fore-and-aft curve of a vessel's deck line.

SHEER, TO. To move across.

SHEER-STRAKE. The topmost plank of the ship's side.

SHEET ANCHOR. A spare bow anchor – (hence, colloquially, an invaluable standby).

SHEETS. A rope or ropes controlling the clews of sails.

SHELL. The outer casing of a block.

SHIFT, TO. To change clothes, sails, etc.

SHIP, A. A fully square-rigged vessel.

SHIP, TO. To take anything on board.

SHOAL. Shallow.

SHORE, TO. To buttress.

SHROUDS. Lateral stays to the mast.

SKEG. The metal socket that supports the base of a 'rudder'.

SKIN. The outer planking of a vessel.

SLACK WATER. When the tidal stream is stationary.

SLANT. Wind in a favourable position.

SLOOP. A sailing vessel with one mast and two sails, 'mainsail' and 'headsail'.

SNATCH BLOCK. A block, the side of the shell of which is cut away to facilitate reeving.

SNIED. Crooked.

SNUB. To check suddenly.

SOLDIER'S WIND. A fair wind.

SOUND, TO. To ascertain the depth.

SPAR. A piece of timber on which a sail is set.

SPELL. An interval.

SPIDER HOOP OR BAND. A metal band round a mast containing belaying-pins.

SPILL, TO. Of a sail, to empty it of wind.

SPINNAKER. A light weather triangular sail boomed out from the mast on the opposite side to the mainsail.

SPLICE. To unite by interweaving strands.

SPRINGS (*of tides*). The maximum range of a tide cycle. Mooring ropes leading from forward to a jetty bollard further aft, and vice versa.

SPRIT. A spar set diagonally from the lower part of the mast to the peak of a (boomless and) gaffless mainsail.

SPRITSAIL. The sail set on a sprit.

SPRUNG (*of a spar*). Injured by straining.

SQUALL. A sudden gust.

STANCHION. A supporting column or pillar.

STAND ON, TO. To maintain one's course and speed.

STANDING. Permanent.

STARBOARD. The right-hand side looking forward.

STARBOARD TACK. Sailing with the wind blowing on the starboard side.

START, TO. To loosen.

STAVE, TO. To crush in.

STAYS. Supports to a mast.

STAYSAIL. Sail 'set' on a 'stay' and named from it, ie 'fore staysail' – sail 'set' from the 'forestay'.

STEADY. Order to a helmsman to stay on the course the vessel is on at the moment of the order being given.

STEM. The foremost vertical timber or plate of a ship.

STEM THE TIDE, TO. To sail against the current without losing ground.

STEP. A socket cut in the keelson to receive a mast heel.

STEP, TO. To put in position.

STERN. The after end of a vessel.

STERNDRIVE. An inboard engine with an outboard drive unit containing reverse/reduction gearbox, steering swivel and propeller-shaft.

STERNPOST. The aftermost vertical timber of a vessel.

STERNWAY. Movement through the water, stern first.

STIFF. Standing up well to the wind under canvas.

STOPS. Pieces of rotten yarn used to secure a sail tightly about its own luff.

STORM. Force 10 and 11, Beaufort Scale; a wind 48 to 65 knots.

STRAKE. Side plank.

STRAND. A number of yarns hove up together in rope making.

STRATUS. Layer cloud.

STREAM ANCHOR. An anchor let go over the stern when mooring stem and stern in a tide-way.

STREAM, TO. To cast overboard a log or an anchor buoy.

STRETCHER. Foothold for an oarsman.

STRIKE, TO. To lower.

STRONG WIND. Force 6 and 7, Beaufort Scale; wind of 22 to 23 knots.

STROP. A band of rope or metal.

SURGE. To allow a rope to render round a revolving winch or capstan.

SWALLOW (*of a block*). The groove for the sheave in a block.

SWIFT IN. To tauten up rigging.

SWING SHIP, TO. To turn a ship through all the points of the compass to ascertain and record the deviation.

TABERNACLE. The housing in which the heel of a lowered mast rests.

TABLING. The double seam round the edges of a sail.

TACK. The foremost lower corner of a fore-and-aft sail; a board or leg when beating to windward – hence starboard tack, a board made with the wind on the starboard side of a vessel; the rope or purchase attached to the foremost lower corner of a sail.

TACK, TO. To work a vessel to windward by sailing alternately close-hauled with the wind on the starboard side and close-hauled with the wind on the port side; to alter course through the wind when beating to windward; to change course from the port to the starboard tack, and vice versa.

TACKLE. A combination of pulley blocks forming a purchase.

TACK-LINE. Short lengths of signal halyard about 6 feet long used to separate groups in a long hoist of code flags.

TAFFRAIL. The rail round the stern of the ship; the capping of the bulwarks on the stern.

TAIL. A length of rope spliced on to the blocks of a tackle, or on to the hauling end of a wire sheet or halyard.

TAKE-OFF (*of tides*). The steady decrease in the rise and velocity of tides from springs to neaps.

TAKE-UP (*of gear*). To shorten; to tighten (of gaping seams in planking); to shrink tight when the boat is immersed in water.

TAN, TO (*of sails*). To treat with a preparation of cutch, or of oil and ochre.

TAUT. Tight; stretched tightly under a severe strain.

TENDER. A small vessel, such as a yacht's dinghy, used to attend on her parent vessel.

THIMBLE. A grooved metal ring, circular or heart-shaped, used to line an eye in a rope.

THOLES (THOLE PINS). Pegs fitted in a rowing boat's gunwale to act as fulcra to the oars.

THOROUGHFOOT, TO. To coil down a rope in figure-of-eight-shaped flakes.

THROAT. The end of a gaff or boom nearest to the mast; the upper inner corner of a gaffsail or spritsail.

THROUGH FASTENINGS. Fastenings of a ship which are driven through the planking and frames.

THUMB CLEAT. A small projecting piece of wood secured to a spar to prevent a strop from slipping.

THWARTS. Seats running from side to side of an open boat.

TIDAL STREAMS. The periodic horizontal movement of the sea.

TIDE. The periodic vertical movement of the sea caused by solar and lunar attraction.

TIDE RIP OR RACE. Disturbed seas caused by tidal eddies or the passage of a tidal stream over an uneven bottom.

TIDE-RODE. The situation of a ship anchored in a tideway when, the strength of the tide being greater than the strength of the wind, she lies head to tide.

TIERS, TIES. Short lengths of rope or canvas used to secure the furled sail to its yard.

TIGHT. Watertight.

TIMBERS. A collective name for the skeleton and unplanked frame of a yacht; timber – the vertical frame of a yacht.

TINGLE. A patch of lead or copper put on the outside of a vessel over a hole in the planking.

TONNAGE. The measurement of a ship's internal capacity.

TOP HAMPER. Gear above decks.

TOP, TO–UP. To lift one end of, eg of a yard, etc; to fill up.

TOPPING LIFT. A rope which tops up one end of a spar and also takes the weight of the spar.

TOPSAIL. A sail set above a course in square-rigged vessels and above the gaffsail with fore-and-aft rig.

TOPSAIL SCHOONER. A schooner-rigged vessel carrying square topsails on her foremast.

TOTAL LOSS. When the underwriters agree to pay the whole amount for which a vessel is insured.

TOW, TO. To pull a vessel through the water.

TRACK, TO. To haul a vessel through the water using man-power or horse-power for the work.

TRANSOM. The stern planking of a square-sterned vessel.

TRAVELLER. A ring travelling along a spar and to which a sail is secured.

TREENAILS, TRENNELS. Wooden pegs used as ship's fastenings and held firmly in place by a small wedge driven into splits in either end.

TREND. Direction.

TRESTLE-TREES. Pieces of timber at the hounds which support the crosstrees and topmast-fid.

TRIATIC STAY. A stay connecting the foremast and the mainmast head in a schooner.

TRICE UP. To hoist.

TRICING LINE. A rope, one end of which is secured to the tack of the sail, rove through a block at the hounds or gaffjaws, used for tricing or trussing the tack of a loose-footed gaff sail (*see* 'Scandalise').

TRIM. The horizontal balance of a ship.

TRIM, TO (*of sails*). To adjust; to manipulate the sheets so that a vessel's sails are used to best advantage.

TRIMARAN. A vessel with three hulls, the outer two being joined to, and smaller than, the centre.

TRUCK. Circular piece of wood at the masthead which contains a sheave for flag halyards.

TRY, TO. To heave to.

TRYSAIL. A three-cornered sail usually part of a yacht's storm canvas and forming the after sail-spread when heaving to in heavy weather.

TUCK, TO (*of rope strands*). To splice; to interweave.

TURN, TO. To beat to windward; to tack.

TURN IN, TO. To go below to sleep; to make an eye in the end of a rope round an object such as dead-eye, etc.

TURN, TO TAKE A. To pass a rope once or twice round anything; to secure round a cleat or bollard.

TYE (TIE). A member of the ship's framework securing vertical to longitudinal timbers, etc; a piece of rope or chain on which the bunt of a square yard is suspended or hoisted.

UNA RIG. An up-river rig, consisting of a single balanced lugsail set on a boom and gaff.

UNBEND. Undo; untie; cast off; remove sails from their yards, etc.

UNDER WAY. Having movement through the water.

UNRIG, TO. To take the standing and running rigging and sails of a vessel; to dismantle.

UNSHIP. Remove; cast off.

UP HELM, TO. To put the tiller up to windward; an order requiring the ship's head to be turned away from the wind.

VANGS, VANES. Ropes controlling the lateral movement of the after end of a gaff or sprit.

VEER, TO (*of the wind*). When it shifts with the sun, ie clockwise; (*of a ship's movement*) to sheer away from; (*of a cable*) to pay out, link by link, by reversing the drive of a capstan; to ease slowly and steadily while retaining control.

VEER AND HAUL, TO. Literally to ease and then haul on a rope – but sometimes used colloquially to express shifting opinions; fair-weather views: vacillation.

WAKE. The disturbed water left behind in the path of a moving vessel.

WALE. A fore-and-aft strengthening timber in a vessel's framework and which supports the outer edge of the gunwale; a plank fastened to the outside of a ship's topside to act as a rubbing-band.

WARP. A rope by which anything is hauled along; the rope cable of an anchor in small craft; (*of sailcloth*) the lengthwise measurement, the lengthwise threads.

WARP, TO. To move a vessel forward by hauling on a hawser or warp attached to a mooring buoy or to posts on shore. (*Of timber*), to curl, to lose shape.

WASH. The wave-form created by a boat moving through the water.

WASHBOARD OR WASHSTRAKE. A movable plank superimposed upon the lee sheer-strake of an open sailing boat to increase the height of side when sailing.

WATCH-BUOY. A buoy specially moored to mark a fixed position at sea.

WATCHES. The division of a ship's company into suitable parts for general duty. These are generally formed of the port watch and the starboard watch, and each in turn is responsible for all work on board for a period of four hours – except during the dog watches from 4 p.m. to 8 p.m., when the period of duty lasts for two hours only.

WATER LAID. Left-handed.

WATER-LINE. The horizontal plan of a ship on the level at which she floats; the length of a vessel, between perpendiculars on this horizontal plan; the ship's side on the level of the water.

WATERLOGGED. Full of water, but still floating.

WATERWAYS. Navigable channels; the deck, under the bulwarks, grooved to act as a gutter to lead water off the deck and out to the scuppers; that part of a small yacht's upper deck between the bulwarks and the sides of a raised cabintop.

WAY. Momentum, movement through the water.

WAYS. Baulks of timber across which a ship is launched or any weight is moved.

WEAR. To go round stern to wind from the starboard tack to the port tack and vice versa, instead of through the wind (head to wind) as in tacking.

WEATHER. Windward – eg weather side, weather bow, weather roll, etc.

WEATHER, TO. (*Of an object*) to pass safely to windward of it; (*of a gale*) to come safely through.

WEATHER-BOUND. Unable to leave harbour, by reason of bad weather.

WEATHER EYE OPEN, TO KEEP A. To keep a good look-out to windward.

WEATHER HELM, TO CARRY. Of a vessel when it is necessary, in order to maintain a straight course, to keep the tiller a'weather because of the vessel's tendency to turn up into the wind.

WEATHER-SHORE. The land to windward of a vessel.

WEATHER TIDE, WEATHER-GOING TIDE. A tidal stream setting to windward.

WEED. Any marine life – animal or vegetable – adhering to the underbody of a vessel.

WEFT. A small pennant-shaped flag; (*of canvas*) the width measurements, the across threads.

WEIGH, TO. To raise the anchor from the sea bottom.

WELL. Cockpit, the sunk part of the deck in which the helmsman sits to steer.

WELL-FOUND. With all the necessary gear on board and in good condition.

WEST COUNTRY WEATHER. A possibly libellous term synonymous with continuous drizzling rain and overcast, lowering sky.

WESTERING. Of the sun between noon and sunset.

WESTING. Distance made good to the westward.

WHEEL. An upright wheel used for steering instead of a tiller. The top of the wheel is usually moved in the same direction in which it is intended the ship's head is to turn; hence the order 'Starboard wheel' or 'Hard a starboard' in a wheel-steered ship is an order to the helmsman to move the wheel clockwise – top spokes to starboard in order that the ship's head shall be turned to starboard.

WHEEL-ROPES. Wires or chains which run from the axle of a steering wheel to the tiller.

WHIP. A rope rove through a single block; (*of a mast*) spring.

WHIP, TO. To bind the end of a rope to prevent it from fraying; (*of a mast*) to bend.

WHISKERS. The athwartship spreaders fitted outboard near the gammoning of a long bowsprit to extend the lead of the bowsprit shrouds.

WHITE HORSES. Breaking wave crests.

WHITE SQUALL. A sudden squall which whips the sea into a mass of foam.

WHOLESOME. Comfortable and seaworthy in a heavy seaway.

WINCH. A species of small windlass in which a drum is revolved by the action of a ratchet lever or bar.

WIND-BOUND. Unable to proceed by reason of adverse winds.

WINDLASS. A machine of the wheel and axle order used for hauling in the chain cable, etc; it is operated by means of handspikes or, more usually, by a crank handle.

WIND-RODE. The position of a ship anchored in a tideway, when the strength of the wind being greater than that of the tide she lies head to wind.

WIND-SAIL. A canvas tube used to direct the wind into the body of the ship in hot weather.

WIND'S EYE. The 'eye of the wind' – the direction from which it blows.

WINDWARD. On the side upon which the wind is blowing; the direction from which the wind is blowing.

WIRE. Wire rope.

WIRING. In a small boat, a stringer upon which the thwarts rest.

WITH THE SUN. Clockwise in direction.

WITHIE. A willow; a stake or perch, sometimes used to beacon the navigable channel of a small river or creek.

WORK, TO (*of an object*). To become slack or loose: to sail, to keep moving – eg to work to windward; (*of a ship's fabric*) to strain open in a seaway.

WORK A VESSEL, TO. To handle or manoeuvre a vessel.

WORKING GEAR. Gear in general use; the sails used by a ship when working to windward in ordinary weather.

WORKING STAYSAIL OR FORESAIL. One whose sheet travels across the deck on a horse.

WORM, TO. To fill in the lay of a rope with small line in order to make a smoother, rounder surface for parcelling and serving. Worming is done with lay of a rope.

WRACK. Anything cast up on the shore and left behind by the receding tide.

WRECK. The destruction of a ship by the sea or by an unpreventable accident, or what is left of a vessel after destruction has occurred.

WRING, TO. To twist; to subject to twisting strain.

YACHT. A vessel used for pleasure only.

YARD. A spar suspended from a mast for the purpose of spreading the head of a sail.

YARD-ARM. The outer end of a yard, especially of a square-sail yard.

YARN. A number of fibres of coir, sisal, hemp, cotton, etc, twisted together, usually right-handed.

YAW, TO. To swing or swerve from side to side of the course ordered, usually as a result of bad helmsmanship.

YAWL. A two-masted vessel, having a mainmast and a short mizzenmast, the latter stepped abaft the sternpost.

YOKE. A flat plate secured athwartships to the rudder head and used for controlling the rudder (*of a mast*); the lower cap or ring through which the topmast runs.

YOKE LINES. Pieces of rope leading from each end of the rudder yoke for turning it and the rudder.

YOUNG FLOOD. The first movement of a flood tide.

ZULU. A Scottish (fore-and-aft rigged) fishing vessel.

CHAPTER FOURTEEN

Glossary of Useful Seaman's Words in Ten Languages

CRUISING: SAIL OR POWER

ENGLISH	FRENCH	GERMAN	DUTCH	SWEDISH
Anchor	Ancre	Anker	Anker	Ankar
Anchorage	Ancrage	Ankergrund	Ankergrond	Ankarplats
Anchorage dues	Droits d'ancrage	Ankergeld	Ankergeld	Ankringspennengar
Boat	Canot	Boot	Boot	Bat
Ballast	Lest	Ballast	Ballast	Ballast
Beam (Breadth)	Bau	Breite	Breedte	Bredd
Bowsprit	Beaupré	Bugspriet	Boegspriet	Bogspritt
Boom	Bout-dehors	Spiere	Boom	Bom
Bow	Avant	Bug	Boeg	Bog
Bill of Customs	Declaration d'entrée	Zolleingangschein	Douaneverklaring	Tullförklaring
Bill of Health	Patente de santé	Gesundheitsattest	Gezondheidpas	Sundhetspass
Bill of Sale	Acte de vente	Verkaufsnote	Verkoopsbrief	Försäljningkontrakt
Breakage	Rupture	Bruch	Breuk	Brott
Breakwater	Brise-lame	Wellenbrecher	Breekwater	Boljabrytare
Broker	Courtier	Makler	Makelaaar	Mäklare
Brokerage	Courtage	Courtage	Makelarij	Mäklarelön
Buoy	Bouée	Boje	Boei	Boj
Consul	Consul	Konsul	Consul	Konsul
Cable	Câble	Kabel; Tau	Kabel	Kabel
Cutter	Cutter	Kutter	Kotter	Kutter
Cargo	Cargaison	Ladung	Lading	Last
Cancelled	Annulé	Annulliert	Geannuleerd	Annulerad
Certificate	Certificat	Attest	Certificaat	Certifikat
Charter party	Charte partie	Charterpartie	Charterpartei	Certeparti
Charterer	Affréteur	Befrachter	Bevrachter	Befraktare
Charts	Cartes (marines)	Seekarten	Seekaarten	Sjökarter
Clearance (customs)	Acquit de douane	Ausklarierung	Uitklaring (bewijs)	Klarering vid Tullen
Collision	Abordage	Zusammenstoss	Botsing	Sammanstötning
Compass	Compas	Kompas	Kompas	Kompass
Compass-card	Rose des vents	Windrose	Kompas-roos	Kompass-ros
Crane	Grue	Kran	Kraan	Kran
Crew	Équipage	Mannschaft	Scheepsvolk	Besättning
Custom House	Douane	Zollamt	Douanekantoor	Tullhus
Custom Officer	Douanier	Zollbeamte	Douanier	Tullbetjänt
Customs duties	Droits de douane	Zoll	Inkomende rechten	Tull
Deck	Pont	Deck	Dek	Däck
Derrick	Mât de charge	Ladebaum	Laadboom	Ladebom
Deviation	Déviation	Abweichung	Afwijking	Deviation
Diver	Scaphandrier	Taucher	Duiker	Dykare
Dock	Bassin	Dock	Dok	Docka
Draught (ship's)	Tirant	Tiefgang	Diepgang	Djupgående
Dry-dock	Cale sèche	Trockendock	Droogdok	Torrdocka
Ensign	Enseigne	Fahne	Vaandel	Flagga
Engineer	Mecanicien	Maschinist	Machinist	Maskinist
Engine	Machine	Maschine	Machine	Maskin
Error	Erreur	Fehler	Fout	Fel
Fathom	Brasse	Faden	Vadem	Famn
Flotsam	Épaves flottantes	Treibgut	Zeevond	Strandgods
Freeboard	Franc-bord	Freibord	Vrijboord	Fribord
Fuel	Combustible	Brennstoff	Brandstof	Bränstoff
Fee(s)	Droits	Gebuhr	Loonen	Belöning
Fore-	De misaine	Fock-	Fooke-	Fock-
Gale	Tempête	Sturm	Windvlaag	Storm
Harbour	Port	Hafen	Haven	Hamn
Harbour dues	Droits de port	Hafengeld	Havengeld	Hamnutgift
High-water	Pleine mer	Hochwasser	Hoogwater	Hogflod
Hulk	Hulk	Hulk	Hulk	Holk
Hemp	Chanvre	Hanf	Hennep	Hampa
Hull	Coque	Rumpf	Romp	Skrof
Insurance	Assurance maritime	Seeversicherung	Zeeverzekering	Sjöförsäkring
Inventory	Inventaire	Inventar	Inventaris	Inventarium
Invoice	Facture	Faktur	Fakfuur	Faktura
Jetty	Jetée	Hafendamm	Havenhoofd	Kajdam
Length	Longuer	Länge	Lengte	Langd
Leakage	Coulage	Leckage	Lekkage	Lackage

266

NORWEGIAN* Danish in Brackets	PORTUGUESE	SPANISH	ITALIAN
Anker	Ancora	Ancla	Ancora
Ankerplads	Ancoragem	Anclaje	Ancoraggio
Ankringsavgift (ankeringsafgift)	Direito de ancoragem	Derechos de anclaje	Diritti d'ancoraggio
Baat (Baad)	Barco	Bot	Lancia
Ballast	Lastro	Lastre	Zavorra
Bredde	Largura	Anchura	Larghezza
Bogspryd (Bugspryd)	Gurupés	Bauprés	Bompresso
Sperrebom	Botalo	Botalon	Boma
Boy (Bov)	Proa	Proa	Prua
Toldangivelse	Anúncio de entrada	Declaración de llegada	Bolletino d'entrata
Sundhetspass (Sundhedspas)	Patente de salude	Patente de sanidad	Patente di sanità
Kjöpekontrakt (Købekontrakt)	Contrato de venda	Contrato de venta	Lettera di vendita
Brud	Fractura	Rotura	Rottura
Bölgebryder (Bølgebryder)	Quebramar	Rompeolas	Frangionde
Maegler	Corretor	Corredor	Sensale
Maeglergebyr	Corretagem	Corretaje	Sensaria
Böie (Bøje)	Bóia	Boya	Boa
Konsul	Cônsul	Cónsul	Console
Tov	Cabo	Cable	Cavo
Kutter	Cutter	Lancha	Cotter
Ladning	Carga	Carga	Carico
Annuleret	Anulado	Anulado	Annullato
Certifikät	Certificado	Certificado	Certificato
Certeparti	Carta partida	Contrato de fletamiento	Contratto di noleggio
Befragter	Fretador	Fletador	Noleggiatore
Sjökärter (Søkort)	Mappa marinho	Cartas de navegación	Carte marina
Udklarering	Despacho	Despacho (aduana)	Soaziamento
Kollision	Collisão	Abordaje	Investimento
Kompas	Bússola	Brújula	Bussola
Kompas-rose	Rosa dos ventos	Rosa de los vientos	Rosa de venti
Kran	Guidaste	Grúa	Gu
Besaetning	Equipagem	Tripulación	Equipaggio
Toldkammer (Toldboden)	Alfândega	Aduana	Dogana
Toldbetjent	Garda	Agente de aduanas	Doganiere
Told	Direitos de alfândega	Derechos de aduana	Diritti di dogana
Daek	Coberta	Cubierta	Coperta
Lade bom	Perigalho	Gúra	Albero de carico
Deviation	Desvio	Desvi amiento	Deviazione
Dykker	Merfulhador	Buzo	Palombaro
Dok	Dique	Dique	Bacino
Dypgaaende (Dybgaaende)	Caledo	Calado	Pescaggio
Tördok (Tørdok)	Dique sêco	Dique scco	Bacino dicaren aggio
Flag	Bandeira	Bandera	Bandiera
Maskinist	Machinista	Maquinista	Macchinista
Maskine	Machina	Máguina	Macchina
Felj	Erro	Error	Errore
Favn	Braça	Braza	Braccio
Vraggods	Fragmentos de maufrágio	Restos flotantes	Galleggianti
Fribord	Franco bordo	Franco bordo	Franco bordo
Braendstof (Braendstof)	Combustível	Combustible	Combustible
Avgift (Afgift)	Gratificaçao	Gratificación	Competenze
Forreste-	De proa	De trinquete	Di prua
Storm	Ventania	Viento fresco	Temporale
Havn	Porto	Puerto	Porto
Havneavgifter (Havneafgift)	Direitos de porto	Derechos de puerto	Diritti di porto
Hoivande (Højvande)	Mare alta	Plenamar	Alta marea
Holk (Hulk)	Asco	Ponton	Pontone
Hamp	Canhamo	Canamo	Canapa
Skrog	Casco	Casco	Scafo
Sjöforsikring (Søforsikring)	Seguro marítimo	Seguro maritimo	Assicurazione marittima
Inventar	Inventário	Inventario	Inventario
Faktura	Factura	Factura	Fattura
Landingsplads	Molhe	Muelle	Molo
Laengde	Comprimento	Longitud	Lunghezza
Laekage	Rombo	Derrame	Colaggio

ENGLISH	FRENCH	GERMAN	DUTCH	SWEDISH
Letter	Lettre	Brief	Brief	Brev
Letter of credit	Lettre de credit	Kreditbrief	Credietbrief	Kreditbrev
Lighter	Allège	Leichter	Lichter	Pråm
Lighthouse	Phare	Leuchtturm	Vuurtoren	Fyr
Log-book	Journal du bord	Journal	Logboek	Loggbok
Master	Capitaine	Kapitän	Kapitein	Kapten
Money	Argent	Geld	Geld	Penningar
Main-	Grand	Haupt-	Groot-	Stor-
Mizzen-	D'artimon	Besan-	Bezans-	Mesan-
Mast	Mât	Mast	Mast	Mast
Mainsail	Grande voile	Schonfahrtsegel	Grootzeil	Storsegel
Motor vessel	Moteur vaisseau	Motorschiff	Motorschip	Motorskepp
Neap tide	Morte d'eau	Nippflut	Dood tij	Lågflod
Oar	Aviron	Ruder	Riem	Åre
Oil	Huile	Ol	Olie	Olja
Owner	Propriétaire; armateur	Reeder	Reeder	Skeppsredare
Passport	Passeport	Pass	Passpoort	Pass
Passenger	Passager	Passagier	Reiziger	Resande
Pier	Jetée	Hafendamm	Havendam	Kajdam
Pilot	Pilote	Lotse	Loods	Lots
Pilotage	Pilotage	Lotsenkunde	Loodsen	Lotspenningar
Policy	Police	Police	Polis	Polis
Price	Prix	Preis	Prjs	Pris
Propeller	Hélice	Schraube	Schroef	Skruv
Protest (sea)	Rapport de mer	Verklarung	Zeeverklaring	Sjoprotest
Provisions	Vivres	Proviant	Proviand	Proviant
Port! (side)	Babord	Backbord	Bakboord	Babord
Petrol	Essence	Benzien	Benzine	Bensin
Paraffin	Pétrole	Erdöl	Paraffine	Petroleum
Quarantine	Quarantaine	Quarantäne	Quarantaine	Quarantän
Quay	Quai	Kai	Kaai	Kaj
Railway	Chemin de fer	Eisenbahn	Spoorweg	Järnbana
Rate of exchange	Course de change	Börsenkurs	Wisselkoers	Kurs
Receipt	Quittance; reçu	Quittung	Quittantie	Kvitto
Repairs	Reparations	Reparaturen	Reparatie	Reparation
Rudder	Gouvernail	Steuerruder	Roer	Ror
Sailing vessel	Voilier	Segelschiff	Zeilschip	Seglate
Sail	Voile	Segel	Zeil	Segel
Sale	Vente	Verkauf	Verkoop	Salu
Sheet (sail)	Écoute	Schote	Schoot	Skot
Shipwright	Charpentier	Schiffzimmermann	Scheepstimmerman	Skeppstimmerman
Shipbuilder	Constructeur de navires	Schiffbauer	Scheepsbouwmeester	Skeppsbyggare
Stern	Arrière	Stern	Achterschip	Akterskepp
Starboard! (side)	Tribord	Steuerbord	Stuurboord	Styrbord
Salvage	Sauvetage	Bergung	Berging	Bergning
Seaman (sailor)	Matelot	Matrose	Matroos	Sjöman
Seaworthy	En bon état de navigabilité	Seetüchtig	Zeewaardig	Sjöfast
Ship	Navire; vaisseau	Schiff	Schip	Skepp
Ship chandler	Fournisseur de navire	Schiffshändler	Verkooper van scheepsbehoften	Skeppshandlare
Ship broker	Courtier maritime	Schiffsmakler	Scheepsmakelaar	Skeppsmäklare
Shipwreck	Naufrage	Schiffbruch	Schipbreuk	Skeppsbrott
Smuggling	Contrebande	Schmuggel	Smokkeln	Smuggleri
Sold	Vendu	Verkauft	Verkocht	Sålt
Steam vessel	Vapeur	Dampfschiff	Stoomschip	Angskepp
Stores	Approvisionnement	Vorräte	Vooraad	Förråd
Stowage	Arrimage	Stauung	Stuwage	Packning
Survey	Expertise	Besichtigung	Expertise	Besiktning
Surveyor	Expert	Besichtiger	Opzichter	Besikthingsman
Telegram	Télégramme	Depesche	Telegram	Telegram
Tide	Marée	Flut	Getij	Ström
Ton	Tonne	Tonne	Ton	Tunna
Tonnage	Tonnage	Tonnengehalt	Last	Ton
Towage	Remorquage	Schleppen	Sleepen	Släpning

GLOSSARY OF USEFUL SEAMAN'S WORDS

NORWEGIAN* Danish in Brackets	PORTUGUESE	SPANISH	ITALIAN
Brev	Carta	Carta	Lettera
Kreditbrev	Carta de crédito	Carta de crédito	Lettera di credito
Laegter	Gabarra	Gabarra	Piatta
Fyr	Farol	Faro	Faro
Log-bok (Logbog)	Livro do log	Diario	Giornale di bordo
Skibsförer (Skibskaptajn	Capitão	Capitan	Capitano
Penge	Dinheiro	Dinero	Danaro
Stor-	Grande	De mayor	Maestra (o)
Mesan-	De Mezena	De mesana	Di mezzana
Mast	Masno	Palo; árbol	Albero
Storseil (Storsejl)	Vela Grande	Vela de mayor	Vela maestra
Motorskib	Motor-barco	Moto; navio	Motoscafo
Niptid	Agua morta	Marea muerta	Marea del quarti
Aare	Remo	Remo	Remo
Olie (Olie)	Azeiteno	Aceite	Olio
Reder	Armador	Naviero	Armatore
Pas	Passaporte	Pasaporte	Passaporto
Passager	Passageiro	Pasajero	Passaggiere
Mole	Embarcadouro	Muelle	Molo
Lots (Lods)	Pilôto	Practico	Pilota
Lotsavgift (Lodsafgift)	Pilotagem	Piloto	Pilotaggio
Police	Apólice	Póliza	Polizia
Pris	Preco	Precio	Prezzo
Skrue	Hélice	Hélice	Elice
Sjöprotest (Søprotest)	Declaração de avarias	Protesta	Testimoniale
Proviant	Víveres	Víveres	Commestibili
Bagbord	Bombardo	Babor	Sinistro
Benzin	Petróleo	Esencia	Benzina
Petroleum	Parafina	Petróleo	Paraffina
Karantaene	Quarentena	Cuarentena	Quarantena
Kai (Kaj)	Caes	Muelle	Banchina
Jernbane	Estrada de ferro	Ferrocarril	Ferrovia
Kurs	Preço de Câmbio	Tipo de cambio	Corso di Cambio
Kvittering	Quitação	Recibo	Ricevuta
Reparationer	Reparos	Reparaciones	Riparazioni
Ror	Leme	Timón	Timone
Seilskib (Sejlskib)	Veleiro	Velero	Veliero
Seil (Sejl)	Vela	Vela	Vela
Saig	Venda	Venta	Vendita
Skjode (Skøde)	Escota	Escota	Scotta
Skibstömmermand (Skibstømmer- mand)	Carpinteiro de navios	Carpintero naval	Costruttore navale
Skibsbygmester (Skibsbygger)	Construtor de navios	Arquitecto naval	Costruttore navale
Agterende	Pôpa	Popa	Poppa
Styrbord	Estibordo	Estribor	Tribordo
Bjergning (Bjœrgning)	Salvamento	Salvamento	Salvataggio
Sjömand (Sømand)	Marinheiro	Marinero	Marinaio
Sjödygtig (Sødygtit	Bom para o mar	En estado de navegar	Atto a navigare
Skib	Navio	Buque	Nave
Skibsandler	Fornecedor	Proveedor de buques	Fornitore navale
Skibsmaegler	Corretor maritimo	Corredor marítimo	Mediatore in noleggi
Skikbrud	Naufrágio	Naufragio	Naufragio
Smugleri	Contrabandismo	Contrabando	Contrabando
Solgt	Vendido	Vendido	Vendita
Dampskib	Navio a vapor	Vapor	Piroscafo
Proviant	Provisãos	Provisiones	Proviste
Stuvning	Arrumacão	Estiba	Stivaggio
Bisegtelse (besigtigelse)	Vistoria	Reconocimiento	Perizia
Besigtelsemand (Besigtigelsemand)	Emprego	Perito	Perito
Telegram	Telegramma	Telegrama	Telegramma
Tidevand	Maré	Marea	Marea
Ton	Tonelada	Tonelada	Tonellata
Tonnage	Tonelagem	Tonelaje	Tonnellaggio
Slaepning (at Burgsere, Slaebning)	Reboque	Remolque	Rimôrchio

CRUISING: SAIL OR POWER

ENGLISH	FRENCH	GERMAN	DUTCH	SWEDISH
Tug	Remorquer	Schlepper	Sleepboot	Släpbåt
Underwriter	Assureur	Assekurateur	Assuradeur	Underskriva
Value	Valeur	Wert	Waarde	Värde
Voyage	Voyage	Seereise	Zeereis	Resa
Weight (gross)	Poids (brut)	Gewicht (brutto)	Gewicht (bruto)	Vikt
Wharf	Quai	Kai	Kaai	Varv
Winch	Treuil	Winde	Winch	Vinch
Windlass	Guideau	Ankerspill	Ankerspil	Ankarvinch
Wind	Vent	Wind	Wind	Vind
Wireless	Radio-Telegraph (TSF)	Drahtlose Telegraphie	Draadlooze Telegraphie	Tadlös Telegrafi
Yacht	Yacht	Jacht	Jacht	Jakt

GLOSSARY OF USEFUL SEAMAN'S WORDS

NORWEGIAN* Danish in Brackets	PORTUGUESE	SPANISH	ITALIAN
Slaepebaat (Bigerbaad)	Rebocador	Remolcador	Rimôrchiatore
Assurandor	Segurador	Asegurador	Assicuratore
Vaerdi	Valor	Valor	Valore
Rsise (rejse)	Viagem	Viaje	Viaggio
Vaegt (Brutto)	Pêso (bruto)	Peso (bruto)	Peso (lordo)
Kai (Kaj)	Caes	Muelle	Scalo
Vinch	Manivela	Montacarga	Verricell
Spil (Ankerspil)	Cabrestante	Molinete	Mulinello
Wind (Blaest, Winde)	Vento	Viento	Vento
Traadlos Telegrafi	Radiotelegrafia	Radiotelegrafia	Radtelegrafia
Jacht (Lystbaad, Lystjacht)	Iacht	Iate	Yacht

*Where no Danish word is given it is the same as Norwegian